DISCARD

Bullying in the Arts

Bullying in the Arts

Vocation, Exploitation and Abuse of Power

ANNE-MARIE QUIGG
Jackson Quigg Associates

GOWER

Gower Applied Business Research
Our programme provides leaders, practitioners, scholars and researchers with thought provoking, cutting edge books that combine conceptual insights, interdisciplinary rigour and practical relevance in key areas of business and management.

Published by
Gower Publishing Limited
Wey Court East
Union Road
Farnham
Surrey
GU9 7PT
England

Gower Publishing Company
Suite 420
101 Cherry Street
Burlington
VT 05401-4405
USA

www.gowerpublishing.com

British Library Cataloguing in Publication Data
Quigg, Anne-Marie.
  Bullying in the arts : vocation, exploitation and abuse of power.
  1. Performing arts--Psychological aspects. 2. Personality
  and creative ability. 3. Bullying in the workplace.
  4. Bullying in the workplace--Prevention. 5. Bullying in
  the workplace--Law and legislation. 6. Entertainers--
  Attitudes. 7. Entertainers--Psychology.
  I. Title
  302.3'0887-dc22

  ISBN: 978-1-4094-0482-8 (hbk)
  ISBN: 978-1-4094-0483-5 (ebk)

Library of Congress Cataloging-in-Publication Data
Quigg, Anne-Marie.
Bullying in the arts : vocation, exploitation and abuse of power / Anne-Marie Quigg.
  p. cm.
Includes bibliographical references and index.
ISBN 978-1-4094-0482-8 (hbk) -- ISBN 978-1-4094-0483-5
(ebook) 1. Arts--Great Britain--Management. 2. Arts facilities--Great Britain--Employees.
3. Bullying in the workplace--Great Britain. 4. Cultural industries--Great Britain--Personnel
management. I. Title.
NX770.G7Q54 2011
700.68'3--dc22

2010049006

Printed and bound in Great Britain by the
MPG Books Group, UK

Contents

List of Figures

List of Tables

About the Author

Dr Anne-Marie Quigg is a director of Jackson Quigg Associates Ltd, consultants specializing in arts management, creative industries and community development, based in Yorkshire in the UK. She is a guest lecturer on MA courses in Cultural Policy and Management, at City University, London. Dr Quigg has a BA in English from Queen's University, Belfast – her native city – and a Postgraduate Diploma in Arts Administration from City University, London, where she also gained her PhD in the Department of Cultural Policy and Management for her research into workplace bullying in the arts.

Anne-Marie Quigg has been a regional and community arts officer at the Arts Council of Northern Ireland, and has held chief executive officer posts in theatres and arts centres. She has been and is a committee member, trustee and chair of, and an adviser to, a large number of community and arts organizations throughout the UK. She has written articles for a variety of periodicals, and papers for international conferences and journals.

Jackson Quigg Associates (www.jacksonquigg.com) specializes in strategic management solutions and capital project delivery for the community and voluntary sectors, having expanded from its initial concentration on the arts. As a director of the company, Anne-Marie is closely involved in all aspects of the company's work, in particular business and financial planning, human resources management, strategic development and fundraising. The company has delivered both large- and small-scale capital projects and has raised over £10 million – both capital and revenue – for clients.

Dr Quigg welcomes emails from those interested in her research and can be contacted at amquigg@mac.com. She lives in West Yorkshire, UK, with her husband and business partner Piers Jackson.

Foreword

This book looks at the experience many of our members have faced, that of being bullied or of seeing colleagues and friends being bullied. As a trade union, BECTU supports its members when faced with such abusive practices. Bullying by definition is behaviour that occurs on more than one occasion and means that the work environment can become toxic for all. Arts organizations are especially at risk as the pressure to 'be all right on the night' can mask a bully's wish to control and humiliate. This book and its research shows that the problem can be a direct result of lack of skills in management and lack of a commitment to creating a workplace that values all employees equally. BECTU represents members in the theatre, arts centre, cinema, film and television communities and knows that our members can provide the best of their skills and vision when the workplace respects them.

Anne-Marie Quigg's research can help raise the awareness of these issues, develop the dialogue that can create a better work environment, and show methods of resolving the problems. BECTU is pleased to have been able to help with this work. As in the commercial world, companies that are rated as the best to work *for*, are often the best able to fulfil their goals. We believe that a work environment that respects all and knows how to handle issues of bullying is a work environment that supports the arts and creative industries. Trade unions have a key role in supporting members and helping to create workplaces that all employees enjoy working in, and this book will help us achieve that goal.

Christine Bond
President,
Broadcasting Entertainment Cinematograph and Theatre Union
December 2010

Preface

About Bullying

Bullying, mobbing or harassment is a set or series of behaviours, recurring regularly, which results in one person or body consistently intimidating and oppressing another. It is perhaps most familiar as a feature of childhood and of the school playground, and there has been a great deal written about bullying in schools, in the United Kingdom (UK) and elsewhere, for example, Olweus (1993), Colvin et al. (1998) and a comprehensive overview in Smith and Sprague (2003).

Since the start of the millennium, however, workplace bullying has become increasingly common and more frequently reported by the media. Adult bullying is destructive conduct that can have a devastating effect on individuals and on the workplace. The ramifications go beyond the personal interconnection between perpetrator and target. One individual can bully another, and two or more people can cooperate to persecute a target. This target is often a subordinate or a vulnerable peer and, as the focus of the negative behaviour, they are put under extreme duress, which has detrimental and sometimes damaging consequences. This is not to deny the existence of upward bullying, where a subordinate tyrannizes a superior, although this is much less common. Frequently, colleagues who witness bullying behaviour are adversely affected too.

When an organization bullies its workforce via unfair employment terms and conditions, often workers are not, or feel they are not, empowered to object. They perceive that objections are frequently dismissed, apparently without reasonable consideration, and, being financially dependent on their employers, often they regard themselves as being coerced. In the current straitened times, the swingeing financial cuts being made across the whole of the economy in the United Kingdom are placing increased pressure on individuals and companies, to the extent that a sharp upsurge of bullying behaviour in the workplace is highly likely.

In all cases, whether bullying takes place at an individual, group or corporate level, the efficiency and effectiveness of whole departments can suffer, organizational performance can slump and sectors where bullying is known to be rife earn unfavourable reputations. The status of entire professions can be badly damaged. Workplace bullying has been identified and investigated by researchers in a range of disciplines and fields, including the armed forces, the police, prisons, further and higher education, the church and the health services. Now, for the first time, research into bullying provides information on the extent of coercive behaviour across the cultural sector. No previous study of workplace bullying in the arts has taken place in the UK, beyond the inclusion of a single London dance company in a study that ranged across a number of employment sectors (Hoel, Cooper and Faragher 2001). As of the end of 2010, no evidence has come to light of such research having taken place outside the UK.

The research originated because of my personal experience of being bullied, and the fact that, as a consultant, I realized I was increasingly witnessing bullying behaviour in a number of different arts organizations. As soon as I began to question what was taking place, more and more colleagues came forward with stories of similar incidents occurring in the cultural sector. As a result, the initial guiding question was whether the behaviour represented isolated, rare occurrences in specific creative environments, or whether, as I suspected, it was indicative of a more widespread problem in the arts and cultural sector as a whole. Ultimately, the quantitative research findings revealed that two in five arts workers report being the target of a bully in their place of work – the highest level of bullying recorded in any single employment sector, as at the end of 2010.

About the Research

Ethnographic research is centred on gaining the worldview of a particular community of interest – here, people working in the arts – in order to achieve an understanding of how social or cultural phenomena are perceived – here, bullying behaviour. Every research journey has the potential to develop as it proceeds – an answer often begets another question. Alongside establishing that bullying does indeed exist, and is widespread, in order to comprehend how the practice is socially constructed, or how bullying behaviour is regarded, understood and/or tolerated among arts workers in the UK, it was logical to enquire further about how arts practitioners in the UK recognize and counter this behaviour in the workplace.

Modern anthropological ethnographies are studies based on long-term site-specific field research in the context of a particular society, history and culture and provide ways of obtaining a comprehensive and thorough look at everyday life and issues of special interest to the researcher (Schein 2003). These focus on a central guiding question that connects the specific area of study to larger questions about how culture works (Hall 2001). The central guiding question of the arts research evolved into: why do we in the cultural sector tolerate bullying? The connection to larger questions, for example about how culture works, is reflected both in terms of the place of the arts and the cultural industries in contemporary society, and in our expectations of those managing human resources in the arts. Guiding questions can encode within them larger questions regarding culture or social practice and, by refining and reducing, the focus of the interrogation became: does the arts environment permit or encourage bullying behaviour?

The cultural sector research establishes both its relevance to, and its commonality of interest with, other employment sectors. Examining a phenomenon such as workplace bullying is a delicate process and potentially raises contentious issues. Undoubtedly, an honest appraisal presents us with an uncomfortable reality; however gaining a clear understanding of bullying in the arts, and the ability to recognize and acknowledge it, is an important step towards finding ways to deal with it effectively. Enthusiastic and motivated arts workers are the lifeblood of creative organizations: bullying depresses, demoralizes and damages people. It is imperative, therefore, that the harmful and negative effects of this behaviour are resolved without further loss or detriment to the cultural sector.

About the Arts

Working or participating in the arts engenders excitement: to be involved in the imaginative creation of something new, or in an inventive new version of something old and (perhaps) revered, is an extraordinary experience. Enthusiastic arts workers are passionate about their work, notwithstanding the emotional roller coaster that often accompanies the creative process. This is evident from the personal histories recounted in the book. Many arts workers experience the arts as a calling, and this seems to be sanctioned by leading agencies in the field. According to Peter Hewitt, Secretary General of Arts Council England in 2003, as quoted by Davies and Lindley (2003):

> The arts are a growing source of employment and an increasingly important part of our economy ... The growth in employment opportunities in the arts has not seen any reduction in the personal commitment or the powerful sense of vocation of individuals working in the arts.

Traditionally, then, the arts have been regarded as a profession for which participants nurture a passion rather than the more prosaic desire to make money or advance a career. This love of the arts may go some way towards explaining the fact that earnings in cultural occupations are substantially less than those of similarly qualified professionals working in other fields and also that 73.5 per cent of arts workers perceive their pay to be low. Sadly, arts workers are very used to dealing with a lack of resources, so that although the current cuts in funding will have severe consequences on many of our companies, arts organizations have a history of resilience that is likely to enable many of them to deal with the hard times.

Notwithstanding the negative ramifications of the appendage of industry to every aspect of working life today, as in leisure industry, tourism industry and creative industry (Protherough and Pick 2002), a touch of romanticism still lingers about working in the arts and might be held to contribute to the assertion by arts managers that the arts are *different*. However, a detailed examination of the arts, in terms of how people behave and how they are treated, suggests that this sector is not so different from other employment fields. In considering those who govern, those who manage, and those who are employed – including those who are deemed to be *creative* – I found that very few real differences emerge.

I hope this book will make a modest contribution to the growing body of academic work on the topic of workplace bullying, offering some insight into bullying in a sector that has not previously been investigated. The case studies offer real-life examples of negative practice – a steer on 'what not to do' – and the research may be of interest to students of management, human resources, leadership and organizational behaviour, as well as of use to practitioners, managers and those who govern in the cultural and other sectors. For those who are campaigning against, or working towards solutions for, workplace bullying, I hope that the quantitative data about bullying in cultural organizations will be welcomed as a supplement to that from other employment sectors. I have no doubt that some of the incidents reported by survey respondents or contained in the case studies will reflect the experiences of some readers: if you have been a target of bullying and need help, please use the appendix to find appropriate support.

Acknowledgements

Heartfelt thanks to the many colleagues and friends in the arts, including those who participated in the early pilot studies, and the members of the Broadcasting, Entertainment, Cinematograph and Theatre Union (BECTU) who participated in the national research. Those who were willing to share their personal stories, particularly those who had direct experience of being bullied, displayed remarkable courage and fortitude, and will always have the author's respect and unstinting admiration as models of endurance in times of adversity. They have provided both inspiration and support in this endeavour and, ultimately, this book belongs to them: you know who you are.

Thanks, also, to the UK professional bodies who contributed appropriate information: Equity; the Independent Theatre Council; The Musicians' Union; and the Theatrical Management Association; as well as the Arts Councils in England, Northern Ireland, Scotland, and Wales. Thanks also to the UK-based anti-bullying campaigners, and to those from many different parts of the world, who have been generous with their information and with permission to cite examples of the important work they do. Particularly, thanks to those in the United States of America and Canada: the Domestic Abuse Intervention Project, Duluth, Minnesota, USA; Dr Elizabeth Englander, Director of the Massachusetts Aggression Reduction Center, USA; Anton Hout, Founder of OvercomeBullying.org, North America; Tamara Parris of Business Accountability, Toronto, Canada; Tom Starland, editor and publisher of *Carolina Arts*, USA.

A special thank you to Val and Terry in Languedoc Roussillon, France, who gave up their home for a month so that the author could enjoy the peace and solitude needed to complete the work. Martin West made it possible for this book to be written: he and his professional colleagues in the production team at Gower Publishing provided invaluable and comprehensive practical advice and assistance throughout the process, making constructive suggestions about the chapters and approaching the editing task with great care and skill. Thank you all.

I owe the biggest debt of gratitude to my husband and partner, Piers Jackson. His selfless encouragement and support has never wavered, even momentarily. He has been subjected to endless requests to read and reread drafts, and has done so without complaining – always making useful, perceptive and knowledgeable comments along the way. I could not have accomplished anything without him.

Anne-Marie Quigg Jackson
December 2010

CHAPTER 1

Bullying, Mobbing and Harassment

Bullying is offensive, abusive, malicious, insulting and/or intimidating behaviour that occurs on more than one occasion. The frequency of bullying behaviour precludes one-off incidents of aggression or violence; the most common type of bully encountered in the arts is the *serial bully* who picks on one employee after another and attempts to destroy them. A serial bully identifies a target and proceeds to systematically bully that person until they are forced to move on, either to another role in an organization or to another workplace altogether. Sometimes a serial bully is bullying more than one person at a time and when, usually, the bully has succeeded in destroying the target(s), another target is selected and the cycle of bullying behaviour begins all over again. In the case study below, a director in a privately owned company with a strictly hierarchical structure targets the Chief Executive Officer (CEO). Both perpetrator and target are mature, well-educated and relatively high-powered people in their individual circles.

THE ART GALLERY: HIERARCHICAL BULLYING/SERIAL BULLYING

In a small town, a privately-funded commercial gallery was opened to provide educational exhibitions, workshops and installations. The gallery's owner was London-based and the Board of Directors included a local, retired financial executive, Alastair. The owner appointed an art gallery manager: an intellectual, Hazel had experience in managing large exhibition centres and was a distinguished curator, a personable individual and an accomplished professional. From the time of her arrival to take up her post, Alastair made himself known to Hazel as the *eyes and ears* of the owner. In the early weeks following her appointment, he began to take a particular interest in the day-to-day running of the gallery, as well as the policy and governance issues appropriate to his remit as a company director.

A retired executive with time on his hands, Alastair developed the habit of ringing Hazel daily, often with trivial queries ostensibly connected with the work of the gallery, or to question her about income streams and expenditure. This continued for several weeks and then Alastair began to appear on site, often turning up unannounced. At Board meetings, it became apparent that Alastair had been *reporting back* to the owner, without consulting Hazel, on a number of different issues. His reports were not always accurate.

Hazel made it clear that his continual interference was having a serious effect on her ability to manage. As a result, Alastair reported to the owner that Hazel had admitted she was not coping with the job and, six months into her tenure, he moved himself into an office in the gallery, full time.

Alastair was extremely polite and courteous to all the gallery staff, including Hazel when other people were present, and he made a particular point of letting everyone know of his important role as sentinel for the owner. However, in Hazel's absence, he often made insulting and belittling remarks about her to other members of staff, especially about her intellectual capacity – describing her as a *know-it-all* – and her appearance. When alone with Hazel, his polite façade disappeared and he continually found flaws and weaknesses in the systems and procedures she had introduced, sometimes becoming angry and loud, and threatening that he could *have her sacked any time*.

Hazel's attempts to inform the owner of Alastair's actions and explain their effects were met with incredulity: the owner believed Alastair to be *looking after things properly*. During the following three or four months, Hazel's behaviour began to change. She became increasingly isolated from the rest of the staff and ceased to make her customary tours of the gallery to greet staff and visitors, only venturing out of her own office to leave the building. She was fearful of meeting Alastair and being drawn into one of his *discussions*, during which he took the opportunity to find fault with something she was doing, or not doing. Knowing that he was in regular contact with the owner, discussing topics to which she was not privy, she did not feel in a position to disagree when he suggested doing things in a different way. Other staff began to be affected by Alastair's constant patrolling of the gallery, and his tendency to draw them into conversations during which he often would make offensive and malicious remarks about Hazel.

Hazel became more and more withdrawn and began to worry incessantly about company meetings where, increasingly, Alastair adopted the role of reporting on every aspect of the organization's performance. Without her knowledge, he tabled financial papers he had drawn up and *evaluations* of staff performance, including her own, which contained negative personal comments, none of which were justified.

Unable to bear the situation any longer, Hazel left the gallery abruptly, and shortly afterwards so did several of her colleagues.

A new art gallery manager was recruited. The absentee owner's reliance on Alastair increased as he made it clear that he could provide consistency and stability during the handover period. His status and influence was enhanced and the incoming manager, Helen, although not apprised of the situation at interview, found that she had inherited a *live-in* company director. Helen had worked abroad for several years and had an array of qualifications in arts management. She was a bright and lively individual with an inquiring mind. After a few weeks, she had begun to get to know how the gallery operated, had met the remaining staff and had instigated recruitment procedures for new employees. Alastair had been abroad on holiday. When he returned he again began to take a particular interest in the day-to-day running of the gallery.

What followed was a duplicate of the type of behaviour and events that had resulted in Hazel's departure. After repeated bouts of sick leave, Helen, too, left abruptly and, shortly afterwards, so did several of her recently recruited colleagues. Alastair *held the fort* pending the next appointment.

(*Names and environs have been changed to protect confidentiality.*)

The relationship between employees and their managers is a crucial factor in determining the effective management of many arts organizations. In this case, the absentee owner placed all trust and confidence in a company director who happened to live locally, rather than in the professional CEOs who were employed. Both Hazel and her successor, Helen, were well qualified for the post they held. They had strong track records at national and international level, and were popular with staff. Initially, Alastair may have had a genuine interest in being *more involved* in the business of running the gallery; however his behaviour indicates that there was a high level of confusion about the respective roles of company directors and staff members within the organization – evidence of a lack of constructive leadership (Einarsen, Raknes and Matthiesen 1994, as reported in Rayner 1999: 34). Also, Alastair patently enjoyed his privileged access to the owner and, rather than use this to *build bridges* between staff and directors and to encourage incoming managers to share aspirations and concerns, he embraced management as personal politics (Watson 1986, as reported in Bratton and Gold 1999: 13), employing Machiavellian intelligence to render himself indispensable to the owner. Needless to say, Alastair's actions seriously impaired the succession strategy of the gallery: the arts world is a small world, and this post developed the reputation of being a *poisoned chalice*.

Bullying

Bullying is also known as mobbing, victimization or *le harcèlement moral* (moral or psychological harassment). These are the terms most commonly employed among researchers and they are almost, although not entirely, interchangeable. They can refer to destructive, harmful and intimidating behaviour among schoolchildren, in places of work and in militarized organizations. The physical environment in which intimidation takes place plays a part in determining the terminology used in different parts of the world.

The issue of workplace bullying has been investigated by a growing body of researchers, for example, Adams with Crawford (1992), Randall (1997), Rayner Hoel and Cooper (2002) and Lewis (2002); and the predicament of bullying targets has been exposed by champions seeking to give prominence to the issue, for example Field (1996, 1999, 2001) and Wheatley (1999). Adult bullying behaviour has resulted in court cases involving large sums of money (*The Guardian* 2005) and are making headlines, particularly where high-profile people or organizations are involved – such as the disclosure of bullying behaviour by UK television presenter Esther Rantzen, which received national publicity in 2006, and in 2010, the alleged bullying at the office of the former UK Prime Minister Gordon Brown. Trades unions and employers' organizations have been drawing attention to the issue — for example the Trades Union Congress (TUC 1999), the Public Service trade union (Unison 2003), Broadcasting, Entertainment, Cinematograph and Theatre Union (BECTU 2005), the Manufacturing, Science and Finance union (Amicus MSF 2006) and the Chartered Institute of Personnel and Development (CIPD 2006) – and against this background of validated research, confessional interviews and headline-grabbing, expensive, courtroom battles, awareness of workplace bullying is rising in many employment sectors.

The body of available knowledge is constantly growing, and as researchers have learned more about the underlying complexity of bullying behaviour and its implications, frequently a multidisciplinary approach is being taken and evaluation is becoming increasingly sophisticated. Research into workplace bullying now incorporates elements of psychology (Olweus 1993; Hoel and Cooper 2000), sociology (Lewis 2002) and social anthropology (Edgar and Russell 1998), as well as theories of management and organizational development (Rayner 1999; Ishmael with Alemoru, 1999). Important contributions to the growing body of literature continue to be made by psychologists in the psychosocial sciences, for example Ståle Einarsen and Dieter Zapf, those with a background in clinical psychology, such as Ruth Namie, and those in counselling, education, and training, such as Gary Namie. Methodologies now employ elements of anthropology, sociology and psychology, as well as theories of management and organizational development, thus promoting better understanding of the behaviour and an increasingly sophisticated evaluation.

One of the early pilot studies in the arts research was with arts managers in theatres and arts centres, almost all of whom were experienced line managers or employee supervisors. It revealed that 46.2 per cent of managers were aware of bullying behaviour; none stated that they had been targets or witnesses of bullying, although a few had been asked to take action on behalf of a complainant or management, or had been accused of bullying by a colleague. The managers who declared themselves to be unaware of bullying actually may have been so, or they may have been denying the existence of the phenomenon: most bullies are managers, and the later, national, survey found that half of those who had been targeted by bullies were line managers themselves.

A website survey enabled other arts workers to contribute their views, and the range of case histories compares and contrasts the experiences of bullied arts workers in eight separate settings. A major study in conjunction with BECTU involved a wide range of employees, including managers, in theatres and arts centres in the UK, and investigated whether arts organizations were guilty of corporate bullying because of unfair terms and conditions, such as working hours, rates of pay, attention to employee welfare, policies and organizational culture. This was particularly relevant in light of the fact that the arts managers considered some of the cultural sector's working terms and conditions to be *traditional*, with all that this implied.

The evidence gathered during the statistical research supports the existence of bullying in the performing arts. This is perpetrated by individuals – in the main by managers – and is widespread: in the national study two in every five people working in theatres and arts centres reported being targeted by a bully. Half of the members of the arts workforce were told of bullying by a colleague and over 46 per cent reported witnessing bullying at work.

The research literature tells us that bullying is destructive and damaging (Leymann 1996; Wilkie 1996; Field 1999; McKeown and Whiteley 2002) and there is ample evidence that this applies to individuals working in the performing arts specifically, and also to those in other arts organizations. There is an impact on physical health and/or mental welfare, and it is clear that there is sometimes permanent damage that affects the professional and personal development of some individuals. Bullying also has an economic impact on organizations – it mars organizational effectiveness, morale, attraction and retention of employees, and reputation. The arts sector comprises a range of small, medium and large organizations, and the damaging nature of workplace bullying is particularly hazardous in terms of personal and organizational welfare in those companies at the smaller end of the scale.

The majority of cases of workplace bullying regularly reported to the UK National Workplace Bullying Advice Line until January 2004, and thereafter to The Field Foundation and Bully Online, involve an individual being bullied by their manager, and these account for around 75 per cent of cases reported. Approximately a quarter of cases involve bullying and harassment by peers – often with the collusion of a manager, either by proactive involvement or by the manager refusing to take action. A small number of cases (around 1–2 per cent) involve the bullying of a manager by a subordinate. Serial bullies like to tap into hierarchical power, but they also generate their own power if they are enabled to bully with impunity, and successfully justify or deny their behaviour through rationalization, manipulation, deception or lying.

In 1996, Swedish psychologist Heinz Leymann noted that researchers in Australia and England used the term *bullying* to refer to intimidating behaviour whether in schools, the workplace or in military establishments, whereas elsewhere in Europe and in the USA *bullying* referred only to school settings and *mobbing* was used for workplaces. In France and French-speaking Canada, the terms *le harcèlement moral* and *le harcèlement psychologique* place special emphasis on attacks on the integrity of the individual and the psyche. The terminology used in courts in English-speaking Canada is *psychological harassment* or *mental harassment*. Other common terms used in different parts of the world include *psychological terrorization* and *horizontal violence*. The latter is used to refer to peer-to-peer bullying.

The earliest publications about bullying in schools appeared in Scandinavia in the early 1970s. Professor Dan Olweus, of the Research Centre for Health Promotion, University of Bergen, Norway, carried out an extensive, long-term research project on bullying in Sweden in 1970. In 1997–1999, he led a group in a substantial study that introduced the widely respected Olweus anti-bullying programme to schools in Norway (from 2003, this became the Olweus Bullying Prevention Program, or OBPP). Publications about mobbing in workplaces appeared over a decade after the 1970 study in Sweden (Gustavsson and Leymann 1984). Generally, mobbing was considered to have connotations of mental and emotional harassment, whereas a strong element of physical coercion was always included in definitions of bullying.

Today in the United Kingdom, Australia and New Zealand, growing awareness about bullying behaviour in the workplace has led to the term becoming synonymous with the more covert and subtle intimidation among adults, traditionally associated with mobbing and with psychological harassment. For example, the definition of bullying given in the Dignity at Work Bill, the UK employment legislation bill first introduced in 1997, which then ran out of parliamentary time is:

- behaviour on more than one occasion which is offensive, abusive, malicious, insulting or intimidating;
- unjustified criticism on more than one occasion;
- punishment imposed without reasonable justification; or
- changes in the duties or responsibilities of the employee to the employee's detriment without reasonable justification.

The definition does not contain any references to physical threats specifically; it covers behaviour between individual adults and also between employers, and their representatives, and employees. It provides greater clarity for individuals who use employment tribunals to seek redress against bullying (Ball 1998) and is the term most commonly used in the UK by:

- researchers, for example: Adams with Crawford (1992); Field (1996); Rayner (1997); Wheatley (1999); Salin (2001);
- campaigning organizations, for example: the Dignity at Work Partnership – a project jointly funded by Amicus and the Department for Trade and Industry; Bully OnLine – a project of The Field Foundation; Harcèlement Moral Stop – a French association for the fight against bullying at work;
- the media, for example: Cath Janes in *The Guardian* (February 2010); Colin Brown in *The Independent* (April 2010); Michael Herman in *The Times* (May 2010); Web pages, for example: BBC (2010) 'Manchester head teacher sacked after bullying claims.'

Tim Field's definition of bullying is expressed in the catchphrase *Those who can, do. Those who can't, bully,* which is repeated on every page of the extensive Bully Online website. This emphasizes factors associated with the personality of the bully, such as inadequacy and incompetency (Field 1996). The comprehensive information on the website outlines the drive by the perpetrator to act in a hostile way and describes how that is accomplished:

> *Bullying is a compulsive need to displace aggression and is achieved by the expression of inadequacy (social, personal, interpersonal, behavioural, professional) by projection of that inadequacy onto others through control and subjugation (criticism, exclusion, isolation etcetera).*

Further, and most importantly, Field (1999) goes on to explain (on the website) what enables the behaviour to continue and what nourishes it:

> *Bullying is sustained by abdication of responsibility (denial, counter-accusation, pretence of victimhood) and perpetuated by a climate of fear, ignorance, indifference, silence, denial, disbelief, deception, evasion of accountability, tolerance and reward (for example, promotion) for the bully.*

The case studies in this book provide examples of bullies who are often incompetent and unsociable in the workplace, and who target highly capable and popular individuals. The notion of what sustains bullying behaviour is also borne out: the absence of support in the arts workplace, in particular the lack of understanding and action on the part of management, emerges as a key factor in determining the outcome of the target's experience of bullying behaviour. Some arts managers also exhibit a Pontius Pilate approach – repudiating the existence of, and therefore any responsibility for, workplace bullying in their organization. At the same time many remove the bully to a new location, sometimes through promotion, rather than challenging, or dealing effectively with, the situation.

Types of Bullying

Definitions of bullying behaviour invoke subtle and slightly different meanings depending on our cultural backgrounds, the local connotations of the terminology, the perceived balance of physical and psychological factors, the number and status of the people involved as perpetrators and the nature of the place where the behaviour is happening. The term bullying continues to be used in the United Kingdom irrespective of the location of intimidation. Originally, Field identified 12 types of bullying – the number of definitions has now expanded – some of which overlap in one way or another. He employed qualifying prefixes for purposes of clarification, as in *serial bullying* – targeting one person after another– or *pair bullying* – joint action by two perpetrators and where a sexual link is often involved. Sometimes the sexual link is between the perpetrators, sometimes someone is bullied due to a former sexual link between them and one, or both, of the perpetrators.

Group or *gang bullying* – bullying by more than two people – is described here as *collective bullying* and is also known in the UK as *mobbing*. Collective bullying is common among children and young people, where often a gang leader emerges surrounded by acolytes who are in thrall through admiration, fear or both. Psychologist Professor Dan Olweus describes this core group of one or two henchmen (Smith and Sprague 2003) as *passive bullies*.

Among arts organizations, evidence of collective bullying as described by Olweus was not prevalent, although the case studies cite instances where bullying by a perpetrator was observed by others who were in a position to intervene – that is, who had sufficient status or power – but did not do so. Rather than passive bullies, these external onlookers might be defined as *accessories to bullying* in the sense that they witnessed bullying behaviour by a colleague and chose not to take action.

The other types of bullying identified are:

- *pressure bullying* or *unwitting bullying* – where the stress of the moment causes behaviour to deteriorate; however, generally, this is not regarded as a bullying problem, unless it happens repeatedly;
- *organizational bullying* or *corporate bullying* – where an employer abuses employees with impunity, knowing that the law is weak and that jobs are scarce;
- *institutional bullying* – similar to corporate bullying and arises when bullying becomes entrenched and accepted as part of the culture;
- *client bullying* – employees are bullied by those they serve (such as teachers being bullied by parents or pupils) or employees bully their clients;
- *secondary bullying* – often unwitting bullying which people start exhibiting when there is a serial bully operating who causes everyone's behaviour to decline;
- *vicarious bullying* – two parties are encouraged to engage in adversarial interaction or conflict;
- *regulation bullying* – a serial bully forces their target to comply with rules, regulations, procedures or laws regardless of their appropriateness, applicability or necessity;
- *legal bullying* – the bringing of a vexatious legal action to control and punish a person;
- *residual bullying* – the bullying of all kinds that continues after the serial bully has left, having bequeathed a dysfunctional environment to those who remain;

- *cyberbullying or cyberstalking* – the misuse of email systems or Internet forums, etcetera, for sending aggressive, flame mails.

Hierarchical bullying, peer bullying, horizontal bullying and *upward bullying* all indicate the direction of the behaviour. It is useful to consider these various designations in the knowledge that the first two, *serial bullying* and *pair bullying*, alongside *corporate bullying*, have been encountered most often in arts workplaces, as can be seen in the case studies. In effect, the other designations have more in common than not, and although interpretations may differ slightly, the word bullying serves as a comprehensive and easily recognizable term which is readily understood.

Corporate Bullying and Moral Harassment

As noted above, there is a range of descriptors when more than one person engages in bullying. Sometimes, an organizational regime is actually, or is perceived to be, oppressive. Consider how this relates to the fourth part of the Dignity at Work Bill, which describes the following as bullying:

> *changes in the duties or responsibilities of the employee to the employee's detriment without reasonable justification.*

Many arts workers have expressed the view that, as organizations owe a duty of care to their employees, those organizations that impose unfair terms and conditions should be regarded as engaged in *corporate bullying*. They argue that employees should be protected from oppressive working conditions, whether these are introduced as a result of changes to working practices or are already established as the norm. Elsewhere in Europe – in Sweden, France, Luxembourg, Spain and Belgium – corporate or organizational bullying is included in the legislation governing *moral harassment*. As the European Union (EU) seeks to harmonize national laws via adopting EU-wide directives, it is a positive step forward that the Equality Act 2010 in the UK includes harassment alongside discrimination based on protected characteristics, such as gender or age.

A useful and interesting example is a Private Bill, introduced in France on 14 December 1999, which defined moral harassment.

> *Moral harassment at work is: persecution by deliberate disadvantageous changes to workplace terms and conditions.*

According to this bill, and in the context of a situation where bullying is alleged, the intentional action by an employer or manager which changes workplace terms and conditions in such a way as to reduce the employee's chance of success or effectiveness would be held to be corporate bullying. The law (which was enshrined in the Labour Code) was updated in January 2003 to clarify that the onus is on *an employer* to justify any actions that have been construed by employees as moral harassment, and to introduce mediation procedures.

Terms and conditions are normally taken to refer to rates of pay, hours of work and entitlement to leave. However, they also apply to status, job title, location, physical environment and quality of working environment, including the social climate of the workplace (Hirigoyen 2000). In this light, the action of a manager, a board of directors or any governing body in altering any of these elements to the detriment of an employee may be judged oppressive behaviour: the perpetrator is responsible for deliberately creating difficulties for the employee, with the result that the employee's chance of failure in the workplace is increased. Several of the case histories in this book reflect instances of such detrimental changes, and actions of this type are recognizable as part of a pattern of bullying behaviour. Both companies and individual managers have been known to use such tactics to force retirement, redundancy or to make someone leave an organization.

In the UK, such actions can and do lead to claims of unfair, wrongful or constructive dismissal. In its 2008–09 Annual Report, the Advisory, Conciliation and Arbitration Service (ACAS) notes that workplace tension is continuing to rise amid an unstable employment landscape, in particular that the recession stimulated:

- a 22 per cent rise in unfair dismissal conciliation cases;
- an increase in other forms of employment tribunal; and that
- the demand for redundancy advice soared by almost three-quarters.

In terms of ensuring corporate responsibility for workplace bullying, however, the definition in the French law has obvious flaws. There are two variables that create difficulties: the elements of intent and change.

When detrimental changes are not deliberate, this could be termed creating disadvantage without intent; for example, an employee is moved to work with a new colleague or superior, perhaps by way of a promotion, and as a result becomes the target of a bully. If management can demonstrate that there was no intent to degrade the employee's working conditions, then this law indicates that management cannot be held responsible for the behaviour or its effects. This may be a relief for management if the bullying has gone unnoticed, but if that is the case, then it suggests that reporting procedures and internal policies are inadequate. Similarly, if management introduces into the workplace a new scheme, with the declared intention of improving the lot of employees – such as performance-related pay linked to specific targets, for example – then, even if some or all employees suffer a reduction in income, it may prove difficult to hold management to account and/or to determine if the targets set were unrealistic. In these circumstances, it may be difficult to establish if unrealistic targets were set in the first place.

Disadvantage may be dictated by organizational culture, or by custom and practice, and this is not necessarily as a result of *change*; for example, an employee, new to an organization, encounters a working environment where oppressive practices have become the established norm. In this case, management has not introduced any changes (saying that things have always worked this way), and the fact that terms and conditions might be held to be disadvantageous, *per se*, is not taken into account in the French law as it currently stands. It does strive to provide a degree of protection, and this should be considered carefully if similar legislation is proposed for the UK, bearing in mind that a more effective definition might read:

Moral harassment at work is: persecution by deliberate disadvantageous changes to workplace terms and conditions, or by failure to protect employees from maltreatment.

Mobbing

In 1996, Leymann noted that the term *mobbing* was used in the USA and in Europe – Sweden, Germany, Italy and elsewhere – to refer to bullying in workplaces. In the UK, however, the term is more likely to conjure up *collective bullying* – images of bullying by a mob or a gang. So, this is another descriptor for an experience involving more than one person who engages in bullying. In an item in *The Observer* (in April 2006), it was claimed that a young woman had been driven to the point of mental breakdown because she was subjected to *mobbing* by four female colleagues in her workplace. The article (Asthana 2006) described mobbing as:

> a non-sexual, non-racial harassment that can have serious consequences such as severe anxiety and post-traumatic stress disorder.

The woman sued her former employer, the global company Deutsche Bank Group Services founded in Berlin in 1870, for £1 million. The woman's case was successful, and it seems that *mobbing* was indeed a more suitable description of the behaviour as what she experienced was collective bullying.

Leymann's (1996: 165) own definition has connotations of bullying by more than one person:

> Psychological terror or mobbing in working life involves hostile and unethical communication … directed in a systematic manner by one or more individuals, mainly toward one individual, who … is pushed into a helpless and defenceless position and held there by means of continuing mobbing activities.

Leymann's definition expands on the abuse of power by the perpetrator in terms of its effect. The terminology – *helpless, defenceless* – and the suggestion that it is the perpetrator who has the capacity to determine the outcome connotes the status of victim. There has been debate among researchers, for example Leymann (1996), Field (1996), Randall (1997), about the use of these terms; that is, whether victim or target is more appropriate. This is further explored in Chapter 5 of this book, 'Being a Target'. He goes on to establish a statistical timeframe for the behaviour:

> These actions occur on a very frequent basis (… at least once a week) and over a long period of time (… at least six months' duration). Because of the high frequency and long duration of hostile behaviour, this maltreatment results in considerable mental, psychosomatic and social misery. (Leymann 1996: 165)

This time frame serves to make the very important distinction between a campaign of bullying behaviour, which is persistent and repeated, and isolated occurrences of bullying in the workplace involving loss of temper or outbursts of anger. The latter are as common in arts workplaces as in any other.

Harassment

Like bullying and mobbing, harassment is not an isolated incident of conflict in the workplace and several factors characterize it: frequency, length of time over which it takes place and severity of the effects on the target(s) of the behaviour. As indicated in the exploration of the French Proposition de Loi du 14 décembre 1999 (Draft Law of 14 December 1999), which deals with moral harassment, the role of *intent* needs to be examined closely. Some researchers indicate that, during and following confrontation about their actions, perpetrators of mobbing or bullying behaviour claim to be largely unaware that they are persecuting others, and that this is understandable (Vartia-Väänänen 2003). Other evidence suggests that bullies engage in campaigns of deliberate, degrading actions, the effects of which are calculated and even eagerly anticipated (Field 1996; Neumanand and Baron 1997).

As previously stated, moral harassment, or *l'harcèlement moral*, is a non-status-based form of workplace harassment recognized by the laws of several EU countries, and one of the most rapidly emerging workplace violence complaints. Although there is no internationally accepted definition of moral harassment, it may be understood generally as repeated, non-physical acts of harassment at the workplace, occurring over a significant time period, that have a humiliating effect on the victim.

In many European countries one or more independent groups combine the functions of lobbying for changes to legislation and providing support, advice and assistance to victims of bullying. One such example is *Harcèlement Moral Stop* (HMS) in France, which uses Marie-France Hirigoyen's definition of moral harassment. Marie-France Hirigoyen is a psychiatrist who has raised the profile of the bullying issue in France through her books about psychological stress in the workplace. She (1998) defines harassment as:

> *Abusive conduct by a superior or colleague, aimed at one or more persons over a period of time and carried out repeatedly and systematically, which is characterized by behaviour, actions, words and/or writing, and constitutes a serious attack on the personality and psychic integrity, deliberately degrading employment conditions, and making it impossible for those persons to continue working.*

Hirigoyen's definition begins by describing workplace harassment at an individual level, where a higher-ranking employee or a peer engages in one or more of a number of bullying activities over a period of time. These activities are not limited to derogatory remarks or verbal threats, either in private or in front of an audience, for example in meetings, rehearsals or other public or group situations. The definition extends beyond deeds and gestures whether these take place in private or in front of colleagues. The inclusion of writing acknowledges that harassment is not confined to real-time activity – it can be conceived and executed by a perpetrator at a distance from a target and may not always involve face-to-face contact. In terms of using the written word, the element of personal attack is key. An even-handed and balanced report about an employee's substandard work is not harassment; however, an unfair attack which disparages them is. An accurate appraisal noting poor performance is not harassment; however, an unjustly negative evaluation is. A terse letter or electronic communication is not necessarily intimidation, *per se*; however, a deliberately insulting or offensive tone in a letter or an email, especially when such a communication is a frequent occurrence or one of a range of abusive behaviours employed, is harassment.

The reference to *intent* is clear: the conscious aim of the action is to pollute the working environment so that it becomes unbearable, and the situation thereby becomes untenable for the target – they cannot continue working. It is as if the perpetrator sets out deliberately to unnerve and eventually *destroy* the target, at least in terms of their ability to continue working in the same place and/or at the same level. The intention is to undermine and to drive out. These are the characteristics of the *serial bully*.

A further section of the definition used by the French anti-bullying campaign, *Harcèlement Moral Stop*, notes that the behaviour can adversely affect the working environment:

> *Any abusive behaviour, particularly words, actions, gestures and/or writing, which attacks the personality, dignity or the physical or psychological integrity of a person, endangering their employment or degrading the social climate of the workplace.*

As above, weight is given to the fact that bullying behaviour can take many forms. Here, there is slightly more emphasis on the effect of conduct that assaults self-esteem or is threatening to the person. In addition to the notion that, in the workplace, it is vital to safeguard the human body from attack, for example via health and safety procedures, the importance of protecting the intellectual and emotional well-being of an individual is recognized. Also acknowledged are the consequences of bullying behaviour in respect of the target's ability to continue to work effectively. This view is reinforced by arts workers themselves who report that the results of bullying behaviour include increased levels of stress, repeated and worsening health problems, including mental health issues, frequent absenteeism and, in many cases, employees eventually leaving their place of employment. On some occasions, targets of bullying behaviour become too ill to work at all, or take an extended period of time to recover sufficiently to be able to work again.

Researchers in other employment sectors make reference to the degradation of the wider social climate in the workplace caused by bullying behaviours. Research in theatres and arts centres indicates that over 50 per cent of respondents were told of a bullying incident by a colleague, and more than 46 per cent had witnessed bullying. It seems that the issue is being widely discussed and witnessed in performing arts workplaces, and this is consistent with the assertion that arts workplaces where bullying is taking place develop a *bad atmosphere*, as related by the case studies.

This deterioration in the employment environment is characterized by intensely strained working relationships in places where bullying is known to be happening, particularly where it is conducted in a surreptitious way. Accounts also report an ambience in the workplace that is patently tense and uncomfortable as a result of workers tiptoeing around colleagues and/or superiors whose tempers are known to flare and where frequently recurring, unjustified public abuse is a feature of the bullying behaviour. In repeated cases, the behaviour of the bully oscillates between extremes: appearing friendly and jovial on one occasion, yet instantaneously capable of switching to being hostile and antisocial on another. This can happen in relation to one individual only or within the workplace as a whole. In both cases, after a number of these Jekyll and Hyde experiences, targets and witnesses become cautious of the apparently positive side of the bully, and the workplace atmosphere settles permanently into an unpleasant one in which the employees are constantly wary. Many survey respondents report that their own behaviour around the bully becomes atypically circumspect, increasing their personal stress levels and adding another layer of discomfort and tension to the already strained working environment.

The Perpetrator: Perspectives on Individuals Who Bully

As the vast majority of research findings on bullying are gathered from targets of bullying, the psychological and physiological distress caused by the behaviour is very well documented (Leymann 1996; Davenport, Elliott and Schwartz 1999; Clifton and Serdar 2000; Mikkelsen and Einarsen 2001). Health problems, both mental and physical, can be caused by bullying and by persistent exposure to other negative behaviours at work (Keashly, Hunter and Harvey 1997; Einarsen, Matthiesen and Skogstad 1998). Mikkelsen and Einarsen (2001) report that the well-being and productivity of other employees who witness, or are aware of, bullying behaviour is also affected, and there are links to rises in negligence, staff turnover and cases of sick leave (Cox 1987; Zapf, Knorz and Kulla 1996). The performing arts research indicates similar characteristics: the impact of an individual bully in the arts workplace is multidimensional and contagious.

There is less evidence on what motivates the perpetrator of workplace violence, although some studies have looked at how bullies and stalkers think and behave, for example, Schell and Lanteigne (2000), and the corrosive effect of the way in which tyrants operate:

> They depend on people giving up; feeling so demoralised that they cannot be bothered to fight. In the cycle of demoralisation, the doubts about oneself, one's motives, what course of action to take, undermines confidence. This plays into the tyrant's hands. They rely on the victim feeling that it is not worth bothering to take any action. (Crawford 1999: 87)

For example, Crawford further asserts that, in pursuit of complete subjugation, a ruthless manager will knowingly exploit a worker's loyalty to an organization and/or their economic dependency on their job. Arts workers have complained of being misused in such a way – being publicly castigated if complaints are made and having their commitment to the arts and to their organization openly doubted and ridiculed.

Archer (1999) noted that in organizations with a military structure, the behaviour of the tyrannical manager could be overtly encouraged and even imitated by others, particularly if the behaviour is perceived as that of *strong management*, which *gets things done*. In the arts case studies there are examples of individuals adopting bullying behaviour on the basis either that it is necessary to ensure that people deliver, or simply that it works – having observed that bullies receive plaudits for results, sometimes including promotion.

It has been suggested that the creation of the bullying personality has its roots in a dysfunctional childhood (Randall 1997: 73–88). Causes include confrontational, rejective, negative or inadequate parental or caregivers' influence, which has the effect of creating an adult with:

> an antisocial personality characterized by the aggressive manipulation of other people. (Randall 1997: 74)

Psychological violence in childhood may be the genesis of adult bullying, and there is evidence of a chain reaction of abuse: the abused child in a loveless environment experiences conflicting emotions, including fear, mistrust of others, envy, self-hatred, and an addiction to self-harm that battles with pent-up aggression (for example, Crawford 1992: 69–71). Many of the traits ascribed to bullies by researchers and observers of bullying behaviour indicate a psychopathic personality (for example, Field 1996: 54, Table 5). In the main, bullies are depicted as insecure, often cowardly, individuals with a high need for control and being right. They can be alternately charming and nasty, and are fundamentally dishonest (Wheatley 1999: 20–24). Beyond this, commentators have explored the themes of bullies as individuals who are socially inadequate and as people seeking to protect their own self-esteem. They have also expatiated on the function of the working environment in bullying behaviour (Einarsen et al. 2003: 168–173). All these factors are represented, to varying degrees, in the arts research. Some of the descriptors noted by Wheatley and Field correlate with the attributes of the creative personality, which is further discussed in Chapters 8 and 9 of this book.

When confronted about their actions, perpetrators of harassment, mobbing or bullying behaviour usually claim to be unaware that they are persecuting others. It is possible that bullies may not realize what they have done, or how their behaviour affects other people, given that it is difficult to admit to bullying as aggressive behaviour is socially indefensible (Vartia-Väänänen 2003). In the UK, for example, the Musicians' Union acknowledges that 'some individuals do not realize that what they are doing is being perceived as bullying' (Personal email to the author: 2010). In the main, however, the research suggests that many arts bullies engage in campaigns of deliberate, degrading actions, the effects of which are calculated and eagerly anticipated (as represented in Field 1996; Randall 1997). Particularly, the case studies support the notion that bullies deliberately and aggressively project their own social, interpersonal and professional inadequacy onto the person they target, who is usually competent and popular (Field 1999). The projection seems to enable the bully to avoid facing their own inadequacies, serving to distract and divert attention away from them, the effect of which is often to focus unfavourable attention on the behaviour of other staff. Here is the testimony of one arts worker:

> *The Board only ever gets the version of events as presented by the Chief Executive. I am quite sure that the Board would not condone bullying if they perceived that it was happening. A feature of many bullies is that they have a very plausible manner, such as their superiors cannot believe them capable of unpleasant behaviour. This leaves the employees in impossible situations; it appears that THEY are the problem.*

A number of issues highlighted in this example are repeated in other arts case studies: this Chief Executive is in a powerful position at the top of the staff team, accountable to the Board, to which the Chief Executive presents a subjective account of proceedings. The mechanism for other staff to present alternative views is not in place. The respondent believes that the Board would not sanction bullying behaviour; however, as all its information comes through the Chief Executive, she is also convinced that the Board lacks knowledge or awareness of the issue. The trait here attributed to the bully – of being skilled at producing persuasive arguments, especially ones intended to deceive – is a recurrent theme in descriptions of bullies. Normally, the Board of an arts organization appoints its Chief Executive and entrusts that person with the prime leadership role. A serious failure on the part of a Chief Executive reflects badly on the Board. During the research, several arts workers indicated that they had sought to inform senior personnel, including Board members, of bullying behaviour carried out by managers. They reported being faced with patent disbelief and stated that their complaints had been rebuffed out of hand. In many cases where one member of staff took a lead to coordinate approaches to management, the upshot was that this person was deemed to be an agent provocateur, and was labelled as a troublemaker. This echoes the experience of teachers who encounter unexpected, unusually disruptive, behaviour in a child who is normally well behaved. If the child has been subjected to bullying, the troublesome behaviour may be a presenting problem – masking their often frustrated attempts at retaliating a bully (Wilkie 1996).

When challenged, bullies often cite *incompetence* as a reason for repeated criticism of a particular employee – particularly if this is a subordinate. In fact, the research indicates that arts bullies discredit others because they are either seeking power or covering their own incompetency, or both. Status/position is the most-quoted reason employees give for bullying in theatres and arts centres, and 50 per cent of arts workers cite *competence* as the second most common reason for bullying behaviour; however, they are referring to *incompetent managers* who bully to cover their own lack of ability – sometimes this alludes to their skills at the job, and sometimes to social inadequacy.

Some bullies are loud, blustering and overtly aggressive; some are cold and manipulative, adept in social situations and able to charm superiors, whilst using subtle, indirect methods to bully others – a reason why complainants of bullying are often disbelieved. Arts workers noted, in particular, bullying by individuals who had been appointed to a variety of roles within arts organizations, especially in the voluntary sector, and who had a non-arts background. These included financial controllers – often accountants with no experience of working in an arts organization – and managers whose marketing or other relevant experience had been gained in the public or private sectors. This connects with the self-esteem factor identified by Zapf and Einarsen (2003), who note that social incompetence is one of three characteristics of bullying related to the personality of the bully (as reported in Vartia-Väänänen 2003: 16). Anecdotal evidence suggests that interactional difficulties are a feature of the personalities of bullies in the performing arts, and that the transfer of hostility to a target who is popular and competent is common. Another feature of of character-related bullying is that perpetrated by bullies who act to gain status or authority within an organization, rather than according to matters of principle – micropolitical behaviour. This was identified in the performing arts findings by 51.4 per cent of all respondents and was the most cited reason for bullying behaviour. Finally, character-related bullying can occur when self-esteem is threatened, and the perpetrator takes steps to regulate the situation by engaging in a campaign to subjugate and control – arts workers describe this as the bully's need to *punish* someone external to them, rather than take responsibility for their own feelings of low self-worth. These types of character-related bullying indicate poor management skills and demonstrate unconstructive leadership on the part of perpetrators (Rayner 1999: 34).

Beyond the dysfunctional childhood cited by Randall as a cause of bullying in adults, increasingly researchers are making links between adult bullies and other violence and conflict scenarios, including experiences of school bullying both as perpetrator and as target (Tattum and Tattum 1996), domestic violence (Rathus 1996) and personality disorders; and it is claimed that personality disorders, which cover a wide range of behavioural abnormalities, affect up to 13 per cent of the UK population (Batty 2004). Exposure to negative behaviour in childhood may result in adult bullying, especially if a child is subjected to humiliating behaviour by a dominant adult or other individual (for example, Randall 1997; Ishmael with Alemoru 1999; Clifton and Serdar 2000). School bullies have been found to have a high level of self-confidence, often characterized as *bravado*, and to tend towards aggression in many situations. They are also impulsive, reacting and responding to situations without prior thought or consideration (Olweus 1991). Further, studies of school bullying have explored inherited cycles of violence, making links between childhood, adolescent and adult bullying (see Figure 1.1):

> *A cycle of violence appears to occur in which children exhibit bullying behavior at an elementary school age, turn to more serious forms of harassment, dating abuse, and sexual abuse at high school age, and ultimately, to serious acts of violence as adults. These adults, in their own families, model the same behaviors to their children who in turn become bullies at school; thus the cycle continues. (Colvin et al. 1998)*

Opportunities to study bullying from the perspective of those who bully are not as plentiful as opportunities to access those who have been targeted. It does not require a great leap of the imagination or intellect, however, to begin to make connections between different types of aggression and the resulting abuse or violence, whether the behaviour presents itself as intimidation in the schoolyard, adolescent vandalism, hostility towards a partner, bullying in the workplace or political terrorism.

The Domestic Abuse Intervention Project in Duluth, Minnesota, developed the model of the Power and Control Wheel (Figure 1.2) to illustrate how (usually, male) perpetrators employed a variety of methods to dominate their partners (as reported by Rathus 1996: 132–134). At the hub of the wheel is the power and control to which the perpetrator believes they are entitled; at its perimeter, the violence, physical and sexual, which back up the tactics described in the segments. Radiating towards the perimeter are the actions themselves, many of which are familiar in the context of workplace bullying. The perpetrator is able to control the environment to such an extent that the targeted person is objectified, isolated and intimidated. Abusive behaviour promotes powerlessness in the targeted person and assists the perpetrator in the home to employ threats relating to children or to underline financial dependence.

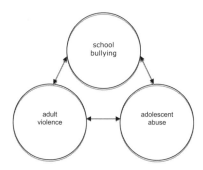

Figure 1.1   Cycle of violence

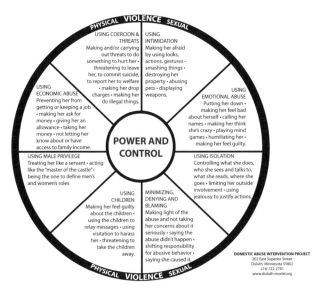

Figure 1.2   Original power and control wheel

If the model is adapted to reflect workplace bullying, it clearly indicates the psychological harassment endured by targets (Figure 1.3). Elements of emotional, political, social, economic and technological abuse are used in the workplace, and in some cases bullying is overlaid with racial, sexual or disability discrimination. This adapted model serves to illustrate the shared features of domestic violence and workplace bullying: in this instance the perpetrator's aim in the place of work is to trivialize the target's role and to destroy their sense of fulfilment and job satisfaction, usually with the ultimate aim of making them leave their employment.

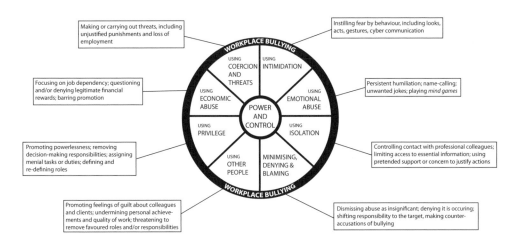

Figure 1.3   Power and control wheel modified for workplace bullying

Source: Adapted from the Power and Control Wheel developed by The Domestic Abuse Intervention Project, Duluth, Minnesota, USA.

The elements that characterize domestic abuse are very relevant to workplace bullying, as outlined in the comparative table, Table 1.1, where features of domestic abuse are aligned with their counterparts in a bullying scenario. In Table 1.1, threats relating to colleagues and other people connected with the workplace supplant those relating to children. Similarly, privilege connoted by status or position supplants male privilege in the domestic abuse model.

Table 1.1   How workplace bullying parallels domestic abuse

Behaviour	Domestic Violence	Workplace Bullying
Using intimidation	Making her afraid by using looks, acts, gestures; smashing things; destroying her property; abusing pets; displaying weapons	Instilling fear by behaviour, including looks, acts, gestures, cybercommunication
Using emotional abuse	Putting her down; making her feel bad about herself; calling her names; making her think she's crazy; playing mind games; humiliating her; making her feel guilty	Persistent humiliation; name-calling; unwanted jokes; playing mind games
Using isolation	Controlling what she does, who she sees and talks to, what she reads, where she goes; limiting her outside involvement; using jealousy to justify actions	Controlling contact with professional colleagues; limiting access to essential information; using pretended support or concern to justify actions
Minimizing, denying and blaming	Making light of the abuse and not taking her concerns about it seriously; saying the abuse didn't happen; shifting responsibility for abusive behaviour; saying she caused it	Dismissing abuse as insignificant; denying it is occurring; shifting responsibility to the target; making counter-accusations of bullying
Using children or using other people	Making her feel guilty about the children; using the children to relay messages; using visitation to harass her; threatening to take the children away	Promoting feelings of guilt about colleagues and clients; undermining personal achievements and quality of work; threatening to remove favoured roles/responsibilities
Using male privilege or using privilege	Treating her like a servant; making all the big decisions; acting like the 'master of the castle'; being the one to define men's and women's roles	Promoting powerlessness; removing decision-making responsibilities; assigning menial duties or tasks; defining or redefining roles
Using economic abuse	Preventing her from getting or keeping a job; making her ask for money; giving her an allowance; taking her money; not letting her know about or have access to family income	Focusing on job dependency; questioning and/or denying legitimate financial rewards; barring promotion
Using coercion and threats	Making and/or carrying out threats to do something to hurt her; threatening to leave her, to commit suicide, to report her to welfare; making her drop charges; making her do illegal things	Making and/or carrying out threats, including unjustified punishments and loss of status and/or employment; making official false accusations; ensuring complicity in dubious activity

Source: The information under the headings Behaviour and Domestic Violence is from the Original Power and Control Wheel (see Figure 1.1) from the Domestic Abuse Invention Project in Duluth, Minnesota. The information under the heading Workplace Bullying is that of the author.

Profile of an Arts Bully

Randall's (1997: 16–17) description of dysfunctional childhood, the cycle of violence outlined by Colvin et al. (1998) and the Power and Control Wheel adapted from the Domestic Abuse Intervention Project's model offer important information about how oppressive behaviour can be learned and the techniques that perpetrators use. In the arts research, one manager admitted to bullying 'when necessary'. An analysis of the survey data yielded the following characteristics about her (her comments are reproduced as quotes):

White female, 25–34 years old, working in arts management full time in the north-west of England. She has been in her current post for six–ten years, has had on-the-job work-related training and is directly line-managing one or more of the 50–100 employees in the organization where she works. She rarely works longer than 40 hours per week – once or twice a year – and when this is required she normally gets less than one week's notice. In her organization, taking time off is not encouraged, and opinion is divided in the workplace about whether employees could complete their work without working longer hours. In her opinion, management looks upon objections to working hours with hostility and resentment, and whilst there have been objections to working hours, these were informal, and 'never discussed with management'. She does not know what happened to the objectors afterwards.

This manager considers her average weekly pay to be high – there have been no complaints about pay in her organization – and she acknowledges that, 'sometimes', other people's pay is less for the same job. She 'rarely' receives other benefits that add value to her salary and believes that 'often' management cannot afford to pay higher wages. No one in her organization would be afraid to complain about pay, and scarcity of work would never be a reason to accept any wage offered. She would not prefer to work longer hours because overtime is payable ('rarely'), although, 'often', with overtime, her average weekly pay is generous. If wages were increased she would prefer not to work overtime at all, 'sometimes'.

This manager states that workplace bullying is 'not uncommon' – the chief reasons, in her view, being ethnic origin/race, sexual orientation, popularity, religion and 'socialists/commies'. The frequency of bullying has not changed in the past 12 months or five years and, besides bullying people herself 'when necessary', she has witnessed one or more bullying incidents. Complaints of bullying behaviour have been settled satisfactorily by management and to the satisfaction of the complainant, 'sometimes', but this varies. Her organization has written policies covering: direct insults in front of colleagues; arbitrary withholding of information, cooperation or arrangements; and physical assault, for example, throwing objects. Her organization does not condone bullying, but has not given any consideration to having a bullying policy. She does not think there is a role for BECTU in helping to stamp out bullying behaviour in the workplace and states instead that 'BECTU must be dissolved'.

Of note here is the lack of job-related training beyond what has been learned in office, despite the line-management responsibilities. This manager considers herself fortunate to be employed in a high-paid position requiring little additional time beyond her normal working week of 40 hours maximum: she is satisfied with her terms and conditions of employment. Whilst she acknowledges that her employers are unsympathetic to complaints about working hours, she confidently asserts that scarcity of work should 'never' be a reason to accept any wage offered.

She is familiar with bullying behaviour – it is 'not uncommon' – and besides the blatant reasons she offers for this occurring – that is, evident physical and cultural differences such as race, gender, creed and politics – she identifies popularity as a cause. During the research, 'status, popularity and competence' were cited as the principal reasons for bullying by both bullied and non-bullied arts workers alike. Bullies may be seen to be prone to personal and professional jealousy, which in this context can be described as experiencing one or more of the following emotional reactions:

- feeling bitter and unhappy because of another's social, educational or professional advantages, their personal attributes, or their real or perceived good fortune, especially in terms of opportunities for advancement;
- feeling suspicious or mistrustful of a colleague's influence, especially in regard to an issue or an individual that is perceived to be of central importance to the instigator, to the extent that this colleague is judged to be a rival or competitor;
- possessively watchful of someone in everything that they do.

This last reaction is reminiscent of stalking, whereby one individual persistently and obsessively harasses another with inappropriate attention. In the UK, the Protection from Harassment Act 1997, which was initially used occasionally, but in the last five years has been used more frequently, for bullying cases, was heavily used when it first came into force to deal with domestic violence, including stalking offences. Finally, this manager dismisses any role for the trades unions in dealing with workplace bullying; in effect she dismisses trades unions altogether, and in the context of her remarks about bullies targeting socialists and 'commies', it is clear she resents the union's status and influence in her arts workplace. It must be emphasized that this last view is not a common view among the respondents in the national survey, 84.3 per cent of whom wanted BECTU to have an active role in stamping out bullying behaviour. One comment in this respect from another manager was that 'the trades union should be encouraging employees to approach management in confidence'. The desire of this arts bully to see the trades union 'dissolved' should give pause for thought, even if the view expressed was a bizarre attempt at humour or sarcasm. This is not an attitude that reflects good governance, best practice in arts management or quality leadership, and it does the arts and cultural sector a considerable disservice.

2 *Researching the Bullying Experience*

Researchers have employed a variety of approaches to workplace bullying, resulting in a multiplicity of studies in many different contexts and a diversity of interpretations of the findings. Across a range of research fields, these perspectives include views on individuals who bully (Chapter 1) and on the bullying organization (Chapter 4). In social research generally, the basic core assumptions about the nature of the social world encompass premises that are metaphysical – concerned with the ultimate nature of reality; epistemological – concerned with the nature and scope of knowledge and belief; and moral – concerned with the lesson to be learned from a phenomenon or an event. Social theory refers to the use of theoretical frameworks to explain and analyze social action, social meanings and large-scale social structures.

Social Theories

The field is interdisciplinary, drawing ideas from, and contributing to, branches of knowledge such as anthropology, economics, history, literary theory, philosophy, sociology and theology. Some social theories make philosophical attempts to answer the question What is? rather than What should be? Other analytical social theories, such as neo-Marxist theories and feminist theories (see below), argue that as theories are generally based on premises that entail normative positions (what should be), it is necessary to assess the ideological aspects of theories. Sociological theory is often complementary, so that one frame of reference works alongside another to give a fuller picture. Some of the major general sociological theories and disciplines (and their variants) include the following theories and disciplines.

CONFLICT THEORY

This emphasizes the role of power and persuasion using force or threats to enable one individual or social group, at variance with another, to successfully compete. It suggests that society consists of different interest groups striving to gain control of resources; that even where there is apparent cooperation between those controlling different assets and means of production, there is always a constant power struggle going on; and that social groups will use their influence and power to their own advantage, often placing their opponents at a disadvantage as a result. The dominated groups will then contend with others in an effort to gain control; however most of the time the controlling group, which of course has the most resources, will maintain their position or gain new power.

In the cultural sector, arts organizations are in competition for funds because these are limited, and they are in competition with each other in the sense that part of the remit they share is to attract quality people as members of staff, funds, media attention and audiences. It is extremely rare, however, for arts organizations actively or overtly to work against each other. In fact, in recent years, companies have begun to work increasingly collaboratively. Conflict theory may apply to the internal workings of specific organizations – what we may regard as office politics – and, in these circumstances, it would contribute towards an explanation of the prevalence of workplace bullying.

ETHNOMETHODOLOGY

This is a discipline that enables the study of how people make sense of what others say and do in the course of day-to-day social interaction; it is concerned with how human beings sustain meaningful interchanges with one another. The goal of ethnomethodological investigations is to arrive at a description of the methods employed by human beings – real people in real settings – in the production of the orderly character of everyday life. It is different to statistical and analytical sociological methodologies – its focus is on description.

As a way to research human behaviour in the cultural sector, a longitudinal ethnomethodological study would provide the opportunity to observe and record at first hand how arts workers interact in the workplace and how behaviour, both positive and negative, is perceived. Such a study may yield a unique insight into views on behaviour in the creative environment and provide a route to comprehending the reason why bullies are often in denial about their behaviour, choosing to attribute it to misinterpretation on the part of the target.

FEMINIST THEORY

Feminist theory focuses on gender inequality and seeks to understand how male dominance has shaped society. Themes include oppression, objectification, patriarchy and stereotyping, and these have an obvious connection with *macho management*, which has a strong correlation with bullying. However, bullies are not exclusively male, nor are targets exclusively female, and bullies appear just as often to be covert and manipulative (which could be held to be a feminine trait) as they appear to be overtly aggressive.

INTERPRETATIVE SOCIOLOGY

This is a process in which outside observers (such as anthropologists) of a culture relate to a subcultural group or an indigenous people on the observer's own terms. It relates to a non-empirical, empathic approach to understanding social phenomena. Such an approach may provide useful insights to help in the understanding of how bullying behaviour affects specific individuals and groups in their own settings; however it would be unlikely to provide a verifiable empirical analysis of, for example, the frequency of bullying behaviour, and similar quantitative evaluations.

RATIONAL CHOICE THEORY

The main thrust of this theory is that all action is fundamentally rational in character, based on reason and logic, and that people calculate the likely costs and benefits of any action before deciding what to do.

SOCIAL CONSTRUCTIONISM

This is a sociological theory of knowledge – or an epistemological position – that considers that social phenomena develop in particular social contexts: we create the society in which we live, so our social life is one that is actively and creatively produced by human beings. There are many variants.

Social phenomenology

This is, literally, the study of phenomena, that is, how things appear in our experience, or the ways in which we encounter things. Thus it represents the significance things come to have according to our experience of them. Phenomenology studies conscious occurrences from the subjective or first-person point of view.

Social positivism

Social positivism is the belief that social processes should be studied in terms of cause and effect, and using the scientific method. It is a position that holds that the goal of knowledge is simply to describe the phenomena that we experience; thus, the purpose of research is focused on what we can observe and measure, and knowledge of anything over and above that, a positivist would hold, is impossible.

Structural functionalism

This is also known as a social systems paradigm. It addresses what functions various elements (microcosms) of the social system perform in regard to the entire system – the macrocosm. By restoring equilibrium and increasing social cohesion, functionalists believe that most social problems can be solved.

Symbolic interactionism

Symbolic interactionism examines how shared meanings and social patterns are developed in the course of social interactions. The goal of social interaction is communication with others and, in particular, the meaning of objects, events and behaviours is believed to come from the interpretation people give them, and interpretations vary from one individual to another, and from one group to another.

Dramaturgical perspective

This is a specialised symbolic interactionism paradigm, developed by Erving Goffman, an American sociologist and writer (1922–1982), that sees life as a performance. Goffman uses phenomenology to understand how humans perceive the interactions that they observe and take part in. To Goffman there is no single underlying truth, but interpretations that are real to each individual: we might say that each human being constructs their own personal reality.

Sociological Theories and Disciplines in Bullying Literature

Some of these theoretical positions are particularly interesting and relevant in relation to bullying. Conflict theory argues that society is not about solidarity or social consensus, but rather about competition, and in constant conflict over resources. It was developed in part to illustrate the limitations of structural-functionalism. The structural-functional approach holds that society tends toward equilibrium and focuses on stability at the expense of social change. One of the primary contributions conflict theory presents over the structural-functional approach is that it is ideally suited for explaining social change, a significant problem in the structural-functional approach.

In reviewing the bullying literature, Keashly and Nowell (2003) note that Hoel, Rayner and Cooper (1999: 221) argue from the perspective that it is important to view bullying as conflict, and describe severe bullying as destructive conflicts going beyond the point of no return, and that Zapf and Gross (2001: 499) describe bullying situations as long-lasting and badly managed conflicts. Glasl (1994) set out a model for conflict escalation in which nine stages of conflict are described, ranging from initial irritation between parties to a total war of destruction. Other researchers have also sought to map the conflict domain. Einarsen (1999) asserts that there are at least two types of bullying: predatory and dispute-related (Keashly and Nowell 2003: 339). The former type of bullying became familiar territory during the arts research process, and is exemplified by perpetrators seeking out targets where no prior conflict or provocation has been evident. Examples are found in the case studies, notably The Ensemble, The Art Gallery, The Theatre Project and The Playwright.

Einarsen (1999) proposes that dispute-related bullying arises out of a grievance where retaliatory action is taken, sometimes resulting in one party dominating and becoming more powerful than the other. Again, the imbalance of power in the bullying scenario is evident from the arts case studies, and Keashly and Nowell (2003) investigate the similarities and differences between bullying and conflict through analysis of behaviour, strategies for managing conflict, status of perpetrators and targets, and the escalation of conflict. They conclude that describing bullying solely in terms of a conflict situation is harmful to the target:

> Applying the label of conflict wholesale without qualification also creates the sense of shared responsibility for the bullying, and the victim may be expected to manage the situation on his/her own or, in some cases, be held accountable for the hostility exhibited by the other person. (Keashly and Nowell 2003: 355)

This notion of shared responsibility for bullying is evident in the literature on school bullying (for example, Olweus 1993, Randall 1997) and, on balance, Keashly and Nowell (2003: 356) advise that bullying should not be described as a conflict, but rather they urge researchers, practitioners and others to consider what a conflict perspective might offer in terms of reaching an understanding of this extremely hostile and devastating phenomenon. The arts case studies indicate that bullying is a result of conflict in some cases – where a disagreement arises in The Contemporary Dance Studios, for example – but, as previously stated, not in others. Conflict theory may offer useful guidance in terms of techniques to address some circumstances in which workplace bullying takes place, but it cannot be held to be applicable universally to bullying situations.

The more familiar assumptions within social theory include positivism and antipositivism, materialism and idealism, determinism and free will, individualism and collectivism. Positivism is described as the belief that the existence of objects stems solely from their measurement (Cook and Payne 2002). This includes, for example, calculative analysis of written contributions, as well as numerical data. Zapf, Einarsen, Hoel and Vartia (2003: 122) carried out a systematic analysis of empirical findings on bullying in the workplace across European studies, demonstrating converging results in the various European countries. Their findings identify similarities between the various types of research that have been undertaken, and a set of conclusions which broadly supports the conclusions of others, although they also call for more rigorous studies to further substantiate the concept of bullying in the workplace. In the arts research, the quantitative data gathered during the national survey proved a useful source of baseline information and further empirical studies would add value to this initial work.

Whilst the collection of quantitative data has its place, those social scientists concerned with antipositivism or phenomenology seek to create and to use scientific methods to study human behaviour and society, and those are methods used in the field of the natural and the formal sciences. Phenomenology is a philosophical stance, rather than a research method, but of course it may well influence the research methods chosen. Although quantitative methods can be used to assess the impact of bullying behaviour by analysing language, for example, qualitative researchers, and especially phenomenologists, argue that these measurements lack depth and therefore do not really get to the essence of the bullying experience. Phenomenologists hold that research should focus on how people experience a phenomena such as bullying, what it means to the individual and how that meaning is constructed. This is a view that is in direct opposition to the more positivist (quantitative) perspective common to most of the sciences. Whereas positivism sees the world objectively and seeks to discover absolute truths or scientific theories that explain these truths, phenomenologists reject this objective approach, emphasizing the importance of interpretation on the part of the researcher. The research approaches that phenomenologists tend to adopt are known as emergent designs in which the question under investigation may actually change as the research proceeds and the data is analysed. It is argued that phenomenological approaches offer ways of understanding the world that other research methodologies do not. It is more interpretative – some have even argued poetic – than the so-called objective approaches characterized as scientific method.

Bullying is a problematic subject because, at an individual level, it deals with interpersonal differences that can be held to be open to a variety of interpretations and, at the corporate level, acknowledgement of its existence is an indicator of the abuse of power, and of socially unacceptable disharmony and conflict. The investigation of bullying behaviour is, therefore, a delicate task for the researcher, requiring a great deal of sensitivity, because bullying involves experiences of violence, exploitation and negative behaviours. Research into bullying calls for the identification of appropriate methods of eliciting and validating data and incidents. When dealing with self-professed targets of bullying behaviour, the researcher must be conscious of the severity of the distress caused by the experience, which often re-emerges in the retelling. When examining information presented by alleged bullies, or observing negative behaviours, an objective assessment is vital if the evidence is to be accurately represented. In the corporate domain, the context in which information is presented is essential, as employers' and employees' views of the same set of circumstances are likely to diverge.

During the arts research both quantitative and qualitative information from targets was relatively easy to obtain via respondents to surveys, both online and written, and through formal structured interviews, as well as informal non-structured interviews. Colleagues in the arts have also contributed personal histories, and candid views, providing a focus on a number of key areas of the issue. Overwhelmingly, there has been a willingness to contribute information, and for many people a sense of urgency aligned with the importance of doing so, alongside a strong reluctance to be identified. This was notably the case where the interviewees' experiences were particularly painful and/or relatively recent; however, even when incidents had happened some time in the past, some people simply found it was too daunting to relive their trauma and they were advised and encouraged to withdraw from the process.

Objectivity and Ethics

Anthropologists have long since acknowledged that ethnographic research is not objective research because we bring to any research project ourselves, complete with personal histories and identities, and our own 'interpretive lenses' (Hall 2001). Despite this, the sensitive nature of workplace bullying as a research topic was such that apparent or perceived non-objectivity would have been to the detriment of the validity of the work. The only ethical approach to the research was to aim to be, as far as possible, completely transparent, objective and fair.

In research and analysis it can be difficult to establish true objectivity or impartiality as researchers have a stake in the results of their work; this means that the type of objectivity that is promoted is intended as a check on partiality. In this sense, objectivity means reproducibility – an objective test is one that produces the same results regardless of who scores it. Thus, to be objective, the data gathered during the arts research had to be analysed in accordance with standard, acceptable procedures, and the mechanisms used to achieve this had to be above reproach.

Transparency is another important aspect of objectivity: the data had to provide sufficient information to allow others to test the findings through replication. Often, openness can extend to the sharing of data sets, as long as all necessary confidentiality can be maintained; however, in this research into bullying behaviour a high degree of privacy was requested by or offered to participants, a fact which might compromise the sharing of baseline information. It was therefore necessary to be fair, in the sense of not exhibiting any bias (objectivity, again). In early pilot studies two different routes were taken to canvass opinion from managers and arts workers, and the findings varied considerably. In the national study, therefore, it was important to ensure that both managerial and non-managerial arts workers were included in the sample, that they were asked exactly the same questions and given the same opportunities to contribute additional information as they so wished.

In pursuit of an equalitarian approach, it is necessary to consider whether arts managers in the pilot study who stated that they had no awareness of bullying behaviour in the workplace might be:

- accurately describing their reality, because bullying did not exist in their workplace;
- inaccurately describing their reality, because bullying did exist in their workplace, but they were ignorant of its existence;
- inaccurately describing their reality, because bullying did exist in their workplace, but they were dissembling in order to protect themselves or their organization.

In the same spirit of openness, it has to be recognized that respondents to the online pilot survey were self-identified victims of bullies, with all that this implies. Without this objectivity or supposed distance it is difficult to claim insight into cultural practices and the basis of ethnographic authority under these conditions is unclear.

It is unlikely that there is only one single truth to be discovered in a research situation (Rayner, Sheehan and Barker 1999) and adopting a single standpoint from which to judge all cultures and ways of being in the world is to deny cultural relativism, which is the principle that we should not judge the behaviour of others using the standards of our own culture, and that each culture must be analysed on its own terms. With regard to workplace bullying, it became essential to see various perspectives as positioned (Abu-Lughod 1991), and the things learned in the field as partial truths (Clifford 1986). This goes some way towards explaining that, during the early pilot studies, there seemed to be a huge gap in understanding, knowledge and experience between the participants who reported bullying to be common and increasing in frequency, and the managers who denied its existence except on rare occasions. Also, it begins to explain why bullies often do not see their own behaviour as oppressive in any way.

Reflexivity impacts on the ethics of conducting such research. The desire to be seen to be objective was increased as a result of being an investigator who had direct experience of bullying, and had witnessed it within a range of arts organizations. In designing the methodology, two-tier triangulation offered a means to ensure results and conclusions were based on more than one research activity: on level one, the research comprised the bifurcated pilot (website survey and postal survey) plus unstructured interviews; and on the more profound level two, it comprised the pilot, plus the survey of Broadcasting, Entertainment, Cinematograph and Theatre Union (BECTU) members, plus comprehensive case studies. The combined research methodology offered the opportunity to give lengthy, and at a distance, consideration to the topic.

Cloaking and Confidentiality

In considering the guiding questions about workplace bullying it was apparent at the earliest stages that there was likely to be resistance to free and open discussion of such an uncomfortable topic. Accordingly, a light touch was used.

Bullied adults, or those who report having witnessed or heard about bullying behaviour, were considered to be vulnerable interviewees because bullying is a form of abuse. This vulnerability places targets and witnesses in the category of individuals in a dependent or unequal relationship because their experience has rendered them powerless. Employees who perceive that they are targets of corporate bullying are economically dependent on their employers (Crawford 1999; see also Biderman's Stages of Oppression, Chapter 5, and the Power and Control Wheel, Chapter 1, Figures 1.2, 1.3 and Table 1.1). Even if a balance of power exists among individuals, this is no longer in place following bullying behaviour (Einarsen 2000; Knorz and Zapf 1996, as reported in Zapf and Gross 2001).

Researchers are morally obliged to be honest and open about their work; however, in some instances it is recognized that there is a need to prevaricate, for example, with some types of medical research:

> As a general rule, deception is not acceptable when doing research ... Using deception jeopardizes the integrity of the informed consent process and can potentially harm your participants. Occasionally exploring your area of interest fully may require misleading your participants about the subject of your study. For example, if you want to learn about decision-making practices of physicians without influencing their practice-style, you may consider telling them you are studying 'communication behaviors' more broadly. The IRB [Institute Review Boards for the Protection of Human Subjects] will review any proposal that suggests using deception or misrepresentation very carefully. They will require an in-depth justification of why the deception is necessary for the study and the steps you will take to safeguard your participants. (Callahan 1998)

So when is it permissible to deceive? There does not appear to be a simple answer; however, psychologist Michael Eysenck proposes that the less potentially damaging the consequences of the deception, the more likely it is to be acceptable.

In terms of research into workplace bullying, exposure of a bully could be damaging for both individual and collective perpetrator(s), potentially in terms of reputation, cost and legal action. However, the behaviour being investigated is acknowledged to be damaging also, arguably more so because of its profound and long-term effects on individuals and organizations. The purpose of the research was not hidden; however, it was put into a context deemed acceptable to each particular group involved. This cloaking of the research topic, in the sense of shrouding or wrapping the issue of bullying, rather than not revealing its presence at all, was intended to dilute the effect or impact temporarily rather than to deliberately mislead. For example, in the pilot study of managers, the topic of workplace bullying was introduced as part of an examination of stressors in the arts workplace, the other stressors being hours of work and complaints procedures. Responses in all these areas were duly analysed and, although bullying was the issue of central concern to this research, comments on the other stressors also provided valuable responses that informed the later appraisal of terms and conditions that apply to working in the arts.

Although the central subject matter was cloaked in this way, a definition of workplace bullying was provided in order to clarify and to aid recognition of the behaviour. With hindsight, this was an important and useful definition to have provided. In the absence of that definition, it could have been assumed that the failure of managers to recognize the existence of bullying might have been due to ignorance of the precise nature of the behaviour. Instead, the definition enabled respondents to avoid the tendency to report minor differences of opinion, practical jokes or general disagreements in the workplace as bullying. Rather, such instances can be described as:

> *Pressure bullying or unwitting bullying ... where the stress of the moment causes behaviour to deteriorate; the person becomes short-tempered, irritable and may shout or swear at others. Everybody does this from time to time ... This is 'normal' behaviour and I do not include pressure bullying in my definition of workplace bullying. (Field 1996)*

As it was, the designation was clear and unambiguous, and the failure to recognize its existence must be interpreted differently.

From the outset, it was apparent that participants in the research, particularly targets of bullies, would need to be confident that there would be no adverse or damaging consequences as a result of their participation. Preserving their anonymity was critical to securing their involvement, and it was considered ethical to offer anonymity to all participants. Thus assurances of confidentiality were given to interviewees, online respondents and national survey participants alike. This decision is upheld by psychologists who, like Eysenck, emphasize the need for researchers to protect those who take part in a study. Nonetheless, the need to protect participants from stress – however this might be created (Eysenck 2004) – leads to another ethical dilemma for researchers of workplace bullying: how to justify the level of psychological, emotional, social or physical distress that may be incurred by allowing or encouraging participants to relive negative experiences, with all that this implies.

Eysenck's view prompts the question: are the consequences of *not* investigating bullying behaviour more damaging than the effects of the research? In a paper on research methods in psychology, he explores some of the difficulties of telling the truth about the purposes of certain types of research; whilst obtaining consent and avoiding deception is a key ethical issue in research with human participants, he concludes that to deny the ability to deceive altogether would put a halt to many valuable research programmes and that many forms of deception are entirely harmless:

> *For example, some memory researchers are interested in incidental learning, which involves people's ability to remember information they were not asked to remember. This can only be done by deceiving the participants as to the true purpose of the experiment until the memory test is presented. (Eysenck 2004a)*

Eysenck also proposes that it is easier to justify the use of deception in studies that are important in scientific terms than in those that are trivial. It is essential and logical that research into bullying behaviour should be scientific, in that it should conform to science or its principles, and it should proceed in a systematic and methodical way. Finally, Eysenck states that deception is more justifiable when there are no alternative, deception-free ways of studying an issue. The difficulties inherent in researching bullying, in particular the denial of perpetrators, and the issue that management is perceived as condoning the behaviour if no action is taken to prevent or deal with it, means that alternatives to cloaking the subject matter are particularly difficult to find.

Key Findings

Following the pilot studies, the national survey collated information from 249 BECTU members from across England, Scotland and Northern Ireland. The participants worked in theatres and arts centres that collectively employed more than 22,000 people. Of the participants, 65 per cent described bullying behaviour as occurring 'commonly' or 'not uncommonly', and only 6.4 per cent had never encountered any of the bullying behaviours listed. A subgroup of 99 employees – 39.7 per cent – stated that they had been the target of a bully; this became the bullied group, and the views of its members are positioned alongside the main sample and the other subsample of managers (10.8 per cent) in the reporting of the results. Levels of awareness of bullying behaviour among managers in this survey showed a significant increase compared with levels of awareness exhibited in the earlier pilot study.

Targets of bullies were found in performing arts organizations in all UK regions, with a particularly high rate of bullying in the London houses outside the West End. Bullying was prevalent in every participating employment category: administration, box office, cleaning, front-of-house, management and production. More box office staff reported bullying than those in any other work area. Fewer people working in management reported bullying than in any other work area. More young women than men were found to be bullied, and the bullied group contained a smaller percentage than the norm of those who identified themselves as being from ethnic minority backgrounds. No disabled people reported being targets of a workplace bully. The findings demonstrated that the individual most likely to be bullied would be a young, white woman working in a box office in London, outside the West End.

Profile of Participants

The research encompassed the responses of all employees, and analysed findings according to specific groups; for example, managers, targets in the bullied group, witnesses who had seen bullying happen to colleagues in the workplace, or those who had heard about bullying – hearsays. There was a degree of crossover within these groups. Broadly, the

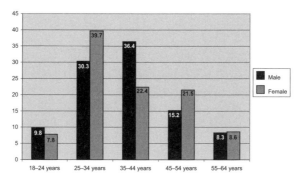

Percentages are based on 'male' (132) and 'female' (117) within 249 observations

Figure 2.1   Participants by gender and age

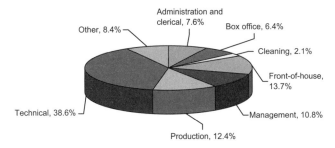

Percentages are based on 249 observations

Figure 2.2   Areas of work represented

profile was representative of the union's membership: there were slightly more men (132, that is 53 per cent) than women (117, that is 47 per cent). Employees ranged in age from 18 years to 64 years, with the majority being between 25 and 44 years.

BECTU members are employed in administration, box office, cleaning, catering (not represented here), front-of-house, management and production. Other staff in this survey sample included education workers, bar staff, dressers, maintenance, marketing, press and media workers, and a visual arts director. Technical staff predominated in the national survey, comprising more than half of the men and one-fifth of the women, followed by front-of-house and production staff.

One-tenth of the employees worked in management, and there were twice as many men as women. Among the 249 participants there were three disabled people and 6.8 per cent were from minority ethnic backgrounds. The size of the minority ethnic population in the UK was 4.6 million in 2001, or 7.9 per cent of the total population of the United Kingdom, according to the Office of National Statistics (2001), so the level of representation is slightly below the population norm. The preponderance of white workers results in a very small number – 17 people – who can be identified accurately as being from non-white minority ethnic backgrounds.

Table 2.1   Participants by ethnic group

Ethnic group	No. of citations	Per cent
Non-response	3	1.2%
Asian or Asian British (includes Indian, Pakistani, Bangladeshi, other Asian background)	2	0.8%
Black or Black British (includes Caribbean, African, other Black background)	8	3.2%
White (includes British, Irish, other white background)	229	92.0%
Chinese	1	0.4%
Other[†]	6	2.4%
Total observations	**249**	**100.0%**

[†] *Note*: among the respondents, those who identified themselves as 'Other' were people from other ethnic backgrounds who had British citizenship.

Anecdotally, many of those working in the performing arts tend to be freelance, part time or short term; however, less than one-third of all jobs recorded were part time or equivalent (Figures 2.3 and 2.4). In all, 62.4 per cent of women and 72.7 per cent of men worked full time; twice as many women as men worked part time; there were more men in the pool of short-term workers; however twice as many female as male workers were freelance.

The smallest group of female workers was the group on fixed-term contracts; the smallest group of male workers was the freelance group. In terms of permanence and job security, 29.7 per cent of arts workers had served more than 10 years in their current jobs, and 42.6 per cent had worked for between three and ten years (Figure 2.4).

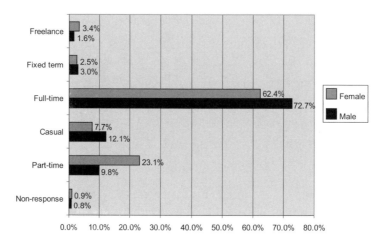

Percentages based on 249 observations

Figure 2.3   Types of post by gender

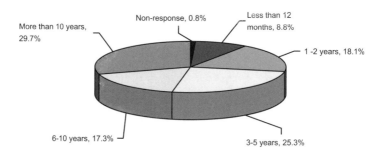

Percentages based on 249 observations

Figure 2.4   Length of service

Approximately 49.4 per cent of the participants had no supervisory or management responsibilities, as opposed to 48.6 per cent with direct line management or supervisory responsibilities, or who worked to the board of their organizations (Figure 2.5) (2 per cent did not respond).

Percentages based on 249 observations

Figure 2.5   Line management responsibilities

During the pilot study, among managers a low level of training in managing people was recorded, and this prompted the inclusion of questions to all respondents in the national survey about access to work-related training generally and within the last three years. Several different types of training provision were listed, and more than one answer could be selected, allowing respondents the opportunity to indicate in a number of different ways whether and how they had undertaken training. In all, 37.3 per cent of respondents had not undertaken any job-related training within the last three years.

Of those who had received job-related training (156 people), 64.1 per cent had received on the job training and 42.9 per cent had attended a day release course or similar (Table 2.2). Overall, evening classes and residential courses exceeded other types of training undertaken.

Table 2.2   Types of training undertaken by respondents

Work-related training	No. of citations	Per cent
Non-response	1	0.4%
None	93	37.3%
On the job training	100	40.2%
Day release course or similar	67	26.9%
Evening classes	11	4.4%
Residential course	12	4.8%
Other	20	8.0%
Total observations 249	**304**	

Note: the number of responses is greater than the number of observations, due to multiple responses (maximum of six per person). Each percentage figure is based on the number of observations, which is why the total exceeds 100 per cent.

Respondents were asked to say whether they had actively sought out training and/ or if training had been offered to them in their current job. In all, 32.9 per cent had not asked for, or been offered, training, and 27.3 per cent had asked for training, but no further action had been taken, whilst 34.5 per cent said training was planned for the future (2.4 per cent did not respond and 2.8 per cent had been offered training but had declined).

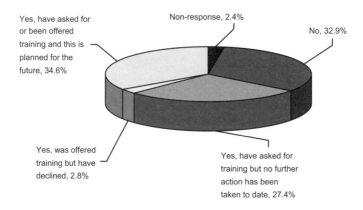

Percentages based on 249 observations

Figure 2.6   Employees' access to training

Information from line managers, revealed that 25.2 per cent of line managers (34 out of 135) and 25.2 per cent and 50 per cent of supervisors of other line managers had not received any work-related training in the last three years. Five out of the nine people working directly to the board of their organizations had not received training in the last three years either.

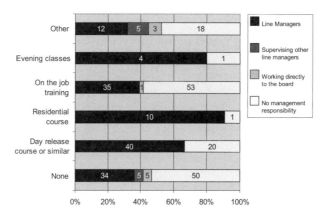

Established on 249 obesvations. More than one response can be selected (to a maximum of 5)

Figure 2.7   Work-related training undertaken by line managers

From the overall sample, responses to questions about bullying behaviour were analysed to give data relating to specific geographical locations. In Figure 2.8 below, the subsample of people who stated that bullying was occurring 'commonly' or 'not uncommonly' (160) was examined in further detail in order to ascertain where there were regional variations. In several regions 'commonly' was used to describe the frequency of workplace bullying by the majority of people, for example in London, the Midlands and in Scotland. In others 'not uncommonly' was the more frequent response, for example in the North West and in Yorkshire and the Humber.

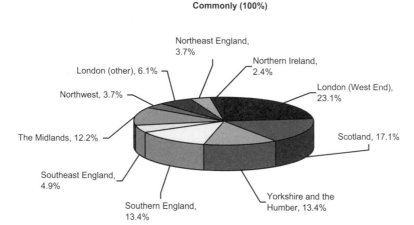

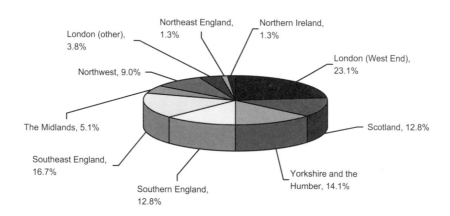

Values are percentage breakdowns of 160 observations from those who cited bullying as occurring 'commonly' or 'not uncommonly' (2 responses as 'commonly', not geographically related, are omitted)

Figure 2.8   Experience of bullying by region

These 160 observations stating that bullying behaviour was occurring 'commonly' or 'not uncommonly', comprised 100 per cent of respondents in the north east of England and Northern Ireland, over 75 per cent of those in the north west of England and Scotland, 67 per cent of those in the south east of England, over 60 per cent of those in London (excluding the West End) and The Midlands, over 58 per cent of those in Yorkshire and The Humber and in the West End, and 50 per cent of those in southern England (excluding all of London). So bullying in performing arts workplaces is familiar to people in all geographical locations within the UK.

The Bullying Experience

Respondents were asked to comment on their personal experience of bullying behaviour, indicating any of a number of stated occurrences that applied to them. In all, the 249 respondents cited 473 different experiences, indicating that individuals had encountered bullying in myriad different ways (Table 2.3).

Three significant and overlapping subgroups emerged:

1. the bullied group of 99 people who stated that they had been the target of a workplace bully – 39.8 per cent of the survey group;
2. the 116 witnesses who had observed bullying – 46.6 per cent of the survey group; and
3. the 125 hearsays who had been told of a bullying incident by a colleague – 50.2 per cent of the survey group.

Table 2.3   Personal involvement in bullying

Personal involvement in bullying	No. of citations	Per cent
Non-response	10	4%
I was involved as a trades union representative (BECTU or other union)	23	9.2%
I was asked to intervene and/or assist someone who complained of bullying	29	11.6%
I witnessed one or more bullying incidents	116	46.6%
I was told of a bullying incident by a colleague	125	50.2%
I was asked to deal with a complaint for the management of an organization	5	2%
I was the subject of a complaint about bullying from a colleague	9	3.6%
I was the target of a workplace bully	99	39.8%
I have had no personal involvement in bullying	47	18.9%
Other	10	4%
Total Observations 249	**473**	

Note: the number of citations is greater than the number of observations due to multiple responses (maximum of seven per person). Percentages are based on the number of observations.

Table 2.4   Three subsamples

Personal involvement in bullying	Bullied group	Witnesses	hearsays
I was involved as a trades union representative (BECTU or other union)	9	11	13
I was asked to intervene and/or assist someone who complained of bullying	10	15	22
I witnessed one or more bullying incidents	57	116	80
I was told of a bullying incident by a colleague	51	80	125
I was asked to deal with a complaint for the management of an organization	2	1	5
I was the subject of a complaint about bullying by a colleague	6	5	6
I was the target of a workplace bully	99	57	51
I have had no personal involvement in bullying	0	5	9
Other	4	7	5
Total Citations	**238**	**297**	**316**
Total Observations	**99**	**116**	**125**

Note: the number of citations is greater than the number of observations in each case due to multiple responses (to a maximum of seven per person).

In Table 2.4 above, the areas where the results intersect reveal that within the largest group, hearsays (125), 80 people had also witnessed bullying behaviour and 51 had been targeted by a bully. Among the witnesses (116), 57 had been targeted by a bully and 80 had been told of an incident by a colleague. Among the bullied group (99), 57 had also witnessed bullying and 51 had heard reports of bullying behaviour from a colleague. A few people stated that they had no personal involvement in bullying; however, some of them then went on to demonstrate that they had either witnessed it (five people) or heard about it (nine people).

Interventions on behalf of management and/or a complainant and trades union roles were explored. Respondents could add comments and 10 people supplied further clarifications that included descriptions of their encounters with bullying. The selection below indicates in which subsamples the commentators occurred:

- as a member of the box office involved with a grievance procedure against a line manager [witnesses];
- constructive bullying by management carried out by staff [bullied group];
- had difficult people in stage management who abused their power [hearsays];
- help and advice given [to a target];
- a management bully [bullied group, witnesses, hearsays];
- [bullied because of] trade union activities .. [bullied group, witnesses, hearsays];
- I was targeted because I am a union member [bullied group, witnesses, hearsays];
- the bully was a drunk/arrogant manager [bullied group, witnesses, hearsays];
- I witnessed indirect degradation ... [witnesses].

Trades union representatives, either current or past, numbered 69 people or 27.7 per cent of the national survey group. Among the bullied group were 19 current and eight former trades union representatives, and all representatives had encountered workplace bullying in some respect or heard about it from colleagues.

As indicated in Chapter 1, more than half the members of the survey group suggested status or position within the organization as the reason behind bullying behaviour, a reason that was closely followed by competence and popularity. More than a quarter gave gender and physical appearance as possible explanations. Participants were invited to add their own comments and additionally cited age, political affiliations, trades union membership, personal dislike and the personality issues of some managers. Among the bullied group, more people (63.6 per cent) felt status/position within the organization was a reason for bullying than in the non-bullied group where 43.3 per cent selected this reason. Most non-bullied people (45.3 per cent) identified competence as an issue and this was also recorded at a high level in the bullied group (57.6 per cent). However, popularity scored 54.5 per cent among the bullied group and only 26.7 per cent among the non-bullied group as a reason for bullying.

Among managers, 59.3 per cent said that the main reason for bullying was competence, followed by status/position (44.4 per cent). It is important to note that managers may have intended to signal that lack of competence in a target is a reason for bullying behaviour, whereas other employees and targets of bullying identify being good at one's job as a factor that attracts the attention of the incompetent bullying manager. No manager identified disability, including learning difficulties, as a reason for bullying, although both non-bullied people and members of the bullied group did.

Trades union representation was cited as a reason for being a target. However, 27.7 per cent of the survey group were currently or had been trades union representatives, compared with 27.3 per cent of the bullied group, so the occurrence of representatives in the bullied group was no higher than that of the survey sample as a whole.

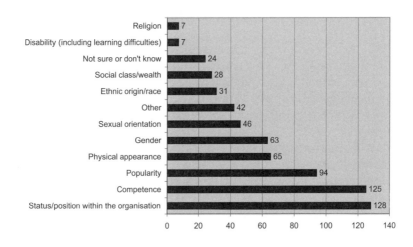

Based on the survey group of 249 observations. The number of citations is greater than the number of observations, due to multiple responses (to a maximum of 11)

Figure 2.9   Reasons for bullying behaviour

Overall, half of the respondents –50.2 per cent – had not perceived any change in the *frequency* of bullying during the last five years: 28.1 per cent felt it was more frequent and 14.9 per cent that it was less frequent (Table 2.5). However, more women than men thought bullying was more frequent (35 per cent of all women), whilst more men than women thought it was less frequent (16.7 per cent of all men) or that there had been no change (56.8 per cent of men). A higher proportion of the bullied group thought the frequency of workplace bullying had increased both in the last five years (41.4 per cent) and in the last 12 months (33.3 per cent), compared to the non-bullied group – 19.3 per cent and 14 per cent respectively; as they had been on the receiving end of the behaviour it is likely they had a more heightened awareness and were more cognizant of increases in frequency.

Interestingly, although the majority of managers thought there had been no change, a substantial number thought bullying had increased both in the last five years (37 per cent) and in the last 12 months (29.6 per cent), and it may be that the high-profile cases in the media and the introduction of dignity at work policies has registered with management more than with other employees, as in the non-bullied group the majority of respondents believed there had been no change in the frequency of bullying during the last five years (58 per cent) or the last 12 months (63.3 per cent). Lower percentages for the no-change option were prevalent among the bullied group.

Overall, a smaller number of people thought bullying was more frequent in the last 12 months (21.7 per cent) than the number who thought it more frequent in the last five years (28.1 per cent), and this was the case also within the bullied group, perhaps indicating a slowing down of the incidence of the behaviour. On the other hand, a

Table 2.5   Perceptions of the frequency of bullying

Time period	Survey group %		Bullied group %		Non-bullied group %	
	Last 5 YRS	Last 12 MOS	Last 5 YRS	Last 12 MOS	Last 5 YRS	Last 12 MOS
Bullying is more frequent	28.1%	21.7%	41.4%	33.3%	19.3%	14%
Bullying is less frequent	15.3%	14.1%	15.2%	14.1%	15.4%	14%
There has been no change	50.2%	56.6%	38.4%	46.5%	58%	63.3%
Non-response	6.4%	7.6%	5%	6.1%	7.3%	8.7%
Total	**100%**	**100%**	**100%**	**100%**	**100%**	**100%**

Note: totals are in-column percentages pertaining to the survey group (249 observations) and its two subgroups, the bullied group (99 observations) and the non-bullied group (150 observations).

smaller number of people also thought bullying was less frequent in the last 12 months (14.1 per cent) than the number who thought it less frequent in the last five years (15.3 per cent), and this was the case also within the bullied group, indicating a growing trend in the reporting of bullying behaviour. As a result, there is no clear indication from the statistical analysis as to whether bullying is increasing or decreasing in arts organizations specifically, although the case studies and the reported experiences of senior arts workers provide evidence that suggests the behaviour is increasingly more frequent and also more prevalent.

The Bullied Group

A number of features emerged that characterize the targets of workplace bullies – the bullied group. The survey dealt with arts employees' experience of workplace bullying as defined by the Dignity at Work Bill 1997:

- behaviour on more than one occasion which is offensive, abusive, malicious, insulting or intimidating;
- unjustified criticism on more than one occasion;
- punishment imposed without reasonable justification, or
- changes in the duties or responsibilities of the employee to the employee's detriment without reasonable justification.

Altogether, two in five of the total number of respondents reported being the target of a workplace bully; this is equivalent to over 9,000 employees in the participating theatres and arts centres, or 304,000 people engaged in cultural occupations in the UK, according to Davies and Lindley (2003). Of the 17 people who identified themselves as being from ethnic minority backgrounds, five were in the bullied group (Figure 2.10).

When compared with the total number of respondents in each work area, the bullied group comprises a significant number of employees from each sector, although some sectors were numerically much smaller than others. For example, 41.6 per cent of technical staff is 40 people whereas 40 per cent of cleaning staff is two people (Table 2.2).

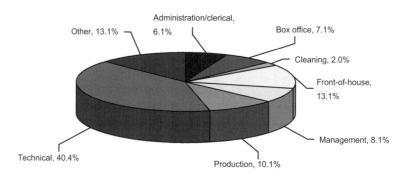

Values are percentages of the sub-sample (99), established according to areas of work

Figure 2.10   Targets of bullying behaviour according to areas of work

Table 2.6   Targets of bullying behaviour and their areas of work

29.6% of management staff	40% of cleaning staff
31.6% of administration/clerical staff	41% of technical staff
32.2% of production staff	43.7% of box office staff
38.2% of front-of-house staff	61.9% of other staff

Other staff were the most frequent targets of bullying behaviour — in this case, those working in education, fundraising, marketing and the media, facilities and bar management, and backstage as crew, dressers or at the stage door. Management staff were the least frequently targeted. All age ranges and types of post were targeted. A slightly higher percentage of the bullied group have attended evening classes and residential courses than the norm. In many respects, the bullied group does not vary significantly from the non-bullied group, apart from – as could be anticipated – in their views on bullying behaviour, management attitudes, employee objections and complaints procedures.

As with the survey group as a whole, the venues in which bullied participants worked were in England, Scotland and Northern Ireland and, although there were representatives from every geographical region within the bullied group, the distribution pattern differed from that of the survey group overall (Table 2.7). For example, whilst only 8.8 per cent of the survey group was based in London (outside the West End), these employees accounted for 15.2 per cent of the bullied group. Southern England constituted 8 per cent of the survey group and only 4 per cent of the bullied group. Compared to the norm, then, employees are almost twice as likely to be bullied if they work in London outside the West End, and half as likely to be bullied if they work in southern England.

Table 2.7   Geographical locations of employees in the bullied group

Location of employee	Survey group %	Bullied group %
Non-response	0.8%	1%
London (West End)	25.7%	23.2%
London (other)	8.8%	15.2%
North east England	3.2%	3%
North west England	10.8%	13.1%
Southern England	8%	4%
The Midlands	15.7%	14.1%
Yorkshire and The Humber	11.8%	12.3%
South east England	2.4%	3%
Northern Ireland	1.2%	1%
Scotland	11.6%	10.1%
Total observations (per cent)	**100%**	**100%**

Note: established on 249 observations and subsample bullied group (99 observations).

The statistics suggest that, compared with the norm, the major London houses have a higher proportion of bullied people than any other type of venue – 19.2 per cent compared with 16.4 per cent elsewhere. In fact, although greater numbers of bullied people were found within larger arts institutions, the distribution is more complex, with targets of bullying being found both in the small-scale venues and in the very largest ones with more than 100 employees (Table 2.8). At both ends of the scale of venue, levels of bullying were above the norm. The major London houses included in the survey were the Royal Opera House, the English National Opera, the Royal National Theatre and the Royal Shakespeare Company.

Types of bullying behaviour were listed and respondents were invited to comment on how often these had been encountered. A very small number (16) had never encountered bullying behaviour and 65 per cent of the national survey group described it as common or not uncommon. This rose to 85.9 per cent among the bullied group (Table 2.9).

Table 2.8   Scale of venue reported by bullied group

Numbers of employees per venue	Survey group %	Bullied group %
Non-response	1.6%	2%
less than 20	4%	5.1%
21–30	8.8%	10.1%
31–40	10.9%	15.1%
41–50	6.4%	5.1%
50–100	27.7%	21.2%
over 100	40.6%	41.4%
Total observations (per cent)	**100%**	**100%**

Note: established on 249 observations and sub-sample bullied group (99 observations).

Table 2.9   Experience of bullying behaviour across subsamples

	Survey group in total	%	Bullied group	%	Non-bullied group	%
non-response	2	0.9%	0	0	2	1.3%
never	16	6.4%	0	0	16	10.7%
very rarely, isolated examples only	69	27.7%	14	14.1%	55	36.7%
not uncommonly	78	31.3%	30	30.3%	48	32%
commonly	84	33.7%	55	55.6%	29	19.3%
Total Observations	**249**	**100%**	**99**	**100%**	**150**	**100%**

Note: sample percentages established on 249 observations: subgroups bullied group (99) and non-bullied group (150).

A higher percentage of the bullied group – 55.6 per cent compared to 19.3 per cent of the non-bullied group – perceived that bullying occurred 'commonly'. Among the managers (10.8 per cent of the survey group), 25.9 per cent described bullying as occurring 'commonly'; however 37 per cent said it occurred not 'uncommonly' – a higher percentage than both the non-bullied group and the bullied group. One-third of managers and 36.7 per cent of the non-bullied group felt bullying was rare; however only one manager had never encountered it. Although the survey group size in the early pilot study of managers was equivalent to only 48.1 per cent of the numbers in the national research, the results are still very striking: in the pilot survey, 53.8 per cent of the managers said they were unaware of bullying behaviour in the arts workplace, compared with four years later when 3.7 per cent of managers said they had never encountered bullying.

Among the bullied group, those who thought bullying in arts workplaces occurred 'commonly' or 'not uncommonly' totalled 85.9 per cent, compared to 51.3 per cent of the non-bullied group and 62.9 per cent of managers. Personal experience is likely to have contributed to heightened awareness of the issue; however it was also the case that employees (whether bullied or not) in all areas of work reported bullying behaviour broadly to the same degree, although management employees maintained that it was less common than did others. More administration/clerical workers (47.4 per cent) felt it occurred 'commonly' than any other employment sector (Table 2.10).

Table 2.10   Experience of bullying by areas of work

Experience of bullying by work areas	Non-response	Never	Rare, isolated examples	Not uncommonly	Commonly	Total % within each work area
Administration or clerical	0%	5.2%	21.1%	26.3%	47.4%	100%
Box office	0%	6.3%	31.1%	31.3%	31.3%	100%
Cleaning	0%	0%	20%	40%	40%	100%
Front-of-house	0%	5.9%	26.4%	35.3%	32.4%	100%
Management	0%	3.7%	33.4%	37%	25.9%	100%
Production	3.2%	9.7%	25.8%	29%	32.3%	100%
Technical	1%	7.3%	30.3%	28.1%	33.3%	100%
Other	0%	4.8%	19%	38.1%	38.1%	100%
Total % across all work areas	0.8%	6.4%	27.8%	31.3%	33.7%	100%

Note: table values are the in-columns percentages established on 249 observations (some totals may have been rounded up or down to accommodate reduction to one decimal place).

Among the bullied group, there was a positive variation from the norm in the survey sample in terms of the percentages of staff working in box office (+0.7 per cent), technical (+1.8 per cent) and other staff (+4.7 per cent), and a negative variation among production (-4.3 per cent), administration/clerical (-1.5 per cent) and management staff (-2.7 per cent). There was an insignificant or nil difference among cleaning and front-of-house staff. With the exception of those working as technicians, there were more women than men working in every other area, with almost three times as many in administration/clerical fields and in production. The bullied group featured higher proportions of staff on freelance and fixed-term contracts, at +1.6 per cent and +1.2 per cent respectively. Numerically, the largest subsets within the bullied group were male technicians (66.7 per cent of bullied males) and female technicians (21 per cent of bullied females). This is the only work area in which more men than women stated that they were bullied, presumably because men outnumber women 134:25.

Gender, Sexual Orientation, Ethnic Origin and Disability

Although early research indicated that bullying was not gender-specific, increasingly, studies have considered bullying in the context of gender and sexual orientation (Costigan 1998; Hoel, Cooper and Faragher 2001; M. B. Lee 2001 as reported in Turney 2003; Lewis 2006). There has been a tendency towards the predominance of women as targets, and Lewis (2004: 296) noted that of the 15 participants in his study of workplace bullying in education sectors, and the impact of shame, only two were men. He urges further research to explore whether men react differently to the constructs of bullying and shame, and whether they employ different coping mechanisms. Hoel, Faragher and Cooper (2004) conducted a national cross-section study (N=5,388) and found that differences between the sexes and between occupational contexts emerged when damage to health caused by bullying was measured. Yet Vartia and Hyyti (2002) conducted a study in prisons in Finland that found no evidence that gender should act as a predictor of stress among victims of bullying.

During the arts research, almost half of the women respondents (48.7 per cent) reported being the target of a workplace bully, compared to less than one-third of the men (31.8 per cent), and 35 per cent of all women (that is, both bullied and non-bullied) thought bullying had become more frequent during the last five years. However within the bullied group, the gender breakdown changed and a higher percentage (57.6 per cent) was female, compared to males (42.4 per cent). The data from the survey demonstrated that more women than men are bullied within every age group. The majority of men in the study, and also in the bullied group, were aged between 35–44 years, whilst the majority of women were between 25–34 years. This appears to indicate that bullying is not age-specific, although lower rates of bullying are returned for both men and women in the 55+ age group. Among the youngest participants, aged 18–24 years, there were more men than women (Table 2.11), yet 23.1 per cent of the men in this age range belonged to the bullied group, compared to 66.7 per cent of 18–24-year-old-women. This may suggest that young females perceive themselves to be, or are actually, commonly targeted by bullies. Alternatively, it may indicate that younger women are more sensitive to negative workplace behaviours than men of the same age.

Table 2.11   Age and gender within the bullied group

National survey gender/age	Non-response	18–24 years	25–34 years	35–44 years	45–54 years	55-64 years	Total
Males	0	13	40	48	20	11	132
Bullied group males (% all males)	0	3	13	17	7	2	42
	(0)	(23.1)	(32.5)	(35.4)	(35)	(18.2)	(31.8)
Females	1	9	46	26	25	10	117
Bullied group females (% all females)	1	6	23	11	13	3	57
	(100)	(66.7)	(50)	(42.3)	(52)	(30)	(48.7)

Note: percentages are based on males (132) and females (117) within 249 observations and the bullied group subgroup (99 observations).

Certainly, women appear to be bullied more than men as a similar pattern, with different absolute percentages, is found among the 25–34 year olds: half of all the women in this category belong to the bullied group, as do 32.5 per cent of the men, which means that the majority of the bullied group (36.4 per cent) is in this age range. Each age band yields similar results: in every case a higher percentage of women than men are in the bullied group, even in the range where men predominate overall – the 35–44 years band.

Compared to men, more women also report having witnessed bullying behaviour. This correlates with evidence from other studies, for example the analysis of a bullied group by Zapf, Dormann and Frese (1996), that indicates that women have a 'greater tendency to report more psychological ill health and distress than men in general' (Hoel, Faragher and Cooper 2004: 370).

Given the high level of bullying described by young females, it might have been expected that employees relatively new to an organization, particularly young women, would report being targeted more frequently than their longer-serving colleagues. Within the bullied group, however, the highest proportion of employees reporting bullying (29.3 per cent) had been in post for between three and five years (+4.0 per cent above the norm), followed by those who had been in post for longer than 10 years (27.3 per cent), which is -2.4 per cent below the norm. So length of service in an arts organization does not appear to make a significant difference to the likelihood of being targeted by a bully, and there is some basis for supposing that the probability of becoming a target increases with career longevity, particularly in view of the findings that it can take some time for targets to realize that they are being bullied, and also that bullying does not necessarily start at the commencement of an individual's employment, as evidenced by the case studies (for example, The Museum and The Theatre Project).

The bullied group displayed a similar breakdown to that of the survey group as a whole in terms of those who had management and supervisory responsibilities; that is 54.8 per cent of men (+2.5 per cent on the norm) and 36.8 per cent of women (-0.8 per cent of the norm) in the bullied group had management and supervisory responsibilities, compared with the survey group baseline of 52.3 per cent of men and 37.6 per cent of women. It would seem that those with line management responsibilities, whether male or female, are just as likely to be targeted by a bully as those without, and this is the case in four of the eight case studies: The Gallery, The Museum, The Theatre Project and The Arts Service.

We have seen that, within the bullied group, there was a 10.6 per cent difference from the survey group in terms of gender breakdown – 57.6 per cent were female, compared to 42.4 per cent who were male. The findings in the national survey indicated that women were observing and/or experiencing bullying more than men in performing arts workplaces and also that a higher percentage of women than men described bullying behaviour as occurring 'commonly' or 'not uncommonly' at 38.5 per cent and 33.3 per cent respectively, compared to 28.8 per cent and 31.1 per cent of men (Figure 2.11). Fairly equal proportions of males and females (47 per cent of the men and 53 per cent of the women) had been told of bullying behaviour by a colleague – the hearsays. Ten fewer women (53) than men had actually witnessed bullying incidents; however the witnesses still comprised 45.3 per cent of the total number of women respondents.

In the case studies, both men and women are both bullies and targets and, as yet, no evidence has emerged to suggest that either men or women are more likely to be perpetrators. Sexual orientation is also not evident as a factor in determining who is more likely to be a bully, although it is acknowledged that individuals are targeted because of their sexual orientation. For example, in May 2005, a gay box office worker in Durham who suffered months of harassment by his manager won a discrimination case (BBC 2005a), and, in July 2009, a former City of London lawyer started an action to recoup record damages of £12m after a tribunal upheld a ruling that she was a victim of sexual discrimination and harassment '... after leaving the company following 18 months of workplace bullying' (Switalski 2009). In addition to sexual harassment, bullying can also be aligned closely with other types of discrimination.

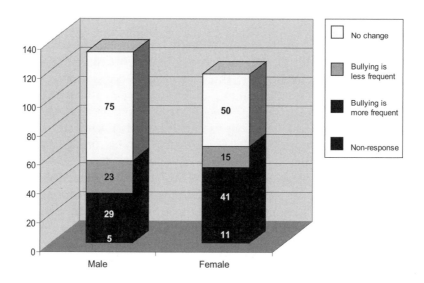

Values are the number of observations in the survey group (249), established according to gender

Figure 2.11 Perceptions of frequency of bullying behaviour by gender

Respondents of non-white ethnic origin – both male and female – reported bullying behaviour occurring 'commonly' (Chinese) or 'not uncommonly' (Asian or Asian British) or both (Black or Black British or other). All but one, who had never heard of or witnessed bullying behaviour, were part of either the bullied group and/or hearsays, and none had been asked to deal with a complaint for management or had been the subject of a complaint by a colleague.

An arts management professional from the USA has related two or three of his experiences, which he believes came about because he is a non-white male. He recounted several examples of bullying behaviour, having observed that the arts sector was 'dominated by White females', and he believes himself to be 'an outlier in a field where there are not many people like me'. He states:

> I have experienced some very agressive/passive-agressive behavior that I believe was meant to intimidate me … In my current position I work with two White females … no matter what idea I have or how good a job I do, I get nothing but resistance from both of them, while my superiors, colleagues, and subordinates give positive feedback.

Certainly, bullying behaviour can result from discrimination – on any basis – and can also exist where no discrimination is in evidence. The same arts professional further reports 'interesting discrimination trends' that have emerged in the US:

> I suspect many men do not want to admit to workplace bullying … however more men are reporting sexual harassment from women. Additionally, more men and women are reporting sexual harassment from people of the same gender …

Four arts workers in the national study declared that they were registered disabled: two men and two women. They worked in administration/clerical, management and technical posts. Three were full-time workers and one a casual worker: three had given more than 10 years' service and one between three and five years. They included employees without supervisory responsibilities, line managers and one who worked directly to the board of the organization. All said bullying occurred 'commonly' or 'not uncommonly', and that they had witnessed or heard about bullying or been asked to intervene on behalf of a colleague who had complained of bullying; however none of them cited disability as a reason for bullying behaviour.

Despite this, however, seven individuals did cite disability as a reason for bullying: five males and two females. They worked as technicians, front-of-house and in production. Three were line managers and three were, or had been, trades union representatives. They worked in some of the largest venues employing substantially more than 100 people, including two of the major London houses and several of the theatres governed by Theatrical Management Association (TMA) agreements, and one worked for a small arts centre employing fewer than 20 people. Their personal involvement in bullying was that two had been targets and three had witnessed bullying, one had been involved as a trades union representative and one had been asked to assist someone who had complained of bullying.

Sometimes, then, for those working in the arts there is a clear correlation between bullying and discrimination, for example, when it occurs as a result of a perpetrator deciding that someone is different, whether because of gender, sexual orientation, ethnic origin, disability or some other factor of the bully's choosing. For the most part, these cases have recourse to legislation, unlike bullying that appears to originate because of status/position, competence or simply because the perpetrator perceives the target as a threat.

3 Pair Bullying and Founder's Syndrome

The profile of workplace bullying in the UK has continued to grow since the early 1990s when, through two BBC Radio 4 documentaries, the late Andrea Adams effectively gave the behaviour and the problem a name. Levels of awareness and interest have accelerated rapidly since 1992 when Adams collaborated with Neil Crawford and published *Bullying at Work: How to Confront and Overcome It* (Adams with Crawford 1992). In the following decade, instances of bullying behaviour began to be described and reported in the media at an increasingly frequent rate – often by those who had suffered at the hands of bullies.

As a research topic, bullying has been studied within a range of disciplines in the behavioural sciences, including psychology, psychiatry, sociology and social anthropology. As a management issue, bullying is germane to studies of organizational behaviour, human resources development, leadership, corporate culture and business ethics. Increasingly, examination of the potential for legal redress and action by employers' associations and trades unions is integral to workplace bullying studies. Research findings on bullying have an impact on the development of management guidelines and policies for staff welfare, notably in terms of motivation and retention of staff, disciplinary and grievance procedures, diversity, managing change and dignity at work. As legal action on workplace bullying becomes more common, employers are faced with more onerous responsibilities for employees' welfare at work and are beginning to make financial provision for harm caused as a result of their negligence.

Researchers into workplace bullying have taken both positivist and phenomenologist stances. A positivist approach makes a significant contribution to bullying research, particularly when this research takes place in a new field, as it focuses on measuring every aspect of the behaviour being studied including, for example, using word counts to analyze speech or text. A phenomenologist approach is also valuable as it seeks to create conditions for the objective study of things that are usually regarded as subjective, such as emotions, perceptions or other conscious experiences. In order to achieve a fully rounded picture of bullying in the arts it was desirable to consider, and to seek to understand, both the measurable data and the quality of the personal experience. By combining the quantitative and the qualitative, a complete and balanced view of bullying in the arts was more likely to be achieved. In discussing and examining the role of combined research methods, Silverman (2000), Morse and Chung (2003) and Gorard and Taylor (2004) make persuasive arguments for a thorough overhaul of the traditional theoretical perspectives and philosophical stances.

Bullying is held to be a destructive, harmful and undesirable phenomenon in the workplace. Positivists identify it and confirm its existence as the truth. In the arts research the national survey revealed that bullying exists in arts organizations, with the numerical data providing measurable evidence of that fact. Postmodernists argue that there can be myriad interpretations of the same scenario – different realities for participants in the behaviour. Indeed, Lewis (2003: 65–81) notes that: '... evidence [from various researchers] can reveal multiple realities of bullying at work: Managerial; Organizational; Between individuals.' In some of the case studies, different people do interpret what occurs in different ways – in The Arts Service, in Chapter 4, for example, the experiences described by target, witness, supervisor and management vary widely. The function of postmodernism is an important one:

> While modernism seeks to understand, postmodernism is continually asking whose view is being supported and whose interests are served. (Liefooghe and Mackenzie Davey, 2003: 219)

Some researchers distinguish between person-related and work-related bullying, for example, Einarsen and Hoel (2001) as reported in Salin (2005). Bullying by individuals and organizational, or corporate, bullying were identified as prevailing issues in the performing arts research. In the case of the former, pair bullying and serial bullying were more common than group bullying. Pair bullying and group, or gang, bullying (mobbing) involves more than one perpetrator:

> ... who victimise[s] an individual until that person is pushed into a helpless and defenceless position and held there by means of continuing mobbing activities. These actions occur regularly over a period of time. (Leymann 1996)

Pair Bullying

The Museum case study involves two founder governors, a couple in a relationship (consistent with the sexual link identified by Field), who dominate a new arts organization and engage in an internal power struggle with the other founder governors. As part of the battle for continuing dominance, the pair bully the CEO, who has created and cultivated an organizational development strategy according to principles of best practice and which would have resulted in spreading the balance of power more evenly among all the governors. Eventually, following a mental breakdown as a result of the stress caused by bullying, the CEO leaves the organization. The pair of bullies prevail for a short time, but eventually lose the confidence of their peers who retreat from involvement.

THE MUSEUM: HIERARCHICAL BULLYING/PAIR BULLYING

A group of local people planned to set up a small museum in a redundant building. These founders included Alexis, a project manager in the private sector, and her partner Sofia. Alexis took the lead in recruiting a board of governors from amongst her personal friends and business colleagues, and became Chair. The founders appointed a curator, James, who recruited two support staff. The initial brief was to raise funds for ongoing repairs and maintenance work, and then to oversee the development of the exhibition spaces, and the museum programme. Previously, James had been an officer in a funding body where he had managed large budgets and initiated new programmes. He had also fundraised for, and managed, arts buildings. The local founders continued to function as a subcommittee of the board of governors, monitoring all aspects of the development of the museum between governors' meetings.

When the fundraising campaign was under way, the time came to put into place a small advisory panel which would function alongside the Board of Governors and deal with the museum's programme of permanent and temporary exhibitions. James was keen to ensure that the advisory panel should comprise individuals with relevant, exhibition-related skills, and Philip, who was an eminent figure in the cultural sector, seemed the most appropriate person to act as Chair, particularly as he was already a member of the founders' subcommittee and therefore very familiar with the project. The new panel was to run in tandem with the Board and would be subsidiary to it.

Alexis and Sofia resented the move to recruit new members to the advisory panel on the basis of relevant skills and areas of expertise, and particularly disliked the suggestion that anyone other than Alexis should hold the position of Chair of any subcommittee or advisory panel. Alexis began popping in to the museum, often with trivial queries ostensibly connected with board matters, but usually to probe James about his current thinking regarding the advisory panel. She made it clear, more than once, that she could command considerable support from her friends on the Board of Governors. Determined to adhere to best practice, however, James appealed to the other founders, Felicity and Grace, on the basis of Philip's suitability and qualifications, and Philip duly became Chair of the advisory panel.

In subcommittee meetings, Alexis and Sofia became rude to, and dismissive of, their former friends and fellow-founders. Outside of museum matters, shared social occasions amongst them ceased. They also openly disparaged any ideas James, Philip and Felicity proposed at meetings. Grace tended to stay silent on these occasions.

During the next six months, James repeatedly tried to convince Alexis and Sofia that the development proposals and the recruitment of new, skilled individuals to the advisory panel were best for the organization as a whole, but he was met with accusations of betrayal, which, although false, he found hurtful and upsetting. Alexis and Sofia began to take every available opportunity to criticize everything he did, often in front of the other staff. He was required to prepare labour-intensive, detailed written statements on unimportant matters, reducing the time available for running the museum, which now operated a programme of occasional exhibitions.

Meetings of the Board of Governors chaired by Alexis became interminable: every agenda item became a debate, and the written reports from James and his staff, on every minor aspect of the museum's activities, were never enough. One day Sofia confronted James at the museum's offices about the lack of respect he displayed for her partner, Alexis. Sofia was extremely aggressive, abusive and rude in front of the other staff, accusing James of deliberately setting out to undermine Alexis. Sofia continued to hurl abuse, demeaning James until, humiliated, he broke down in tears and the other staff fled the office, shocked and, on his behalf, embarrassed.

The unpleasant Board meetings, alternating with confrontational visits from Alexis and Sofia, continued unabated and took their toll. One employee left the organization and was not replaced. James managed to appoint a temporary assistant to relieve some of his workload, but became increasingly isolated; he felt tired all the time and began to suffer symptoms of stress, eventually developing a series of physical stress-related illnesses. He attempted to alert the other governors to the behaviour to which he was being subjected, but was met with expressions of disbelief – they had, after all, been recruited by Alexis. About three months after the incident with Sofia in the office, on medical advice James took the maximum available sick leave.

On his return to work he found that the museum had lost a grant due to funding cuts and was now in financial difficulty. He also found that Alexis and Sofia immediately resumed their behaviour; he was unable to continue in his job. The remaining member of staff also left and the museum closed down for some months during which time founders Philip and Felicity resigned. Alexis and Sofia continued to run both the Board of Governors and the advisory panel, and chose not to recruit a new curator according to the museum's equal opportunities policy. Instead, Grace became the new appointee.

(Names and environs have been changed to protect confidentiality.)

The bullying behaviour is not evident at the outset; it emerges when the founder governors, Alexis and Sofia, perceive that their authority is threatened. What should have been an arts project designed to provide a new local amenity, and run according to professional standards and practice, instead became an example of the destructive effects of power and 'power difference' (Einarsen 1999: 18).

As in the study of The Ensemble, in Chapter 6, at the beginning the parties appeared to be on an equal footing, although Alexis and Sofia can be seen to exert some additional influence initially – Alexis as the Chair of the Board of Governors, and Sofia as her partner. The appointment of the curator, James, is a success. He undertakes and accomplishes the early development work on the project, and works hard to build the amateur committee into a professional arts board, all with the apparent willingness of all the participants.

The proposal to install Philip as Chair of the advisory panel, however, appears to Alexis and Sofia to be a transgression on the part of James, and to represent a threat to their dominant status within the organization. Perhaps there is, as can be seen elsewhere, a sense of inadequacy on the part of the pair who had extensive knowledge of project management, but none of museum programming, unlike James, Philip, Grace and Felicity. They were content to accept help from these partners, because of their specific skills, in the early stages of the development, but unwilling to let them share in any benefits gained, such as enhanced status, as a result of their combined efforts.

Indeed, for Alexis and Sofia, self-interest dominates everything, including the health and future of the organization as a whole. The withdrawal of cooperation by the bullies, and their active resistance to any change and development that would result in a loss of personal power, creates major problems at all levels in the organization, finally causing it to close. The other governors do not take seriously the complaints made to them about Alexis and Sofia, despite the fact that these came from an employee with a track record of major achievements for them over a number of years. This is symptomatic of the nature of bullying at work outlined by Einarsen (1999: 19):

When stepping into the case, upper management ... tend to accept the prejudices produced by the offenders, thus blaming the victim for its misfortune.

The staff members who witnessed the bullying of the curator perceived this as tolerance of the behaviour by management (Rayner 1999) and they left the organization rather than endure the deteriorating atmosphere. Even at this early stage in its development, there are clear indications that the subcommittee comprised of founder governors is operating as a passive-aggressive organization:

congenial and seemingly conflict free, achieves consensus easily, but struggles to implement agreed-upon plans. (Neilson, Pasternack and Van Nuys 2005)

Good Governance and Policy Development

In the case study The Art Gallery (in Chapter 1), and here again in The Museum, the bullying is carried out by individuals in important and very senior positions: those who are charged with the duty of good governance. According to the Office of the United Nations High Commissioner for Human Rights, good governance is participatory, responsible, accountable, transparent and responsive. To augment this: participatory and responsive infers action that is consensus-based; responsible presumes that conduct is efficient and effective; accountable incorporates following the rule of law; transparent encompasses being equitable and inclusive. Good governance works to ensure that misconduct is minimized, that minority views are taken into account and decision-making reflects the needs of the most vulnerable. Richard Eyre, Director of the Royal National Theatre 1987–1997, a respected stage and screen director and a prolific writer on theatre, has lamented the haphazard style in which members are appointed to the boards of trustees governing the top end of management of many UK theatres and arts centres, and he recommends:

No Board should be able to appoint its own members or Chair independent of external consultation ... all new Board members must be given appropriate training. (as reported in Lathan 2001)

Given the experiences outlined in these studies, this is no less important in small- and middle-scale organizations. Eyre's reference to training is particularly significant: in The Art Gallery, the board member who bullies – Alastair – is a retired executive with a non-arts background; in The Museum, the board members who bully – Alexis and Sofia – are experienced project managers, but unfamiliar with the work of curators and the requirements for programming exhibitions.

Given the experiences described in the case studies, board members who come to arts organizations from non-arts backgrounds need to:

1. be aware of the environment in which they will now be working and, where appropriate, how this differs from their previous situation;
2. understand their role as a board member, which is not that of CEO, by being enabled to recognize the difference between the two;

3. be given appropriate training and/or induction so that the first and second requirements are married with the specific needs of the particular organization of which they will have governance.

Of course, this is not a new idea and, fortunately, today in the UK there are many organizations working hard to promote good governance, not only in the arts but also in the third sector generally. For example, the Independent Theatre Council (ITC) manages a board development programme – Governance, Access, Inclusion and Networking (GAIN) – aimed at London-based arts, sports and heritage organizations, which is particularly focused on diversity, and the National Council for Voluntary Organizations (NCVO) promotes good governance using a range of resources. Also, the former Scottish Arts Council's excellent publication *Care, Diligence and Skill: A Corporate Governance Handbook for Arts Organizations* reached its sixth revised edition in September 2008. (It is available from Creative Scotland as a pdf download.)

So, the issue is not whether the knowledge of best practice exists, which patently it does, but whether it is being carried out. Those serving on arts boards are familiar with skills audits and board recruitment procedures that are tailored to the needs of the organization, and these should be updated and reviewed on a regular basis if they are to remain useful and relevant. However, arts workers are calling into question whether, in reality, the theory is being put into practice. Many have confirmed the existence of policies that are meant to deal with issues such as bullying, but have made it clear that these are not, in fact, implemented. A policy that exists in principle, but not in practice, might as well never have been written.

In the survey of arts workers who were BECTU members, 249 respondents were asked to comment on whether their organization had a written policy to govern specific types of bullying behaviour (see Chapter 4). Of these, 99 had stated already that they were the targets of bullies – the bullied group. A few employees, representing each of the areas of work in theatres and arts centres in the survey, stated that written policies to deal with bullying behaviour existed, however almost half of all respondents – 48.6 per cent – did not reply, indicating uncertainty about, or perhaps ignorance of, written policies. As seen in Table 3.1, those who answered identified the behaviours covered by written policies as those most often connected with physical assault, and least often with actions such as arbitrary withholding of information or unwanted/persistent jokes. Physical threats in the workplace may be more tangible, in terms of descriptions for policy documents, than more subtle, insulting behaviour, which acts to harm psychologically.

However, even where written policies existed, the targets of bullying reported a feeling of helplessness when faced with a more powerful chief executive or board, or a corporate culture of bullying within the organization. For example, one respondent to the pilot study commented:

Interestingly I discovered that an organization I had been working for in an executive capacity had breached its constitution and the laws governing incorporated associations. I reported this to the management committee only to be persecuted and slandered and sought to raise this matter at the annual general meeting. At the AGM I was gagged. Prior to the AGM, I was slandered. When I responded I was threatened with legal action.

Table 3.1   Types of bullying behaviour covered by written policies

Written Policies	No. citations	Per cent
Non-response	121	48.6%
Direct insults in front of colleagues	69	27.7%
Shouting or abusive behaviour/bad language	78	31.3%
Persistent unjustified threats or sanctions	55	22.1%
Arbitrary withholding of information, cooperation or arrangements	27	10.8%
Unwanted/persistent jokes	34	13.7%
Behaviour which is threatening to the person	87	34.9%
Physical assault, for example throwing objects	97	39%
Other (please state)	23	9.2%
Total citations from 249 observations	**591**	

Note: the number of citations is greater than the number of observations due to multiple answers, to a maximum of eight per respondent. The percentage figures pertain to the survey group as a whole (249 observations).

In any case, the existence of a policy does not appear to guarantee protection from bullying behaviour or a resolution of difficult relationships, as the comments from a respondent to the pilot study make clear:

> *For nine years my life was made hell, then I left. There is a policy but no one enforces it. They'll [the management] talk to you for a bit, then say try to like them [the bullies].*

Despite a degree of uncertainty about the existence of anti-bullying policies generally, attitudes were more forthright among those from the bullied group. Overall, the view was that policy is not implemented, and that management tends to be both disinterested and inactive about dealing with bullying behaviour. The following is a selection of comments made by respondents to the national survey:

- not aware of a policy;
- don't know what company policy is;
- not sure but would think they have a policy;
- [there is a] written policy but [it is] not supported in practice;
- policy exists but it is not internally applied/adhered to;
- there is a policy, but workers are often too intimidated to use it;
- management need to have far better training in dealing with staff and show respect to all staff, no matter what their grade is.

This theme (of disinterested and inactive management) recurred when participants were asked about terms and conditions, and about how complaints were dealt with by management (see Chapter 4). Many employees felt trades unions could have a useful role in terms of contributing to, or advising on, policy development and in training shop stewards and managers how to deal with bullying behaviour. Specifically, employees said BECTU should:

- [provide] training for stewards leading to them setting an example in the workplace – which some at present do not;
- [convince] organizations to invest in training their managers NOT to be bullies themselves and HOW to deal with bullying in their departments;
- [give] direction to management on how to talk to staff. I don't think that a lot of them are aware of what is right and wrong. Surveys of management by staff once a year may help;
- [educate] the management about the fact that if we are patted on the back, our tails wag!

Founder's Syndrome

The issue of good governance, and the difficulty the CEO in The Museum had in ensuring that the founder governors accepted good governance, can be aligned closely with the concept of Founder's Syndrome, as described by Andrew Gaupp, Associate Professor of Theatre Arts at the University of Texas at Arlington, USA. In a journal article he recounts his own, and others', observations on a predicament experienced by a number of theatre companies in the USA: creative professionals establish new arts organizations that grow and then become so successful that a more complex system of authority is required, the result of which is that the founder becomes a liability and is ousted (Gaupp 1997). This is a familiar phenomenon in the UK, also, and several of the arts case studies illustrate the level of harm that can be caused by the process of driving out someone, whether or not this process is ultimately successful. The Museum also bears the hallmarks of Founder's Syndrome, although in this case the founders prevailed at the expense of good governance and best practice. One UK colleague with considerable experience of a similar syndrome in UK theatre, has dubbed it 'founderitis'. It will be familiar to many experienced arts workers, particularly those in small- and middle-scale arts organizations.

In the case study The Contemporary Dance Studios we see that bullying behaviour is not limited to those who share the same building or work for the same company under a permanent contract. Freelance arts professionals, short-term workers and part-time employees also encounter the behaviour, as shown by the empirical evidence. This is an

---

THE CONTEMPORARY DANCE STUDIOS: CLIENT BULLYING/ UPWARD BULLYING/PAIR BULLYING

Two young dancers, Amanda and Jalal, recently graduated from a London dance school, approached funders for assistance and advice to enable them to set up a studio space dedicated to contemporary dance. The idea was to find suitable premises that they themselves could use as rehearsal space, with additional areas for use by other dancers and dance companies. The funders were interested in the concept, however they felt that the project needed a sound strategic development plan demonstrating that the aspirations were sustainable. They offered seed funding on this basis.

This was not popular with Amanda and Jalal. As emerging artists they believed they were entitled to be supported; they had not given any thought to strategic planning. They felt that the funders' suggestion to employ an advisor was a poor fit with their underlying ideology. Nonetheless, they wanted access to finance and premises, so they engaged a freelance advisor to work with them on the production of a strategic plan. Alongside this, acting on advice from the funders, they began the process of setting up the new company, and recruiting members for a new board of directors. They selected individuals known to them from among members of the dance world, and their friends.

The advisor they chose, Steve, had wide experience of working in a variety of arts environments and had previously worked both as a performer and as an arts manager in a senior capacity with a national performing arts organization. From the outset he was interested in, and enthusiastic about, the proposals put forward by Amanda and Jalal.

Having undertaken market research to establish likely interest in, and potential sources of funding for, the proposed studios, Steve confirmed that the project had every chance of being successful as long as the complex provided facilities to meet the identified needs of local dance professionals and was managed well. However, Amanda and Jalal disliked this assessment, complaining that they were planning a facility for performing artists, not a commercial business, and that neither being landlords, nor being part of management, was of any interest to them. Steve explained further that, to be sustainable, they would have to ensure their overheads and other costs, including any staff they may want to employ, were met by earned income, such as from letting studios, as well as from other sources, such as grants or fees.

The concept of sustainability was new to Amanda and Jalal, and they rejected it, saying they did not plan to employ staff or to manage the spaces; dancers would simply pay a nominal fee for use of space, as needed, from time to time. It seemed they had expected to be supported almost entirely via grant aid and had not thought through the issues around charging other users a realistic price for space – the concept of full cost recovery, whereby every aspect of the real costs incurred are built into the income necessary to sustain a project, was alien to them.

Jalal and Amanda began to frequently question the quality and relevance of the work Steve was undertaking – by phone and by email – remarking that they felt he was not up to the job. They also complained in person, by phone and by email to colleagues and to their new board members that the advisor was useless, and when project meetings were held involving other professional consultants they would ignore Steve completely, embarking on private conversations that excluded him.

This behaviour began to affect Steve adversely. He had been working with Amanda and Jalal for three months and had become increasingly anxious about his relationship with them, and unhappy about their response to him. The quality of his work on other projects declined and, realizing that he was becoming depressed because of the constant harassment, after attempting without success to make progress for a further month, he acknowledged that the working relationship had broken down and arranged for another advisor to replace him.

The new advisor, Maria, checked the work undertaken to date against the brief from the funders and found no omissions. Amanda's and Jalal's complaints about Steve were of a personal nature, and unjustified in terms of the quality of his work.

Maria recognized that Steve was unable to continue, however, and she agreed to complete the work, only to find that Jalal and Amanda had written off all advisors as entirely irrelevant to the arts, and proceeded to say so loudly, and in public, at every opportunity. Defamatory and derogatory emails, now directed at Maria, were often copied to other professionals involved in their project and when the document prepared by Maria was already in their possession, Jalal and Amanda, backed by their new board, refused to pay the agreed fee.

The dancers had broken the terms of their contract and so did not own the information gathered from the research and presented in the document, which remained the intellectual property of Maria and Steve. Notwithstanding this, the advisors were unable to prevent their clients from acting upon the information they had researched and supplied, without recourse to a lengthy legal battle. Therefore, under the terms of the Data Protection Act 1998 (Principle 5), the raw data collected during the primary research period was destroyed – individual responses having been confidential. Steve and Maria contacted dancers and dance organizations to let them know that the information they had contributed would not, after all, be released or published.

The dance studios plan fell through, and an arts reporter, having interviewed Amanda and Jalal about a separate matter, and recorded some of their views, remarked that perhaps they needed to wake up and smell the coffee. More than a year later the development plan was revived, and this time the recommendations, from a different advisor, prevailed. Today, Amanda and Jalal are managers: they look after the premises, rent out dance studio spaces and employ staff. There is considerable capacity remaining within their building.

(*Names and environs have been changed to protect confidentiality.*)

example of upward bullying, a phenomenon more usual in theatres and arts centres than might be imagined, according to anecdotal evidence.

From the start, the potential benefits to be delivered via the founders' vision for this new arts project were jeopardized by their antagonistic attitude to the concept that they had to earn, and/or to justify, the financial assistance they sought. In effect, they had to reconsider the basis of their thinking, which was, essentially, that they had an entitlement to support because they were artists.

The bullying behaviour on the part of the founders seems to materialize as a result of a lack of trust, and of conflicting goals and priorities (Einarsen, Raknes and Matthiesen 1994 as reported in Rayner 1999: 34). The dancers behaved as though financial assistance was their right, and seemed to have gone along, only grudgingly, with the funders' stipulations – which complied with the principles adhering to the distribution of public funds. At first sight, their attitudes and behaviour could be attributed to the arrogance of youth and/or naivety; however, there is a marked difference between, on the one hand, self-assuredness and belief in one's own ideas and, on the other, rigid thinking (dualism) and resistance to change, as exemplified in De Bono's *I am Right, You are Wrong* (1991: 283):

Our understanding of perception helps us to see why there is such resistance to change. Our existing perceptions, concepts, models, and paradigms are a summary of our history. We can look at the world only through such a framework. If something new comes along we are unable to see it. Or, if we do see it, we see it as a mismatch with our older perception so we feel compelled to attack it. In any case we can judge it only through the old frame of reference.

De Bono puts forward a direct challenge to thinking based on inflexible categories, absolutes, argument and antagonistic point-scoring. He makes it clear that this is not creative and is unlikely to help solve problems or improve future situations. This thinking, however, characterizes Jalal's and Amanda's uncompromising attitudes, hostile actions and belligerent behaviour: they display the antithesis of the open mind. In order to understand more clearly their interpretation of the relationship they have with their advisor, their funders and with society, we can benefit from an examination of the concept of humans and infrahumans, as expounded in symbolic interactionism.

This is a theoretical approach to understanding the relationship between humans and society through the exchange of meaningful communication or symbols. In this approach, humans are portrayed as acting – proactive – as opposed to being acted upon – reactive. The main principles of symbolic interactionism are:

* human beings act toward things on the basis of the significance that things hold for them;
* this significance arises out of social interaction;
* social action results from combining individual paths of action.

(Herman and Reynolds 1994: 108).

This approach stands in contrast to the strict behaviourism of psychological theories that were prevalent at the time symbolic interactionism was first formulated (in the 1920s and 1930s) and also contrasts with structural-functionalism. According to symbolic interactionism, humans are distinct from infrahumans (lower animals) because infrahumans simply respond to their environment (that is, a stimulus evokes a response or stimulus > response), whereas humans have the ability to interrupt that process (that is, stimulus > cognition > response). Additionally, infrahumans are unable to conceive of alternative responses to gestures. Humans, however, can. This understanding should not be taken to indicate that humans never behave in a strict stimulus response fashion, but rather that humans have the capability of not responding in that fashion, and do so much of the time.

This perspective is also rooted in phenomenological thought. According to symbolic interactionism, the objective world has no reality for humans, only subjectively defined objects have meaning. Meanings can be altered through the creative capabilities of humans, and individuals may influence the many meanings that form their society (Herman and Reynolds 1994). Human society, therefore, is a social product. Symbolic interactionists advocate a particular methodology: they see meaning or significance as the fundamental component of human/society interaction, and studying human/society interaction requires getting at that significance. Thus, symbolic interactionists tend to employ more qualitative than quantitative methods in their research, and many social researchers prefer qualitative research methods (Gorard and Taylor 2004: 128). However, the most significant limitation of the symbolic-interactionist perspective relates to its primary contribution: it overlooks macro social structures (for example, norms, standards, customs, culture) as a result of focusing on micro-level interactions. Some symbolic-interactionists, however, would counter that if role theory is incorporated into symbolic-interactionism – which is now commonplace – this criticism is addressed.

To return to our case study, then, we can conclude that, unwittingly, Steve entered an arena in which Jalal and Amanda were dealing with unfamiliar territory, but which he, as an experienced practitioner, regarded as a well-known landscape. Amanda and Jalal were unable to exchange meaningful communication with their advisor, and were essentially reactive: the specific issues that Steve raised with them were of no significance to them. Therefore, in the context of their new and strange environment, they had an infrahuman response – we might dub it a knee-jerk reaction – whilst Steve, who was in familiar environs, had a human (cognitive) response.

Undoubtedly, Amanda and Jalal had an aversion to macro social structures, and Steve (and later Maria) may have been symbolic of aspects of the society they abhorred; it could be construed that they believed themselves to be of a new generation, at the cutting-edge, kicking against the traces, et cetera. It might be that the founders were nervous of losing sight of their core objectives through having to conform to rules they perceived as pertaining only to profit-driven organizations. Their preconceptions (De Bono's 'framework') about professional advice and about basic operational principles prepared the way for them to castigate and vociferously reject anything that they believed connoted commercialism and, in their view, threatened their artistic integrity.

As a result of the bullying behaviour, Steve and Maria suffered distress and financial disadvantage; however, despite the fact that they operated as solo advisors in isolation from one another, their ability to share information and to support each other made a significant difference to how they handled the episodes. Others who suffered at a distance because of the bullying were the dancers and dance organizations that willingly participated in the research project, only to find that the achievement of the vision to which they had enthusiastically subscribed was delayed for a long time. Some of these participants were angry at the delay, and unaware that this had happened as a result of Amanda's and Jalal's wholesale rejection of what they believed constituted commercial principles. This rejection was founded on the dancers' belief that management – including arts management – is a function of commercial ideology, and therefore inappropriate for performing artists.

Perhaps due to his considerable experience, Steve was fortunate enough to realize that he was experiencing the effects of the bullying behaviour after a relatively short period – four months. Zapf and Gross (2001: 502) report the views of Leymann (1993) that many victims do not realize for a considerable time what has happened to them, and research supports this. Zapf and Gross also outline the stages of conflict detailed by Glasl (1994) which indicate the tendency for bullies to engage in increasingly severe means to harm the other party as time passes. As indicated in Chapter 2, Glasl (1994: 501) models the stages of conflict from levels one to nine, increasing in severity through all the stages from: 'incidental slips into tensions' to the daunting 'total destruction and suicide'.

Steve was also able to remove himself from the situation. Zapf and Gross (2001: 504) report that in stress research Semmer (1996) has shown that control is an important moderator for successful coping, and, germane to Steve's particular predicament, author and consultant Tom Lambert advises consultants and independent advisors who experience 'personality clashes' as follows:

If the problem cannot be resolved try to have a qualified member of your team or network complete the assignment. (Lambert 1994: 241)

This is what Steve did. Attempts by the second advisor, Maria, to alleviate the situation were to no avail, however. By this stage the bullies were engaged in a 'systematic destructive campaign against the target' – level seven of Glasl's nine levels of conflict escalation (1994: 501). The target extended beyond the individual, Steve, to advisors generally, and beyond this to the *raison d'etre* of business advice and planning and its relevance to the arts.

The clients' ability to withhold payment for already completed work tilts the balance of power in such professional relationships. The advisors did what they were obliged to do by law to protect their intellectual property in the circumstances; however they lost the income they should have earned for work already undertaken. Ultimately, perhaps the reporter's candid prompt for a dose of realism had an impact on the two young dancers; or it may be that the drive to succeed forced them to re-evaluate their preconceived ideas and make a fresh start. Representatives of the funders made it clear that they were not in a position to become involved in a dispute between parties to a contract. Whatever the reason, the organization is now renting space, employing staff and overtly managing premises after all. It may be, however, that the spare capacity in the much-needed studios is an indicator of unconstructive leadership (Rayner 1999) or perhaps the immature approach to management has been maintained, resulting in a difficult or negative workplace atmosphere.

The philosophy these dancers embraced contradicts the fact of the growth and development of creative enterprises; however, it is not uncommon in certain kinds of arts organizations, and among certain artistic types (see Chapter 8). Presumably, as Jalal and Amanda are now doing all the things they rejected at the outset in terms of management, the lesson the young artists learned eventually was that funding and support is not a categorical entitlement that automatically accompanies the status of being an artist.

Entrepreneurship and Role Theory

Arts practitioners describe the phenomenon of being 'driven' by the creative process and this is a central characteristic of a particular type of creative individual: the arts entrepreneur. Four of the case studies describe organizations where the founders were active stakeholders, having been responsible for bringing the companies into existence in the first place: The Ensemble (Chapter 6) and The Theatre Project (Chapter 5), as well as The Museum (Chapter 3) and The Contemporary Dance Studios (Chapter 3). Derek Chong acknowledges that 'there is a case that artists have always been self-promoters' (Chong 2002: 36) and the expansion and development of an arts organization, and its success, brings it own difficulties, which is something that Gaupp (1997: 48) recognizes:

He was greatly admired in his community for his vision, energy, inventiveness and success in overcoming overwhelming obstacles and creating the wonderful local theatre. A few years later the board of directors fired him because of unbearable internal conflict within the theatre.

Andrew Gaupp's account of Founder's Syndrome includes stories of 'spontaneous developers' (Gaupp 1997: 49) – described by him as theatre practitioners who achieve a one-off success but then find themselves in conflict with the organization they have created. Like the CEO in The Theatre Project, founders work long and hard to attain their vision, often battling with difficult situations in hostile environments. Often they do so to great acclaim, finally winning the battle for hearts and minds and frequently obtaining a degree of statutory or other establishment support:

> *These creative founders assume and insist that they have a leadership position, usually the principal one, once the new theatre has been launched. (Gaupp 1997: 50)*

This can be the root of organizational conflict – in Gaupp's examples, founders tend to be driven out; however, in the arts research this is not always the case. Sometimes the conflict results in bullying behaviour and the founders prevail, often creating organizational dysfunction and incurring personal loss, notably where the creation of a new organization has been a team effort, as in The Museum. Understandably perhaps, when a self-appointed founder has succeeded in establishing a new project there is an assumption on their part that they will then take on a key role in the new organization. Often, however, difficulties are created because the role of creative entrepreneur requires different attributes to the role of organizational leader or manager.

Role theory posits that human behaviour is guided by expectations held both by the individual and by other people which correspond to different roles that individuals perform or enact in their daily lives, such as police constable, mother, or friend. Individuals generally have and manage many roles, each role consisting of a set of rules or norms that function as plans or blueprints to guide behaviour. Roles specify what goals should be pursued, what tasks must be accomplished and what performances are required in a given scenario or situation. Role theory holds that a substantial proportion of observable, day-to-day social behaviour is simply people carrying out their roles and it is predictive – it implies that if we have information about the role expectations for a specified position (for example, brother, actor, manager), a significant portion of the behaviour of the persons occupying that position can be predicted.

Role theory also maintains that in order to change behaviour it is necessary to change roles, as roles correspond to behaviours and vice versa. In addition to heavily influencing behaviour, roles influence beliefs and attitudes; individuals will change their beliefs and attitudes to correspond with their roles. For instance, someone overlooked for a promotion to a senior position in a theatre company may change their beliefs about the benefits of management by convincing themselves that they did not want the additional responsibility that would have accompanied the position, or simply that the position was not worth having in the first place. This is cognitive dissonance – as when, in Aesop's fable, The Fox and The Grapes, the fox decides the grapes he cannot reach must be sour anyway.

Many role theorists consider role theory to be one of the most compelling theories bridging individual behaviour and social structure. Roles, which are in part dictated by social structure and in part by social interactions, guide the behaviour of the individual. The individual, in turn, influences the norms, expectations and behaviours associated with roles. The understanding is, therefore, reciprocal. Role theory proposes that human beings spend much of their lives as participants in a variety of groups and organizations, and within these collections of people they occupy different positions. Attached to each of these positions is a role, or a set of tasks undertaken by the individual on behalf of the group or organization. Groups of people will have expectations of an individual, according to their role. These expectations may be expressed informally, or may take the form of norms or even structured regulations, which can include what the rewards will be when roles are successfully accomplished and what the punishments will be when they are not. The norm is that people usually carry out their roles and act in line with existing criteria; in other words, role theory assumes that individuals are primarily traditionalists who try to live up to the norms that accompany their roles. In terms of rewards and punishments, individuals in a group check each other's performance to determine whether it conforms to the agreed standards; the anticipation that other people will apply sanctions ensures role compliance.

Role theory does not explain social deviance when it does not correspond to a pre-specified function, however, so it does not elucidate bullying behaviour in the workplace. For instance, the behaviour of someone who adopts the role of tyrant or dictator can be predicted – they will intimidate and oppress. However, if a manager suddenly and unexpectedly begins to bully colleagues in the workplace, role theory is unable to explain why they do this – although role conflict has been suggested (as reported in Einarsen, Raknes and Matthiesen 1994). Alternatively, one could assume a sudden conversion to management as control – that is, successful managers can exploit and control workers, as reported in Bratton and Gold (1999). Another limitation of role theory is that it does not explain how role expectations came to be what they are, or when and how role expectations change, despite the theorists' argument that individuals and groups engage in reciprocity and influence each other.

In The Theatre Project (Chapter 5), the founder, as CEO, adopts the mantle of leader and achieves national and international success and investment after a 20-year struggle. The arrival of the new Director of Fundraising precipitates the loss of his confidante and puts an end to his highly personal ways of working – Gaupp (1997: 51) refers to this as 'closely kept' or 'kitchen table' administration. The founder in The Theatre Project responds to the bullying by his senior member of staff by ignoring it and retreating, building a protective barrier around his private vision and self-image by employing a personal assistant as gatekeeper. Essentially, he pretends the bullying is not happening – ostrich syndrome – evading the issue on the basis that the negative effects will fade away.

In The Museum, the perception by two founders that their leadership might be diminished led to internal conflict, fuelled by their pair bullying, and eventually to the disintegration of the original core team of founders. One issue was what Gaupp describes as an 'inability to bureaucratize' – the pair bullies could not cope with the changes required as the organization grew and matured because these necessitated the relinquishing of personal control. There is another sense in which this case study reflects aspects of Gaupp's Founder's Syndrome: the curator in this instance was an arts professional who had committed himself to seeing through the early stages of the project and this entailed educating the voluntary committee in the process. He may have regarded himself as the professional founder of the arts organization, with all that this implies. When the point was reached at which significant changes had to be made involving the devolution of power, the professional founder's vision proved inconvenient for, and unacceptable to, two of the voluntary founders and ultimately the curator felt he had to leave the organization.

In The Ensemble (Chapter 5), the bully manages to usurp the principal founder, slowly and surely, ousting his perceived competitor in order to establish his own position of power. Within 12 months this principal founder has lost all the original members of her team, except the bully with whom she appears to have formed an alliance. It is an interesting footnote that, following the conclusion of this particular incident, this alliance developed a sexual connotation, consistent with pair bullying. Anecdotal evidence suggests that, just as Alexis took on the role of Chair in The Museum, with Sofia acting as her sidekick, so Derek eventually dominated The Ensemble, with the principal founder, Claire, becoming his acolyte.

Finally, in The Contemporary Dance Studios the founders experience acute culture shock, confusion and anxiety on finding themselves in an unfamiliar environment. They desperately want financial support, but are confronted by the reality of arts funding requirements which contravene their personal ideology. Gaupp identifies certain characteristics of the personalities of founders: energy, charisma, singular focus, zeal, financial need, ego and spontaneity. He interprets these as: they work hard; they appeal to establishment figures; they concentrate on one goal; they willingly ignore rules to achieve their aims; they hunger after their personal goal; they crave appreciation by others; and, they are concerned with present outcomes rather than future stability. As with The Museum, the founders in The Contemporary Dance Studios experience 'inability to bureaucratize' at a very basic level. Gaupp states that some founders do not actually resist professionalization, instead:

> They recognize the need for change but insist that the changes be on their own terms so they retain control and their vision is not contaminated. (Gaupp 1997: 51)

In the end, the founders in The Contemporary Dance Studios had to recognize the need for change for the sake of achieving a version of their goal. Sigmund Freud might have said that they bullied because they were in simple denial, rejecting the facts with which they had been presented as untrue, despite the evidence. Thus, Steve and his colleague Maria became scapegoats for undeserved condemnation and blame.

Founder's Syndrome is a transferable concept: any of these studies could exemplify the stories of, particularly, smaller enterprises in any field where there is a requirement to manage leadership change. Writers on leadership have identified it in charitable and commercial organizations, and some have suggested remedies for easing the transition from founder to new CEO, (for example, McNamara 1999). McNamara offers constructive advice on courses of action for founders, board members who are non-founders, and staff – he regards the syndrome as primarily an organizational problem, because the organization is not working towards its agreed aims, objectives and mission, but rather responding to the personality of a prominent founder. If we consider the four case studies that feature Founder's Syndrome in the context of some of McNamara's principles, we can conceive that leadership changes could have been handled differently, and surmise whether this might have lessened the bullying, or even prevented it.

Table 3.2   The potential impact of constructive leadership on workplace bullying

	Activity	Result
The Theatre Project	Founding CEO ignores bullying and retreats. Staff unable to cope. Target collapses under the strain.	Bully prevails. Targets leave. Founder achieves vision, but organization is demoralized.
What if?	Founding CEO investigated reports from staff and colleagues and addressed the bullying behaviour.	Positive action might have been taken. Bullying might have stopped.
The Museum	Founders refuse to share power. Set out to remove perceived obstacle. Target collapses under the strain.	Bullies prevail. Target leaves. Two other founders leave and organization closes down.
What if?	Founders adhered to professional standards, and adopted principles of best practice and good governance.	Bullying might never have happened.
The Ensemble	Founder is usurped by bully who flatters her, whilst targeting perceived competitor.	Bully prevails. Organization breaks up, pair bullying may result.
What if?	Founder had made decisions based on organization's aims and mission, appraising others' performance on merit.	Founder might prevail as credible leader. Organization might not break up, although bully might have moved on.
The Contemporary Dance Studios	Founders cling to outdated ideology. Target designated as scapegoat for unpopular, opposing ideas.	Bullies prevail. Target stands down and organization fails. Bullies finally accept same advice after long delay.
What if?	Founders had embraced a professional approach and adopted principles of best practice and good governance?	Bullying may never have happened. Organization may have succeeded at the outset.

A Founder's Journey

This is a contribution from a founder, reproduced almost verbatim. Names and environs have been changed to protect confidentiality.

Before I formed the company Masquerade, I was also a founder member of three other dance companies, the first, Company A (1996–1997), led by Artistic Director Agata, who I danced with for a year, soon disintegrated with a lack of funds, commitment and any kind of administration. She talked a lot, she had great ambition but she didn't see it through … Secretly I thought 'I could do a much better job' and so I set on the path, which a lot of young dancers strive for. I wanted my own company. I wanted to create jobs.

Company number two, Dance B (1997–1998), was then established with two other superb dancers, Vanya and Étienne. The difficulties came when Étienne wanted his friend to join, who in Vanya's mind wasn't right for his choreography and wasn't up to his standards. With two strong-minded characters, ultimately one had to go. I was stuck in the middle of the conflict. [The third company] C Pirouette (1998–1999) was then born as a splinter group. It was short lived but was the most energized time in our existence; it was solely about making and performing truly amazing pieces of work. We ditched the name for Masquerade; it has since traded as a partnership, a sole trader, a company and a charity. Ten years later I understand what all of those are. I wish I had known sooner. I would have applied to become a charity earlier and sought a board of professionals rather than my friends – I remember being put off by many arts professionals who I sought advice from – they said it was far too complicated. I would have also sought an accountant who knew about how arts organizations functioned.

Katy and I ran Masquerade in its early days. We saw each other most days and were totally committed to the company, putting it before everything else in our lives. Katy was an enigmatic dancer and performer, the company was her love and it supported her ambition to succeed as a dancer. Dance came first every time and she was quite obsessive in her need to succeed in her own right. She has always been a very dominant character, inspired many, and had confidence in abundance – or so I once thought. There were also people who were jealous of this success and I witnessed dancers undermine and question the roots of what she believed in.

For years we worked for no or little financial gain and many of our dancers worked on a voluntary basis for long periods. We paid dancers and technicians before ourselves and got by on subsidy from my other job, the odd small grant from the Arts Council and charities. We were good at what we did, and felt that our audience loved and respected the work. Some of the most spontaneous and explosive choreography was created during these early years.

Katy had a very different view to money than I did and agreed that I would manage the financial side of the company, of which I had little experience. We had a small committee of friends and I ran the bank account as a sole trader and later progressed to a formal company. In actual fact this cost me a fortune just in accountant fees, paid to a firm that had no real understanding of arts organizations and of the huge minefield of grants and paperwork that financial management in the arts required.

Katy and I were partners in every sense and trust was at the centre of every decision. It worked through friendship, commitment and belief in our vision. It was a well-balanced company and survived for five years. I was also lucky enough to have some very good advice along the way. We toured nationally in 2005 on a small grant of £10,000 from a charity and it was the most successful tour we have ever undertaken. It could only have happened through the goodwill and ambition of our dancers, who believed in the work and didn't mind subsidizing their career through bar work.

The unfortunate time came when we received our first large amount of funding and we couldn't be more excited about the chance to really move the company forward. After rigorous auditions we chose our company of professional dancers. For the first time the company wasn't made up from our friends, we wanted the best dancers and with that came complications.

We assigned job descriptions for the first time and for the purpose of the tour Katy took on the title of the Artistic Director as principal dancer in the company. Katy didn't really comprehend what was required of her role and hadn't considered the implication of what it really meant. It was a title with responsibility both on a management and on an artistic level. Our inexperience tested our strengths to the limits and we had the biggest learning curve ahead of us. I had to learn quickly and had to get organized.

Katy lost heart when rehearsals for her choreography didn't go as well as expected. Working with new dancers seemed to threaten Katy, particularly in her ability to perform as a dancer in the new choreography. As any dancer, she found it particularly challenging and rigorous. She found the conflict of working full time as a dancer, choreographer and manager too much.

I was busy with administration for the company, creating new choreography and learning new skills to equip me to promote the company on a national level. The all-round support I had provided Katy for so long couldn't be sustained and my time in the studio was limited. Our friendship was threatened and replaced by the realities and demands of the dancers and new choreography. The dancers were hostile to her emotional outbreaks and fears, and doubted the quality of her choreography during the rehearsal process. The fears I think escalated through her own insecurity, and her confidence was attacked.

It was a long tour that tested Katy to the limit to be both physically and artistically inspiring, to lead as a manager and not to mention socialize at the end of the day and share digs. The pressure was immense and over three months of touring it sadly got the better of her and she broke down. I think that it was perhaps a combination of both the artistic/managerial pressure and the hostility of the other dancers. I think that she began by questioning her own ability and, when her dancers confirmed her own fears through their negativity, emotions escalated. She had always been used to positive feedback for her work, and was now finding herself in new territory without the words of her own self-encouragement or from others.

At the end of the tour, there was an unbearable level of animosity which had built up. In my mind it appeared blown out of context, and unfortunately she was beaten by the company's success. There was also a social drug scene, which I think is rife particularly within the dance sector, which only amplified issues outside of work. Love-hate relationships happened within the company for a time and when things were going wrong, spirits spiralled downwards.

Katy described to me that during this time she had felt the same feelings as when she was bullied at school many years before. I was caught in the middle – I had positive relationships with all the staff. Something we had believed in for so long had changed into something new. The lack of respect she felt from the dancers broke down belief in herself as a dancer. At this point I knew that our organization did not have the capacity to deliver what was expected of a successful company.

Until this day I do not know what exactly happened during that time. I feel that perhaps I was partly responsible, striving for a properly managed company. Maybe I had felt a total lack of understanding from Katy on the huge responsibility I suddenly had to undertake to achieve all of our artistic goals. And I am sure that also I had moments of intense anxiety when things went wrong for me.

For a while the company became a lonely place because it was just me running things, but it was also when I learnt the most and that was the challenge which I think I crave. From this experience I developed a clearer vision of what I wanted the company to become. There cannot be any compromise when it comes to the artistic vision, in terms of creating new work, and I don't think that vision can really be shared with another person over a long period of time. I think that it is essential to have total belief in your own ability and goals.

I knew that in order to survive we needed a properly regulated company. I decided to recruit a board to become a charity. People asked me – didn't it bother me to 'hand over my company?' – for me it was a relief to ensure that my company was looked after properly. I have never been one to crave control, which I believe is the root of many people's conflicts. I thrive off providing other people with the opportunity to work and explore their potential as artists and managers. Of course I love being my own boss, but I also need guidance on how to do it right.

Through my business the most important thing I have learnt is that all issues have to resolve one way or the other. What is the worst that will happen? I usually assess this and work back from there. A highly inventive escape plan sometimes helps me get through most crisis periods.

I think that founding a company is viewed as having achieved something highly important by my close circle of college friends, some dedicated reviewers and the founder members of companies who didn't make it as far as I have.

And I suppose my audience just care about what they see, not how we got there.

4 *Institutional Bullying*

As an example of a restructuring nightmare, where confusion, conflict and hostile behaviour are permitted to take hold and flourish, this case study emphasizes that a gap exists between the rhetoric used as justification for organizational restructuring and the reality of participants' experiences (Sheehan 1996). Although there is an identifiable bully at work – one person – this case also illustrates management abdicating its responsibility for staff, and it presents a scenario wherein a specific individual is the embodiment of bullying perpetrated by the whole organization (Zapf 1999).

THE ARTS SERVICE: ORGANIZATIONAL BULLYING/ CORPORATE BULLYING

A local authority department was undergoing relocation and restructuring, during which several staff posts became vacant and were not filled. This resulted in heavier workloads for remaining staff and some gaps in line management. The arts service team delivered a small part of the department's activity, and found itself under the auspices of a new manager, Nina, for whom the arts remit was a new concept. She was an experienced administrator used to delivering reports on the council's service within a framework based on measurable performance indicators. The arts service, on the other hand, specialized in working with disabled people and in disadvantaged communities, and staff had not previously had to work within quantitative parameters.

Soon after her new responsibilities commenced, Nina began to express a dismissive attitude towards the concept of arts provision generally, letting the service staff know that, in the current target culture, it was unlikely they could provide enough hard indicators to secure their continuing existence. During the following months an atmosphere of constant negativity prevailed and the team members became increasingly disconcerted about their future prospects. Nina did not communicate well with them, often failing to disseminate information that was important to the team for the satisfactory completion of their work. It was evident that she lacked knowledge about disability arts work generally and the range and scope of management it required.

One staff member, Jenny, realized that the absence of support for staff during restructuring was having a particularly detrimental effect: it was eroding developments the service had achieved and resulting in staff experiencing embarrassment in public situations, for example when information they should have had, via Nina, did not reach them. In front of Jenny and other staff, Jenny's line manager, Laura, was experiencing unfair criticism and insinuating comments from Nina that her work was not meeting expectations. As a result, Laura became severely emotionally distressed, eventually taking prolonged sick leave. On her return, she found that her responsibilities had been changed and she was to be relocated away from the rest of the arts service team.

Internal relationships deteriorated, and Jenny complained verbally to the personnel department on a number of occasions to no effect until finally she brought a complaint under the council's Disciplinary and Grievance Procedure about Nina's insensitive management style. She took advice from the Citizens' Advice Bureau and copied her complaint to the chair of the leisure services committee, to ensure that it was taken seriously.

Throughout a series of meetings, involving Jenny and senior staff from outside her department, every attempt was made to treat the situation non-officially – the human resources staff indicated that Jenny had not completed the grievance form correctly; she had not detailed specifics of personal hurt; her past verbal complaints had not met with any response because 'comments and actions were tolerated as specific behaviour that could be expected from particular people'; no physical threats had been made; Jenny could not make a complaint under the Disciplinary and Grievance Procedure about the treatment of other people. During the final meeting, which Jenny and Laura attended, Nina expressed surprise at the complaint. No malice had been intended in anything she had said or done.

The human resources staff proceeded to outline their proposal to bring in external consultants to develop a strategic plan that would ensure all staff members were valued and that appropriate systems were put in place. This did not materialize. In some distress, Laura left the organization. Jenny moved to another job as visual arts officer where she assisted local young people in compiling a video about bullying problems in their community. The arts service was wound up, the remaining members of staff were made redundant and Nina moved on to restructure another department.

(Names and environs have been changed to protect confidentiality.)

The background to this case is one of organizational mayhem. Bullying has been found to correlate with:

> ... *dissatisfaction with management, role conflicts, and a low degree of control over one's own work situation (Matthiesen and Einarsen 2001: 469)*

and all three elements are present here. Nina's lack of experience in the field of arts provision is matched by a lack of understanding of the staff and their concerns. She withholds information and bullies the supervisor, Laura, in front of other staff, causing distress in those, like Jenny, who are witnesses. The organization, via restructuring, changes Laura's role and further isolates her on her return from sick leave.

There is inconsistency and disarray about the way in which Jenny's complaints are handled. They are not taken seriously and various, relatively trivial, reasons are cited for them being inadmissible under the council's Disciplinary and Grievance Procedure. The promised strategic plan is held up as some sort of solution, although never put in place, and there is no attempt to address the specific concerns Jenny raises. Management appears indifferent to the complaints. There is no evidence that the council accepts any responsibility for the bullying behaviour: the restructuring takes responsibilities away from Laura, and the bully, Nina, devalues her work, undermining her capabilities. Laura's distress is acute, and this accords with other research findings:

> Exposure to systematic and long-lasting verbal, non-physical, and non-sexual abusive and aggressive behaviour in the workplace causes a variety of negative health effects in the target. (Zapf and Einarsen 2001: 370)

Jenny, who witnesses the bullying, is increasingly distressed to see her line manager intimidated, so much so that she decides to take action. Vartia (2001) notes that the witnessing of bullying was found to be a significant predictor of general stress and mental strain reactions (as reported in Mikkelsen and Einarsen 2001: 394), so Jenny's concerns on her own behalf are valid, and the statement that she could not make a complaint under the Disciplinary and Grievance Procedure about the treatment of other people – which appears to be a literal interpretation of the council's policy – indicates that a review of such policies may be needed to ensure that they protect the welfare of all staff, including those who indirectly encounter personal hurt.

Perspectives on the Bullying Organization

Among possible causes of workplace bullying are the organizational culture and the social system of the workplace (Zapf 1999). Studies have looked at the extent to which traditional organizational cultures tend to permit abuse of power (Archer 1999; Bennett and Lehman 1999) and researchers have noted the tendency for organizations to treat the target of bullying behaviour as the problem (Leymann 1990). Ståle Einarsen, a professor in the Department of Psychosocial Science, University of Bergen, Norway, and author of many books and articles about workplace bullying comments:

> When stepping into the case, upper management, union representatives, or personnel administration tend to accept the prejudices produced by the offenders, thus blaming the victim for its misfortune. Third parties or managers may see the situation as no more than fair treatment of a difficult and neurotic person. (Einarsen 1999: 19).

This mirrors the description of third-stage stress as reported by Wilkie (1996), where schoolchildren who react with uncharacteristic violence to bullying behaviour can be wrongly labelled as troublemakers. It also correlates with the reports from arts workers who attempted, unsuccessfully, to convince management that bullying was taking place. Apparent complicity on the part of management is consistent with the issue of permissibility (Rayner 1999), which is further explored in Chapter 8. Research into conflict in the workplace, how it develops and grows, and how it is managed, indicates that an imbalance of power or strength is necessary for dissension in the workplace to become bullying, although disparity can evolve over time from an apparently equivalent relationship (Zapf and Gross 2001). An example of this in the arts research is in the case study of The Ensemble (Chapter 6), which also provides another ingredient that contributes to bullying in organizations – a situation where there are high demands on collaboration (Matthiesen and Einarsen 2001). As individuals often act and respond at differing rates, the requirement to work in a team may be likely to cause pressure and tension, *per se*, and will be exacerbated if there is unconstructive leadership (Rayner 1999).

Einarsen (1999: 21–22) cites separate studies examining work environments in Ireland, Norway and Finland, which have noted broadly similar reports from bullying targets. An organization undergoing restructuring, managed with an authoritarian leadership style, coupled with a competitive environment and myriad interpersonal conflicts, created highly stressful working conditions for 30 Irish employees (Seigne 1998). In a Finnish study, an authoritative approach to settling differences of opinion, married with an information and discussion vacuum, led to a sense of helplessness among employees who lacked the ability to determine their own future (Vartia 1996). In Norway, respondents also cited a lack of chance for self-determination, coupled with the absence of constructive leadership and a high level of role conflict (Einarsen, Raknes and Matthiesen 1994).

These characteristics were also present in the arts research case studies, particularly The Ensemble, The Theatre Project and The Arts Service. Additionally, one respondent in the pilot survey described the working environment during a period of change thus:

> … *particularly insensitive management style … constant negativity directed at employees …
> undue amount of harassment leading to staff being stressed and absent throughout the year … a
> lack of knowledge by management of the work carried out, and absence of support for employees
> attempting to maintain a service with lack of structure and backing … continual 'put-downs'
> and insinuations that work carried out is not meeting expectations, belies a subversive form of
> demotivation … not conducive to a good working environment and interpersonal relationships
> … my role has been diminished to such an extent that I am indeed threatened with no other
> option than to 'opt out'.*

The working environment described by this arts worker features autocratic leadership, poor management, miserable and demotivated staff who feel helpless, are confused about their roles and aware of only the bleakest possible outlook in terms of their future. The ripple effect of bullying within a workforce can cause absentee levels to increase and morale to plummet. As a result, members of staff lack inspiration, become less motivated and less productive, and organizational effectiveness is reduced. A bullied employee is more likely to leave an organization and high staff turnover can be a reliable indicator of an unhappy workplace as the ripple effect of bullying extends beyond targets to witnesses (UNISON 1997; Rayner 1999). Researchers have commented on the difficulties faced by employees who have tried and failed to address the problem according to existing procedures in their organization and have then resorted to the supreme antisocial behaviour which runs contrary to respect for corporate culture: whistleblowing (Giacalone and Greenberg 1997; Labour Research Department 1997; Richter 2001).

Commenting on corporate culture, McCarthy, Sheehan and Kearns (1995) reported the emergence of a discourse of restructuring and Sheehan (1996) used case studies to identify that when a crisis occurred in capitalist organizations, this was a principal factor in precipitating restructuring, which was often accompanied by bullying behaviour. Sheehan identifies open communication as a first casualty of organizational change, and this is consistent with some of the arts research and with the study in Finland where employees encountered the complete absence of opportunities to obtain information and to engage in debate and discussion (Vartia 1996). Sheehan cites the need for management styles that are compassionate and caring, offering positive support and opportunities for team building.

Organizational or institutional bullying often includes unjustified criticism and punishment and/or changes in the duties or responsibilities of the employee, without reasonable grounds for the change and to the employee's detriment: for example, insisting on an employee undertaking unnecessary menial tasks or duties. Corporate bullying can also involve unfair working terms and conditions, such as unreasonably long working hours (or unreasonably short notice of a requirement to work extra hours) and inadequate rates of pay. An unhappy workplace and failure to deal satisfactorily with complaints are also features of a climate of corporate bullying.

How Organizations Work

If we consider how organizations work we can appreciate the view that, just as with the structure and workings of society, guidelines and directives are useful, if not essential, enabling tools. Functionalists believe that behaviour in society is structural – that is, that rules and regulations help methodize relationships between members of society and that values provide general principles for behaviour in terms of roles and standards. Functionalism is concerned with how interdependent sections of society work together to fulfil the functions necessary for the survival of society as a whole – in microcosm, how members of a team work together to accomplish a task successfully.

Structural functionalism does not account for social change, however, because it focuses so intently on social order and equilibrium. In the case of restructuring of a department or an organization, therefore, such as in The Arts Service, the strict adherence to rules and regulations stated in the disciplinary and grievance procedure may theoretically be intended to ensure the organization's stability, however its effect is to disallow change – to prevent employees from dealing positively with likely, and worrying, changes to their working environment.

There is also the argument that functionalism describes social institutions solely through the extent to which they operate or achieve and, as a result, does not explain the cause of those operations or achievements. This is not unlike the positivist approach that interprets bullying behaviour in terms of what can be measured (for example, Rayner 1997). In some ways structural functionalist theory supports the status quo, and this has a bearing on the issue of how organizations exhibit tolerance of bullying behaviour.

Distinctions about contemporary societies in sociological theory include broad historical trends such as industrialization, underdevelopment, urbanization and globalization, and stages of development such as modernity, postmodernity, post-industrial underdevelopment and the network society. In their discussion of employee accounts of bullying, Liefooghe and Mackenzie Davey (2003: 219) claim that postmodernism challenges the positivist theory that there is an objective truth in all situations:

> by rejecting the taken for granted notions of rationality, order, clarity, truth and realism and the idea of intellectual progress ...

Their desire is to draw attention to:

> *disorder, contradictory explanations and ambiguity ... postmodernism uses deconstructionism to reveal the strategies that are used to represent truth claims ... Postmodernism is thus concerned with the use of language – as such, language becomes the unit of analysis.*

In this respect, then, postmodernists examine and analyse language, as do positivists. However, whereas the measurement made by positivists is held to define the existence of a phenomenon such as bullying, postmodernists are sceptical about the existence of an absolute truth:

> *All interpretations are regarded as equally valid, which implies that our understanding of the truth will always be fragmented, selective and biased. (Liefooghe and Mackenzie Davey 2003: 219)*

When we consider the gulf between how some bullies perceive their own actions and how targets experience them, the relativist viewpoint becomes increasingly justifiable. In The Arts Service, Nina was doing the job she knew and had always done, albeit in other spheres. It is unclear whether she realized the devastating effect she was having in her new department, and also whether those senior managers and HR personnel charged with dealing with the issue were experiencing the same reality as those suffering the consequences.

In the arts sector, organizational culture, custom and practice undoubtedly force some people to comply with unfair or unreasonable working terms and conditions. Trades unions and other agencies representing those who work in the performing arts are particularly protective of employees' rights in respect of hours of work and rates of pay, and they work to combat exploitative terms and conditions, which could be indicators of corporate bullying. Traditionally, arts workers are regarded as overworked and underpaid, not least because they tend not to work office hours (in the UK, 9.00 am to 5.00 pm) as performances, readings and exhibition openings also happen in the evenings and/or at weekends – the inaptly named unsocial hours. Often, this means that arts workers attend to business during office hours and then also cover performance or exhibition requirements to work unsocial hours. Taken together, these are usually more than the standard 37–40-hour week.

One of the aims of the research was to determine if arts organizations were offering fair terms and conditions to employees: were working hours and rates of pay on an equal footing with those in other sectors, or were employers wittingly or unwittingly indulging in corporate bullying?

Working Hours in the Arts

The Working Time Directive provides for a maximum 48-hour working week, unless an employee has signed a waiver to opt out of this condition. In the wake of its submission to the European Commission on the Working Time Directive opt-out, BECTU had a particular interest in surveying members' attitudes to working hours and other terms and conditions offered to employees. In theatres and arts centres, employees reported that such a waiver was routinely included in some contracts of employment, the result being that the worker has no option of working within a 48-hour working week – the opt-out is the compulsory norm. Also, if employees have signed such a contract, does this negate their right to complain, and to have their complaint considered, no matter how many hours they are asked to work? Is this, then, a coercive measure by employers?

Asked whether arts employees worked longer than a 40-hour week, 69.1 per cent of participants gave a clear indication that this is common practice (Figure 4.1). Members of the technical staff team were most likely to work longer hours once or more per month, as were the majority of management, administration and production staff (Figure 4.2).

Most frequently, advance notice of the requirement to work longer hours was less than one week; more than two weeks' notice was rare (Figure 4.3). In some venues, repeated and/or familiar working patterns might provide informal signals to employees as to which weeks they would be more likely to have to work longer hours, however this was not identified during the survey. In Chapter 2, the research results are reported in terms of all of the participants, plus several subgroups, including those who stated that they had been the target of a bully – the bullied group. Within this group 41.4 per cent (+3.6 per cent on the norm) reported that they normally had less than one week's notice

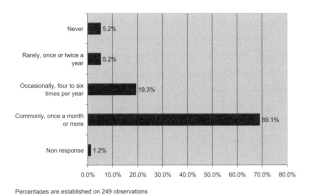

Percentages are established on 249 observations

Figure 4.1   Frequency of working longer hours

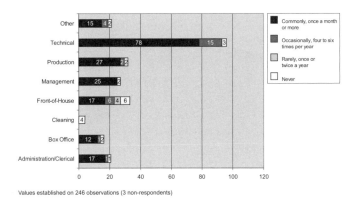

Values established on 246 observations (3 non-respondents)

Figure 4.2   Working longer hours by areas of work

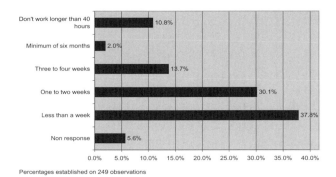

Percentages established on 249 observations

Figure 4.3   Notice of requirement to work longer hours

to work longer hours, and 11.1 per cent (+0.3 per cent on the norm) said they did not work longer hours than 40 hours per week.

In the agreement between BECTU and the Theatrical Management Association (TMA) dated 30 April 2006, the 48-hour working week, where applicable, is averaged over 52 weeks, or over the period of employment if this is less. Employees are entitled to a break of 11 consecutive hours in any period of 24 hours, and 24 consecutive hours in any period of seven days. Where these breaks cannot be given for operational reasons, compensatory rest (or Time Off In Lieu (TOIL)) is given during basic working hours. In 2010 this agreement was due to be changed, however there were no planned changes to these clauses and, further, the TMA now states that, although opt-out causes do exist, they are not included in any standard contract and must be negotiated with management on an individual basis.

For just over 40 per cent of all respondents it was possible to take TOIL after a busy period or later in the year (Table 4.1). However 41.4 per cent (43.4 per cent of the bullied group) stated that taking time off was either not possible because of the workload or not encouraged. A higher percentage of the bullied group (+2.9 per cent on the norm) reported that taking time off was not encouraged.

Those who answered 'Other' to the question about TOIL stated that some employees received overtime payments, worked annualized hours or on a flexible rota. This was also the case among the bullied group, where only one respondent said that TOIL was not

Table 4.1   Time off in lieu (TOIL) of notice

Response	Survey Group %	Bullied Group %
Non-response	7.2%	9.1%
Yes, time off is taken immediately following a busy period	16.1%	14.1%
Yes, time off is added to holidays or taken later in the year	24.1%	24.2%
No, the workload means it is not possible to take time off	24.1%	23.2%
No, taking time off is not encouraged	17.3%	20.2%
Other (please state)	11.2%	9.2%
Total Observations	**249**	**99**

Note: values are based on the survey group (249) and the sub-group, the bullied group (99).

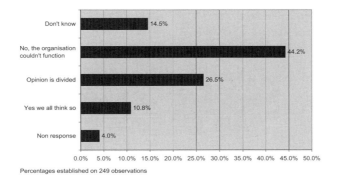

Figure 4.4 values:
Don't know 14.5%
No, the organisation couldn't function 44.2%
Opinion is divided 26.5%
Yes we all think so 10.8%
Non response 4.0%

Percentages established on 249 observations

Figure 4.4   Attitudes to the possibility of working shorter hours

provided. There was also evidence that some theatres and arts centres made no provision for TOIL, and in two cases in London venues the working week was reported as 'always' 48 hours. Some of the staff in theatres or arts centres said that taking time off was not encouraged, and this was common irrespective of location or scale of venue.

Arts employees were asked if they thought the workload could be achieved within shorter working hours (Figure 4.4). A significant 44.2 per cent said their organization could not function without staff working longer hours. Whilst this would appear to justify the opt-out, we need to think about whether this is as a result of long-term custom and practice in the arts; is it a myth promulgated by arts management; or is it the truth? If it is a fact, it reveals that arts organizations are either under resourced, or not strategically managing staff time and workload effectively, or both.

Overall, opinion about shorter working hours was divided, although the majority believed that their organization could not function without employees working longer hours. This held true for the bullied group and for the managers. However more people in the bullied group, and more managers, also believed the consensus of opinion within their organization was that it would be possible to complete the work without working longer hours: 13.1 per cent (bullied group) and 14.8 per cent (managers) compared to 10.8 per cent of the survey group as a whole, and 9.3 per cent of the non-bullied group.

Respondents were asked if anyone in their organization had objected to longer working hours during the last five years. Of those who replied, 44.2 per cent said there had been objections; 32.5 per cent didn't know; 20.3 per cent answered 'No'. Overall, 50.2 per cent said that there were objections, and 66.7 per cent of managers in the group noted that there were objections. Managers may be more likely to know about objections to working hours from all parts of their organizations, than would employees based within particular areas who may only have knowledge specific to their working group.

Notwithstanding the Working Time Directive, arts management does appear to exploit the long hours culture: only 10.8 per cent of employees stated they did not work longer than 40 hours per week; most employees were given less than a week's notice of the requirement to work longer hours; 41.4 per cent of employees said they could not take time off due to the demands of the workload or that it was not encouraged. Some theatres and arts centres make no provision at all for time off in lieu of working extra hours, so if the workload necessitates longer hours of work the employee is unable to offset these against shorter hours on another occasion. More than half of the bullied group, and two-

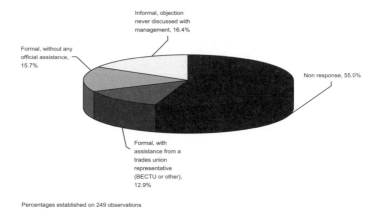

Percentages established on 249 observations

Figure 4.5   How objections to working hours were handled

thirds of arts managers, reported that employees had objected to working hours, and, in the main, that management was considered to be indifferent, at best, to such objections. One third of the managers declined to comment on how these objections were handled. Those who did comment reported that informal objections were dismissed and that only a small number of formal objections were upheld by management – that is, objections brought with trades union assistance.

Knowledge about how objections were handled was evidently limited, and more than half the respondents (55 per cent) did not answer the relevant question (Figure 4.5) – in the subgroups this was 49.5 per cent of the bullied group and 33.3 per cent of managers. A higher percentage of the bullied group had more knowledge of how complaints were handled than those in the survey as a whole. Among managers, 40.7 per cent said these were settled informally and never discussed with management, compared with 16.4 per cent in the survey group as a whole.

The outcome of formal complaints, where known, demonstrated that assistance from a trades union or other official marginally improved the chances of an objection being upheld rather than dismissed by management (Figure 4.6). Informal complaints were dismissed in every case where the outcome was known. This was true of the bullied group

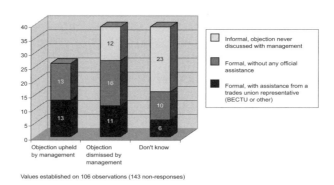

Values established on 106 observations (143 non-responses)

Figure 4.6   Outcomes of objections to working hours

also; however no managers gave any information about the results of a formal hearing (with trades union assistance) and twice as many managers reported that objections were dismissed, as the number who reported that objections were upheld.

A total of 109 respondents (43.8 per cent) commented on what happened to objectors following an objection to working hours. Of these, 18.3 per cent said employees left the organization – this was stated by 25.5 per cent of those who commented in the bullied group – but the vast majority said employees stayed on in the same position. No managers reported employees leaving following objections, although 5.6 per cent of managers who commented said objectors stayed on in a different capacity.

The survey sought to test how arts workers perceived their employer's attitude to complaints about longer working hours (Figure 4.7). Almost half, at 49.4 per cent, did not answer this question – 41.4 per cent of the bullied group. It is not clear whether they did not know their employer's attitude – which seems unlikely as 44.2 per cent knew objections had been made – or whether they were wary of expressing an opinion.

Of those who did respond, half felt that their organization was indifferent to complaints – this opinion was shared by 48.3 per cent of those who replied from the bullied group. Just over one fifth of those who replied felt their organization was sympathetic and understanding about this issue. Among the bullied group, this fell to 15.5 per cent of those who replied. So, only a few respondents felt their employers were sympathetic – even fewer from the bullied group. One respondent described managment as having sympathy but no ability to act, whilst another said management had understanding, but not sympathy!

Other comments indicated that employers' attitudes to complaints included responding with resignation, with annoyance, that the attitudes vary (presumably with the individual), that employers only pay lip service to reducing hours (this from a manager within the bullied group) and that the organization's management team itself does not work more than 39 hours per week. There was acknowledgement that some individual managers understood complaints about long hours, but also references to an organizational position of 'can't function any other way'.

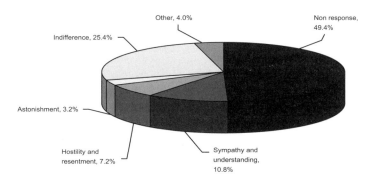

Percentages established on 249 observations

Figure 4.7   Perceptions of management attitudes to objections about working hours

Two-thirds of the managers replied to the question about employers' attitudes to objections about working hours. The majority, at 25.9 percent, cited indifference, however, unsurprisingly, more managers (18.5 per cent) felt their organization responded with sympathy and understanding.

As might be expected, a higher percentage of members of the bullied group (8.1 per cent) recorded hostility and resentment in response to complaints, compared to 7.2 per cent of the arts workers as a whole. Interestingly, 14.8 per cent of the managers also recorded this response. Arguably, managers have a relatively knowledgeable view of their employers' attitudes because they are privy to them; however the bullied group may be nearer to the truth because they may have been on the receiving end of their employer's attitudes to difficult personal circumstances. Some of the bullied group, 7.1 per cent, also reported that employers reacted with astonishment to complaints – almost twice as many as reported by arts workers as a whole. Among the managers, 3.7 per cent shared this view.

According to 18.3 per cent of respondents, complaints about working hours resulted in objectors leaving the organization, although no managers reported employees leaving in the wake of objections. In general, arts workers, including those within the bullied group, were reluctant to comment on management attitudes towards objections and this may have been through fear of negative reports being fed back to their organizations; however the majority opinion of those who did respond was that management was indifferent to complaints. This was also true among managers themselves.

Rates of Pay in the Arts

In considering the issue of corporate bullying by virtue of the terms and conditions of arts employees, levels of pay and the incidence of objections to rates of pay, coupled with management's response to complaints could be indicators. Pay in the arts has been recognized as being below that for comparable jobs in other industries, and in some cases discrimination is gender-based. For example, a survey, which was conducted across 20 countries in 2008 by unions representing nearly 80,000 performers, found that female actors are paid less than men and have fewer work opportunities (Blake 2009).

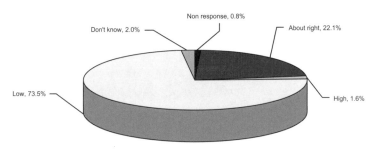

Percentages established on 249 observations

Figure 4.8   Perceptions of rates of pay

There was a high response rate to the questions about current rates of pay: 100 per cent of administration/clerical workers, cleaning staff, managers and other staff; 93.7 per cent of box office staff; 94.2 per cent of front-of-house staff; 93.5 per cent of production staff; and 97.9 per cent of technicians. Employees were asked to consider whether rates of pay were about right, low or high (Figure 4.8). The majority of arts workers (73.5 per cent) considered that their rates of pay were low, even with overtime, and, as with longer working hours, their organization was considered to be indifferent to complaints about pay – the majority opinion being that 'often' or 'very often' employers could afford to pay more. Among the managers, 33.3 per cent felt rates of pay were about right and 63 per cent felt that they were low, whilst 1.6 per cent of the survey group felt pay was high, compared to 3.7 per cent of the managers. The great majority of respondents in each area of work felt that pay was low.

Overall, 22.1 per cent felt rates of pay were 'about right' (24.2 per cent of the bullied group) and 73.5 per cent felt that these were 'low' (69.7 per cent of the bullied group), so a higher percentage of the bullied group was satisfied with rates of pay than of the survey group as a whole. This is of interest when compared with the fact that a greater percentage of the bullied group (12.1 per cent) than of the non-bullied group (8 per cent) felt other benefits added value to wages – perhaps illustrating that those who had been targets of a bully were appreciative of the advantages of time off, flexible working arrangements and a positive working environment.

Most employees did not feel that overtime payments compensated for having to work longer hours (Figure 4.9): when asked to reconsider their opinions of pay when overtime is added, and to state whether this made levels very generous, 11.6 per cent believed this was 'often' or 'very often' the case (8.1 per cent of the bullied group); 15.4 per cent said this was the case sometimes (11.1 percent of the bullied group) and 65 per cent stated that this was never or rarely the case (72.8 per cent of the bullied group).

Of the managers' responses, 22.2 per cent believed that pay including remuneration for overtime was 'often' very generous; 3.7 per cent felt this was the case 'sometimes'; and, as with the bullied group, 74.1 per cent felt that pay plus overtime was 'never' or 'rarely' generous.

Arts employees were asked if overtime payments made longer hours more acceptable or attractive (Figure 4.10): 23.7 per cent of respondents were definite that they did not prefer longer working hours because overtime was payable; 10.8 per cent stated that

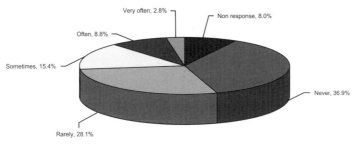

Very often, 2.8%
Non response, 8.0%
Often, 8.8%
Sometimes, 15.4%
Never, 36.9%
Rarely, 28.1%

Percentages established on 249 observations

Figure 4.9   Perceptions of whether, with overtime added, pay is generous

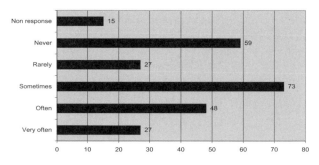

Percentages established on 249 observations

Figure 4.10   Response to overtime payments for longer hours

this would be the case 'rarely'; 29.3 per cent replied that 'sometimes' longer hours were preferable because of increased income; and a further 30.1 per cent positively welcomed longer hours because of the financial reward.

Among the bullied group, responses were similar although more people thought longer hours were preferable 'sometimes' (32.3 per cent) and fewer people (26.3 per cent) felt longer hours were preferable 'often' or 'very often' because overtime is payable. Among the managers, the percentage against working longer hours – those who chose 'never' – rose to 40.7 per cent, and only 25.9 per cent felt this would be preferable 'sometimes'. At 22.2 per cent, a smaller percentage of managers than of those in the bullied group thought it was preferable to work longer hours 'often' or 'very often'. This may be because overtime is not normally payable in management posts or, given that some employees claim that management pays attention to the pay claims of higher-status workers, perhaps managers are in a stronger position to negotiate pay rises and therefore less interested in overtime for longer hours.

More than a quarter of administration/clerical staff (26.3 per cent) did not answer the question about whether overtime compensated for longer working hours (Table 4.2). It is difficult to establish whether this was because they were uncomfortable about considering the question, or whether overtime simply did not apply to their jobs and was deemed to be irrelevant. However, a high proportion of administration/clerical workers (31.6 per cent), the majority of those in other posts (38.1 per cent) and, as previously noted, those in management (40.7 per cent) also felt overtime 'never' compensated for working longer hours. Box office and front-of-house staff most often favoured working overtime 'sometimes' and the views of cleaning staff were fairly evenly split across all the options.

Arts employees were then asked to indicate to what extent they agreed with the statement that increased wages would mean they would prefer not to work any overtime. The most frequent responses were that this would be the case 'often' or 'very often' (46.6 per cent) or 'sometimes' (22.9 per cent). Among the bullied group, there was greater resistance to working overtime and 50.5 per cent said that 'often' or 'very often' they would prefer not to work overtime at all even if wages were increased; 23.2 per cent said this was the case 'sometimes'; and 17.2 per cent opted for 'never' or 'rarely'.

More arts employees commented on complaints about pay than commented on complaints about working hours, and one third of respondents indicated that workers

Table 4.2   Views on whether overtime compensates for long hours – by areas of work

	Non-response	Never	Rarely	Sometimes	Often	Very often	Total per area of work
Administration or clerical	26.3%	31.6%	5.3%	21.2%	10.3%	5.3%	100%
Box office	18.8%	6.3%	6.3%	37.3%	25%	6.3%	100%
Cleaning	0%	20%	20%	40%	0%	20%	100%
Front-of-house	8.8%	20.6%	5.9%	32.4%	23.5%	8.8%	100%
Management	0%	40.7%	11.1%	25.9%	11.2%	11.1%	100%
Production	6.5%	16.1%	16.1%	35.5%	19.3%	6.5%	100%
Technical	2.1%	20.8%	12.5%	32.3%	18.8%	13.5%	100%
Other	0%	38.1%	9.5%	4.8%	33.3%	14.3%	100%
Total across all work areas	**6%**	**23.7%**	**10.8%**	**29.3%**	**19.4%**	**10.8%**	**100%**

Note: table values are the in rows percentages established on 249 observations.

were sometimes afraid to complain about pay, thus indicating another gap between perceptions of employees and perceptions of managers as 48.1 per cent of managers said fear of making complaints about pay happened 'rarely' or 'never'. Complaints about pay may be made for a number of reasons, including disputes about hours worked, inter- and intra-departmental differentiations and/or comparable pay for doing the same job elsewhere. The outcome of formal objections, where known, demonstrated that, generally, complaints about pay were more often dismissed than upheld by management.

It can be seen that among the survey group as a whole 64.7 per cent commented on how complaints about pay were handled (Figure 4.11). Among managers and the bullied group, the response rate was slightly higher at 66.7 per cent. Of those who replied from the bullied group, 47 per cent said complaints were handled formally, that is, with assistance from a trades union representative. Responses from the survey group indicated that such formal complaints totalled just over half (50.9 per cent) of all complaints made. Other formal complaints, made without official assistance, were reported by 28.6 per

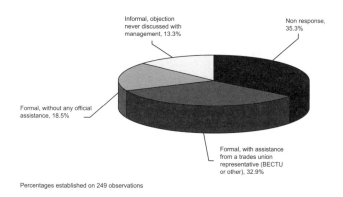

Informal, objection never discussed with management, 13.3%

Non response, 35.3%

Formal, without any official assistance, 18.5%

Formal, with assistance from a trades union representative (BECTU or other), 32.9%

Percentages established on 249 observations

Figure 4.11   How complaints about pay were handled

cent, and informal complaints by 20.5 per cent of those who responded to the question. In terms of objections presented with official assistance, objections to working hours totalled 71, and complaints about pay totalled 128.

Trades union assistance resulted in the same number of complaints about pay as about working hours being upheld by management – 13 reported in each case. Of the bullied group who responded, 14 people reported complaints about pay that they knew were upheld by management, 39 people reported complaints that they knew were dismissed by management and the remaining 11 people reported that complaints had been made, but they did not know the outcome.

Arts workers were asked about their employers' attitudes to complaints about rates of pay. More complaints about pay were reported as having been given a formal hearing (50.9 per cent) compared with complaints about working hours. Complaints made with assistance from a trades union representative totalled just over half of all complaints that were made about pay. In terms of objections presented with official assistance, 71 staff knew about objections to working hours, and 128 knew of complaints about pay. As with objections to working hours, employers dismissed objections to pay more often than they upheld them.

More appears to be known about pay disputes (153 respondents) than about those concerning working hours (109 respondents). Of the respondents, 13.1 per cent said that in the wake of an objection about pay employees left the organization (within the bullied group, this was 18.7 per cent). Inevitably, employees will not always know the detailed outcome of complaints, except perhaps where this concerns formal complaints where agreements or resolutions are published. Neither would they know, necessarily, the precise reason why an employee leaves an organization, even if this is in the wake of a complaint.

A greater number of arts workers commented on their organization's attitude to complaints about pay, than the number who commented on attitudes to objections to working hours (Figure 4.12). On this occasion, two-thirds replied and, once again, the majority view was that employers were indifferent to complaints, including those within the group comprising arts managers (25.9 per cent).

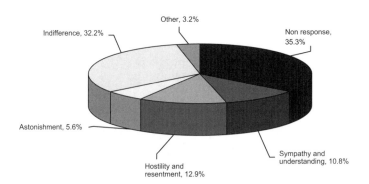

Other, 3.2%

Indifference, 32.2%

Non response, 35.3%

Astonishment, 5.6%

Hostility and resentment, 12.9%

Sympathy and understanding, 10.8%

Percentages established on 249 observations

Figure 4.12   Perceptions of management attitudes to complaints about pay

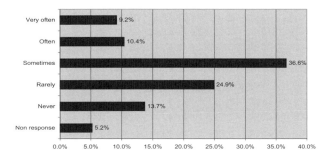

Percentages established on 249 observations

Figure 4.13   Perceptions of whether other people's pay is less for the same job

Among the bullied group, 29.3 per cent felt that management was indifferent to complaints about pay, and 23.2 per cent replied that management reacted with hostility and resentment. Comments on management attitudes indicated that companies say they pay the going rate; however employees perceive that management fabricates sympathy, but is uncompromising when it comes to overheads. One respondent felt that management responded to complaints about pay with 'irritation – entirely reasonable in my opinion'; another believed there was 'some level of understanding'; and yet another that levels of pay were 'studied fairly and professionally'. One member of the bullied group said the company claimed it was paying 'above the going rate'. Collective bargaining was cited as the norm in at least one instance.

Overall, there is an indication that a two-tier system may be operated by some arts organizations in relation to rates of pay: arts workers reported that employers are sympathetic to higher-status employees but 'indifferent' to the concerns of low paid workers. Evidently, arts employees are making comparisons, both within and without their specific areas of work, between other people's levels of earnings and their own, and opinion is divided. Respondents were asked to consider whether other people doing the same job were likely to be paid less than them (Figure 4.13): 36.5 per cent thought this would be the case 'sometimes' (44.4 per cent of managers), 19.6 per cent thought this would be the case 'often' or 'very often' (22.2 per cent of managers), however 38.6 per cent thought that this would 'rarely' or 'never' happen (33.3 per cent of managers).

Among the bullied group, one third thought other people's pay for the same job would be less elsewhere 'sometimes', and 19.2 per cent that this would happen 'often' or 'very often'. As with the issue of working hours, the views about rates of pay within the bullied group, and within the managers' subgroup, are very similar to that illustrated by the survey group as a whole. More than twice as many people in the bullied group (42.4 per cent) than in the non-bullied group (20 per cent) hold the view that other people are 'rarely' or 'never' paid less.

In terms of perceptions of rates of pay, then, the non-bullied group are the most pessimistic, with 80 per cent believing others doing the same job usually earn more than they do. The managers are a close second – 76.7 per cent of them believe other people's pay is usually better than theirs. Finally, and perhaps surprisingly, the statistics from the bullied group indicate that only 57.6 per cent share this opinion. Targets of bullying have been described as tending to report more negative behaviours at work (Rayner 1999);

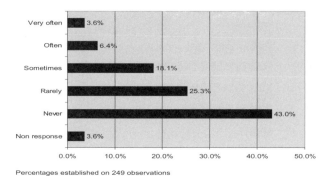

Percentages established on 249 observations

Figure 4.14   Perceptions of whether other benefits add value to wages

however, in this case, that does not appear to extend to a pessimistic view of their own position regarding levels of remuneration.

There is little or no perception among arts workers that they get added value through other benefits – only 10 per cent think rewards or perks of the job add value to wages 'often' or 'very often' (Figure 4.14). Once again, the non-bullied group appears generally less positive than the bullied group: 8.7 per cent of non-bullied respondents felt other benefits 'often' or 'very often' add value to wages, compared with 12.1 per cent of the bullied group. None of the managers subscribed to this view: 51.9 per cent said other benefits 'never' add value; 33.3 per cent said they did 'rarely' and 14.8 per cent that they did 'sometimes'. The majority of employees, especially managers, were acutely focused on their level of remuneration.

Overall in the survey group, the majority of employees (39.8 per cent) said that management was 'never' or 'rarely' unable to afford to pay more; a further 21.7 per cent thought lack of affordability may be the case 'sometimes'; 32.6 per cent thought this was the case 'often' or 'very often' (Figure 4.15). Opinion among managers was divided, with

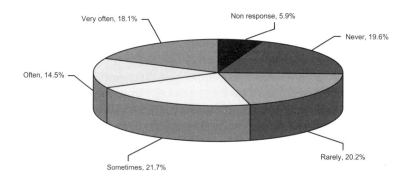

Percentages established on 249 observations

Figure 4.15   Management cannot afford to pay higher wages

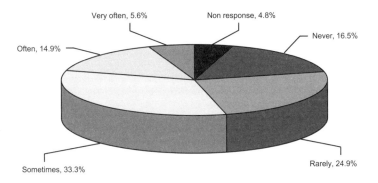

Percentages established on 249 observations

Figure 4.16   Whether workers are afraid to complain about pay

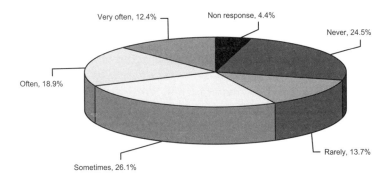

Percentages established on 249 observations

Figure 4.17   Workers should accept any wage offered

one third of this group citing each of the three sets of views. Among the bullied group, 46.5 per cent said that management was 'never' or 'rarely' unable to afford to pay more; 18.2 per cent thought lack of affordability may be the case 'sometimes'; 27.3 per cent thought this was the case 'often' or 'very often'.

Arts employees were asked to comment on the statement that no one in their organization dared to complain about low pay (Figure 4.16). In the majority of cases (41.4 per cent) this was 'never' or 'rarely' the case, (in the bullied group 39.4 per cent); one third answered 'sometimes' (as in the bullied group); and 20.5 per cent replied 'often' or 'very often' (24.3 per cent within the bullied group).

The managers were more positive that employees are 'rarely' or 'never' afraid to complain about low pay, and 48.1 per cent of them stated this; however they are less sure that it does not happen 'sometimes' (29.6 per cent) and 22.0 per cent believe it happens 'often'.

Prior to the current recession in the UK, a surprisingly large number of respondents (57.4 per cent; 67.7 per cent of the bullied group) said it made sense to accept any wage offered 'sometimes', 'often' or 'very often' and it may be that arts workers are put under pressure to accept lower earnings by the perceived or real scarcity of work in their specific disciplines.

Market forces are likely to affect opinions on wage levels; however 24.5 per cent of arts workers felt that, despite the scarcity of work, it was 'never' sensible to accept any wage offered (Figure 4.17). More managers, at 22.2 per cent of the subsample, agreed with this than did members of the bullied group, at 20.2 per cent. The largest number of people in the survey group who answered this question (26.1 per cent), the subsample of managers (29.6 per cent) and the bullied group (31.3 per cent), thought it made sense to accept any wage 'sometimes'.

Regional Variations

Although the experience of bullying is consistent throughout the UK, there are some regional variations on specific aspects of working terms and conditions. Participants in the research worked in venues in Scotland, Northern Ireland and England. The majority of arts workers were based at venues in London, 25.8 per cent in the West End and 8.8 per cent in other venues. Of the participants, 15.8 per cent were from the Midlands and 11.6 per cent from each of Scotland and Yorkshire and The Humber, followed by 10.8 per cent from Northwest England (Figure 4.18).

In the research, larger theatres predominate (Figure 4.19) with 40.6 per cent having a workforce of 100 employees or more and 27.7 per cent having between 50 and 100 employees.

In terms of levels of pay, the majority opinion was that accepting just any wage should be resisted – 38.2 per cent answered 'rarely' or 'never' – although in Scotland the majority view was that 'sometimes' it might be sensible. The majority verdict in the Northeast of England, at 62.5 per cent, followed by London West End at 45 per cent, was that it makes sense 'often' or 'very often' to accept any wage offered. This may reflect the scarcity of work in specific locations, and, of course, the advent of the recession in 2009 is likely to have a marked impact on perceptions about job prospects in all areas.

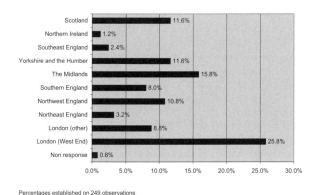

Percentages established on 249 observations

Figure 4.18   Regional location of participants

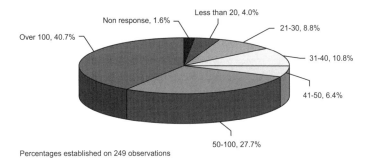

Non response, 1.6%
Less than 20, 4.0%
21-30, 8.8%
Over 100, 40.7%
31-40, 10.8%
41-50, 6.4%
50-100, 27.7%

Percentages established on 249 observations

Figure 4.19   Scale of venue by number of employees

Employees in three of the four major houses, which are the Royal National Theatre (RNT), English National Opera (ENO), Royal Opera House (ROH) and the Royal Shakespeare Company (RSC), were least likely to have to work longer than a 40-hour week. This may reflect the larger staff teams in place in these venues, or a combination of available resources and management expertise in strategic planning, as trades unions strive to ensure that agreements on working practices are uniform. Arguably, however, larger performing arts houses have comparably greater workloads in terms of programme, which in turn can demand more staff time.

We have seen that, frequently, employees were given less than one week's notice of the requirement to work longer hours, and this was true in every venue apart from one major house where longer notice was given. Despite the longer notice, employees at two of the major houses reported that they were not encouraged to take time off in lieu. Some theatres and arts centres made no provision for TOIL and, in two cases in London venues, the working week was reported as 'always' 48 hours.

Only one major house appeared able to provide more than one week's notice on some occasions. Attitudes to workers taking TOIL were analysed across all the venues, and employees in the majority of locations found it difficult to take TOIL due to workload and stated that taking time off was not encouraged. Whilst arts workers in two of the major houses reported no difficulties due to workload, they still stated that taking time off was not encouraged. In the various types of venues opinion differed as to how possible

Values are citations based on 232 observations (17 non-respondents)

Figure 4.20   Whether longer hours are acceptable because overtime is payable

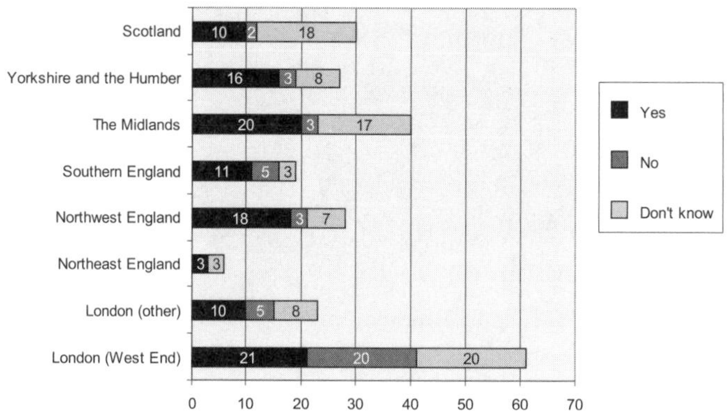

Values are citations based on 241 observations (8 non-respondents)

Figure 4.21   Objections to working hours within the last five years

it might be to work shorter hours: for example, no one in three of the major houses is convinced that shorter working hours are possible. In some regions longer hours are more acceptable because overtime is payable (Figure 4.20), notably in London's West End.

Employees in England and Scotland reported that there had been objections to working hours and rates of pay in their organizations within the last five years (Figure 4.21). In one of the major houses, six times as many objections were dismissed as were upheld by management. In terms of complaints about working hours and rates of pay, the perceptions were that 'indifferent' managements predominate in all types of venue, as well as all geographical locations. The people in the bullied group believed that management's attitude to complaints about pay was one of hostility and resentment.

Respondents from London's West End and the Midlands accounted, in almost equal measures, for 37.6 per cent of all known objections (109 reported) about working hours, and a further 31.2 per cent was shared, again almost equally, between the Northwest of England and the Yorkshire and The Humber region. No respondents from Northern Ireland reported any objections, however validity may be an issue as this represented only three participants.

As well as recording objections about working hours, arts workers recorded objections about rates of pay (Table 4.3). Complaints about pay at 65.5 per cent (67.7 per cent in the bullied group) exceeding complaints about working hours by 21.5 per cent. In all areas the numbers reporting that complaints had been made in the last five years represented a significant majority, with the exception of Northeast England, where 50 per cent of respondents did not know whether or not there had been complaints about pay in their organization. A small number of respondents from Yorkshire and The Humber did not answer this question, indicated in Table 4.3 by the designation non-response' under 'Location of employees'; however this represented only 0.4 per cent of the survey sample overall.

One third of all respondents who knew of complaints about pay were employees in London (London, West End, 39; London, other, 14), followed by 24 in the Midlands, 21 in Northwest England, 19 each in Southern England and Yorkshire and The Humber, and 18 in Scotland. The largest group of venues represented in the research comprised

Table 4.3   Knowledge of complaints about pay during the last five years

Location of employees	Non-response	Yes, there have been complaints	No, there have not been complaints	Don't know	Total
Non-response	0%	50%	0%	50%	100%
London (West End)	0%	60.9%	10.9%	28.2%	100%
London (other)	0%	63.6%	4.5%	31.9%	100%
Northeast England	0%	37.5%	12.5%	50%	100%
Northwest England	0%	77.8%	7.4%	14.8%	100%
Southern England	0%	95%	0%	5%	100%
The Midlands	0%	61.5%	5.1%	33.4%	100%
Yorkshire and The Humber	3.4%	65.5%	6.9%	24.2%	100%
Southeast England	0%	50%	16.7%	33.3%	100%
Northern Ireland	0%	66.7%	0%	33.3%	100%
Scotland	0%	62.1%	6.9%	31%	100%
Total across all regions	**0.4%**	**65.5%**	**7.2%**	**26.9%**	**100%**

Note: table values are the in rows percentages established on 249 observations.

those where an agreement with the TMA was in place (TMA theatres). The TMA theatres employed 39 per cent of arts workers participating in the survey and, accordingly, more complaints about pay were reported by them, and also a larger number of objections were upheld by management than elsewhere. The success rate in persuading management to uphold objections in two of the four major houses was 50 per cent: 7 upheld out of a total of 14 complaints made; in West End theatres it was 35.3 per cent: 6 out of 17 complaints upheld; and in arts centres at 31.2 per cent: 5 out of 16 upheld. These were considerably better results than at TMA theatres where 28.1 per cent – 18 out of 64 – complaints were upheld. Responses for the other two major houses indicated that management was not known to have upheld a complaint about pay.

On the question of overtime, for example, regional responses were mixed everywhere, although proportionately there was more resistance to overtime in Northern Ireland, Yorkshire and The Humber, Scotland and The Midlands than elsewhere. Although most research participants were London-based, there was some representation from all the English regions, as well as Scotland and Northern Ireland. All scales of venue were represented, from those employing less than 20 people, including part-time and casual workers, to those employing more than 100.

Employees were asked to state their views on management attitudes to complaints. The range of options recorded in Tables 4.4 and 4.5 below included sympathy and understanding (A), hostility and resentment (B), astonishment (C), indifference (E), or other. In all, 116 respondents (46.5 per cent) commented on management attitudes to objections about working hours and 161 (64.7 per cent) on management attitudes regarding complaints about pay. Considering the responses from across England, Scotland and Northern Ireland, and amongst all the different types of venues, there is consistent representation of the bullied group among the respondents in each category.

In Tables 4.4 (working hours) and 4.5 (rates of pay) below, the responses from the bullied group are mapped across the regions, and identified alongside the survey group

Table 4.4   Management attitudes to objections to working hours, by region

Location of employee	Non-response	A	B	C	D	Other (please specify)	Total
Non-response	1	0	0	0	(1) 1	0	(1) 2
London (West End)	(12) 39	(2) 4	(1) 3	(2) 3	(6) 15	0	(23) 64
London (other)	(8) 13	(1) 1	(2) 2	0	(4) 6	0	(15) 22
Northeast England	(2) 3	2	0	0	(1) 3	0	(3) 8
Northwest England	(5) 10	(1) 3	3	0	(7) 11	0	(13) 27
Southern England	(1) 9	(1) 5	(1) 1	(1) 1	2	2	(4) 20
The Midlands	(2) 17	1	(2) 3	(3) 3	(4) 10	(3) 5	(14) 39
Yorkshire and the Humber	(7) 11	(1) 6	(1) 3	0	(2) 8	(1) 1	(12) 29
Southeast England	(1) 3	0	(1) 1	0	(1) 2	0	(3) 6
Northern Ireland	(1) 2	1	0	0	0	0	(1) 3
Scotland	(2) 15	(3) 4	2	(1) 1	(2) 5	(2) 2	(10) 29
Total	**(41) 123**	**(9) 27**	**(8) 18**	**(7) 8**	**(28) 63**	**(6) 10**	**(99) 249**

Note: values established on 249 observations and sub-sample bullied group (99) observations.

Key to responses: Tables 4.4 and 4.5
A sympathy and understanding
B hostility and resentment
C astonishment
D indifference

as a whole and displayed in italics in brackets. For example, within the group of 39 West End employees who did not respond, *(12)* belong to the bullied group. Overall, one third of those who did not respond are from the bullied group, as are one third of those who consider management's attitude to objections about working hours to be one of sympathy and understanding. Of those who cite management's characteristics as 'indifference' or 'hostility and resentment', 44.4 per cent are from the bullied group in each case. All but one of those who report management's attitude to objections as 'astonishment' are from the bullied group.

Management response, or perhaps lack of response, exhibiting 'indifference' is the prevailing reaction. This is the majority view of respondents from every venue type in respect of both sorts of complaint. Those who considered that management reacts with 'sympathy and understanding' were found in TMA theatres and arts centres/other venues and in one major house, the last in respect of complaints about working hours, but not pay. These respondents were more common in Yorkshire and The Humber, and Scotland. Evidently, some managements exhibited astonishment that complaints should be made at all – including in TMA theatres, the West End and one of the major houses.

As can be seen in Table 4.5, the bullied group perceived a high degree of hostility and resentment from management to complaints about pay in particular. This is unsurprising as the bullied group constituted 71.9 per cent of those in the survey group as a whole who reported that complaints of pay were met with hostility and astonishment; for complaints

Table 4.5   Management attitudes to complaints about pay, by region

Location of employee	Non-response	A	B	C	D	Other	Total
Non-response	1	0	0	0	1	0	2
London (West End)	28	2	7	4	20	3	64
London (other)	8	1	2	3	7	1	22
Northeast England	5	1	0	1	1	0	8
Northwest England	7	4	5	0	11	0	27
Southern England	1	4	2	1	10	2	20
The Midlands	14	2	8	1	13	1	39
Yorkshire and The Humber	9	7	4	2	6	1	29
Southeast England	3	0	1	0	2	0	6
Northern Ireland	1	0	0	0	2	0	3
Scotland	11	6	3	2	7	0	29
Total	(31) 88	(9) 27	(23) 32	(6) 14	(29) 80	(1) 8	(99) 249

Note: values established on 249 observations and sub-sample bullied group (*99*) observations.

about working hours, only 44.4 per cent of the survey group who felt this way were from the bullied group. Of the 88 employees who did not respond, 31 belong to the bullied group (35.2 per cent). According to the responses, then, indifferent management (D in the table, scoring 63 and 80 in each of Tables 4.4 and 4.5 respectively) predominates in all types of venue, as well as all geographical locations.

Above in this chapter, it was noted that arts workers were sceptical about other benefits that might add value to wages, with only 10 per cent – based in London, Southern England, the Midlands, Yorkshire and The Humber, and Scotland – believing this might be the case 'often' or 'very often'. These respondents were from a variety of venues, including two of the four major houses.

Employees were also unconvinced by management's inability to afford higher wages, with 39.8 per cent claiming this was 'never' or 'rarely' the case (Figure 4.22). The highest number of respondents who believed that management 'often' or 'very often' could not afford to pay higher wages worked in Scotland (58.6 per cent). In other areas opinion was divided as to what management could or could not afford, although more of the people working in London's West End, than in any other area, believed management could *not* afford to pay more. It may be that some of these views will alter as the UK plunges into aggressive cost-cutting, in order to deal with the national deficit.

We have seen that 53.8 per cent of employees in the survey group thought workers were 'sometimes', 'often' or 'very often' afraid to complain about pay (Figure 4.23); this view was held by 57.6 per cent of the bullied group and 51.6 per cent of the managers. It correlates with the bullied group's report of attitudes of 'hostility and resentment' from management towards complaints about pay. In Southern England, the Midlands and London's West End, the largest percentage of respondents stated that people were 'rarely' or 'never' afraid to complain about pay. Elsewhere opinion was divided.

Overall, many arts employees perceive that they endure unfair terms and working conditions, and that management is indifferent to complaints. During the pilot study, managers tended to excuse any shortcomings in terms and conditions in the arts working

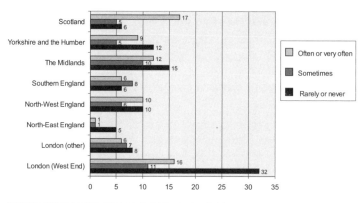

Values are citations based on 232 observations (17 non-respondents)

Figure 4.22 Regional views on whether management can afford to pay more

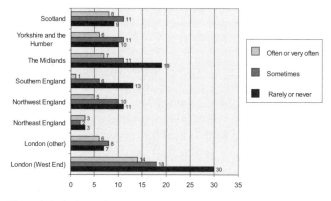

Values are citations based on 235 observations (14 non-respondents)

Figure 4.23 Whether workers are afraid to complain about pay

environment on the grounds that the arts are 'different'. This is explored further in Chapter 8; however it is self-evident that a largely dissatisfied workforce is not a matter to take lightly. Workers who are unhappy with their lot are less likely to give of their best, and more likely to resent a management that appears not to care. Also, a tense atmosphere in the workplace – which must exist, for example, when workers are afraid to complain about pay – is a breeding ground for negative behaviours such as bullying, which then serve to exacerbate any existing problems.

The Effects of Bullying on Organizations

According to a factsheet published by the MFL Occupational Health Centre in Winnipeg, Canada, (MFL Occupational Health Centre 2010: 1), workplace bullying takes a heavy toll on an organization's workplace: 'Bullying in the workplace leads to low morale, fear, anger and depression. This results in many negative effects including:

- increased absenteeism;
- increased turnover;
- increased stress;
- increased benefit costs;
- decreased productivity and motivation.'

The capacity of organizations to deal successfully with conflict resolution, leadership issues, power struggles and bullying behaviour impacts on organizational health and on individual employees, rather than the occurrence of these features *per se*. The ripple effect of a bullying problem in the workplace means it may start with one perpetrator and one target, but it rarely ends there. We have seen that a bullied employee experiences negative stress and will often become ill, with resulting implications for workload management and, often, an economic impact on the organization. Similarly, employees who witness bullying behaviour, or hear of it, share the effects of the unhappy workplace, such as the 50.2 per cent of performing arts workers who had heard of bullying incidents from a colleague. If a serial bully is at work, that person may pick on one member of staff after another, compounding the problem. Randall (1997) argued that the ripple effect can extend to a bullied employee's home environment, and, as outlined in Chapter 1, this fits with the assertion that there is a chain reaction of abuse which may begin in childhood (Crawford 1992: 69–71).

The effects of increased stress levels in a workforce will vary according to the circumstances. Where this is severe on a personal level, traumatic results are evident (Rayner 1999: 31). According to interviewees, these can include prolonged and severe illness, as well as mental and psychological breakdown (Leymann 1996) and even suicide (Field 1999). Rayner, who was the author of the UNISON (1997) report, found no correlation between absence from work and bullying, and there is little information on levels of sick leave in arts organizations specifically. However, there are indicators that by 2004 the UK as a whole was experiencing record levels of work absences when, according to a report by the Confederation of British Industry, workplace absence rose for the first time in five years (Barham and Begum 2005: 149–158). The Barham and Begum's study on sickness absence in the UK also notes the results of research in 2004 by the Chartered Institute of Personnel and Development, which identified the following:

> *The most common cause of sickness absence for both manual and non-manual workers was minor illness, followed by stress for non-manual employees, and back pain for manual staff. Employers believe that almost 20 per cent of absence is not genuine. (Barham and Begum 2005: 157)*

Minor illness aside, according to the Confederation of British Industry (CBI), stress and back pain (another symptom of stress) are the most common work-related illnesses and resulted in 6.5 million lost working days in the UK in 2004, rising to 19 million working days by 2006. The Health & Safety Executive (HSE) publishes annual statistics that reveal the prevalence and incidence of self-reported work-related illness. The 2010 report provides the statistical records for 2008–09 and, as in the previous eight years, one or more of stress, anxiety or depression tops the table, and no clear change has been observed since the base year 2000, although there has been a steady decline in the average days lost due to all health related-illnesses or injuries. In monitoring the population as a whole, HSE found that:

> ... 1.2 million people who worked during the last year [2007–08] were suffering from an illness (long-standing as well as new cases) they believed was caused or made worse by their current or past work. 551,000 of these were new cases. 29.3 million days were lost overall (1.24 days for every UK worker), 24.6 million due to work-related ill health and 4.7 million due to workplace injury. (HSE 2010)

A CBI press release issued in June 2010 commented on the latest CBI/Pfizer Absence and Workplace Health Survey, and stated:

> The impact of staff absence is considerable, with the 180 million sick days costing employers about £16.8bn in 2009, plus indirect costs like reductions in customer service and delays to teamwork. (CBI 2010)

In fact, the CBI/Pfizer survey also found that 15 per cent of manual and 22 per cent of non-manual workers were absent due to work-related stress, anxiety, or depression. In November 2009, The National Institute for Health and Clinical Excellence (NICE) estimated 13.7 million working days are lost each year to poor mental well-being in the workplace – more than half of the number reported by HSE as suffering work-related ill health – at a total cost of £28.3 billion – and well above the CBI level recorded in 2009.

The Australian Council of Trade Unions has calculated that workplace bullying may specifically be costing Australian business up to A\$3 billion (£1.7 billion) annually. Australia's anti-bullying campaigner, The Beyond Bullying Association, estimates that it costs the country between \$6 billion and \$36 billion when hidden factors are taken into account. In the UK, Field has commented:

> The cost of bullying and resultant injury to health to employers, employees and society is estimated to be at least £12bn each year although this doesn't appear in balance sheets. When the consequential costs (impairment to performance, sickness absence, staff turnover, family breakdown, the tribunal system, regulatory bodies, etcetera.) are included, the annual cost to UK Plc could be as high as £30bn – equivalent to around £1,000 hidden tax per working adult per year. (Field 2002)

Bullying is an expensive activity at many levels. In October 2005 the UK Ministry of Defence admitted to paying out more than £895,000 in compensation to 28 complainants in the armed forces since 2000. It paid £516,000 to 13 victims in 2003–04 alone (Press Association 2005). In February 2010, there was a landmark judgement in Victoria, Australia, when a magistrate handed down fines totalling A\$330,000 (£190,000) for workplace bullying. The employer was fined A\$250,000 (£145,000) and the employees who subjected their co-worker to bullying were fined between A\$4,000 and A\$10,000 (£2,300 and £5,800). This was the first major decision of this type in Australia, and set a benchmark for future prosecutions.

Cost estimates of this magnitude make uncomfortable reading for employers, all the more so in the light of one of the conclusions of CIPD research in 2004, which is that employers perceive almost 20 per cent of absences to be 'not genuine' – an increase from 15 per cent in 2003. The CBI/Pfizer study in 2009, however, reported that almost 40 per cent of employers believed there were employees taking non-genuine sickness absences in certain locations and among certain groups of employees. Without further research, it is difficult to establish if more people are actually becoming ill, and if so to what extent this might be stress-related and/or bullying-related. Another possibility is that more people are taking absences from work without valid cause, and a third possibility is that stress-related illness may not be considered by employers as a bona fide illness at all.

A study which considers the extent to which absence from work in the cultural sector mirrors experience of bullying would make a valuable contribution to the literature, given the rise in the rate of absence from UK workplaces as a whole, and the fact that stress is identified as a major cause of sickness. The arts sector is labour intensive, and few arts organizations are in a position to provide cover for employees on sick leave, which means that employee absence can and does create major operational difficulties.

In Finland, researchers have looked at statistics in the health service and concluded that workplace bullying is associated with an increase in the sickness absenteeism of hospital staff (Kivimaki, Eovanio and Vahterra 2000: 656–660). It may be that, in the UK, increasing absenteeism is also a symptom of an increase in workplace bullying. In the performing arts research, as outlined in Chapter 2, more than 28 per cent of respondents felt bullying was more frequent during the previous five years and 15 per cent that it was less so. More women than men thought bullying had increased – 35 per cent of all women, including half of all administration/clerical workers and 44 per cent of box office staff.

Persistent or repeated absences from work cause a range of problems for organizations, including logistical or management difficulties, and unfair workload distribution as other members of staff have to cover for a missing person. Bullying also takes its toll by depriving organizations of people: both targets of bullying and witnesses are known to leave their jobs as a result of bullying behaviour. Rayner states 25 per cent of bullied individuals who leave their employment in the UK in 1999 (Rayner 1999: 32), and Namie and Namie estimate 87 per cent of bullied people leave their jobs within the US workforce (as reported in Glazier 2005). Prior to actually leaving, it is highly unlikely that bullied employees, or their colleagues, are being productive, given the effects that bullying has on people. Employees suffering from feelings of frustration or helplessness, and an increased sense of vulnerability, will lose confidence and may have difficulty concentrating. Co-workers who witness bullying may be confused about an appropriate response, increasing their own sense of concern about how, or if, they should support a colleague who is being targeted. These anxieties and stresses contribute to a toxic workplace environment and are likely to lead eventually to the wholesale erosion of the entire organization's capacity to operate effectively.

5 *Being a Target*

Health and Safety, Equal Opportunities, Diversity

Workplace bullying comes within the sphere of policies governing health and safety at work, and also equal opportunities. An injury sustained in the process of employment is a fundamental health and safety issue and, as noted by Turney (2003), for the majority employment is a captive activity. It is central to an individual's life and sense of self. There is scope within organizational policies and procedures to assist those who have been targeted by a bully; however the capacity varies considerably depending on the type and scale of the organization and the employment sector. Some policies governing abusive behaviour are more universally accepted than others.

Often equal opportunities and diversity policies, created to guard against discrimination and harassment on the grounds of one or more of age, colour, creed, criminal record, disability, gender, sexual orientation, race or religion also can encompass workplace bullying. Although workplace bullying appears to function in the absence of these specific elements, it is sometimes regarded as a form of interpersonal or intra-organizational conflict, or oppression of employees by management, having the same negative effects as status-based discrimination and harassment.

For example, James Cook University (JCU) in Australia has a comprehensive set of web pages about bullying and intimidation. Since its establishment in 1970, it has expanded into a multi-campus institution, having the largest campuses in Townsville and Cairns, smaller study centres in Mount Isa, Thursday Island, and Mackay, and campuses in Singapore and Brisbane. There were over 16,000 students including 4,000 international students of more than 100 nationalities studying with JCU in 2010. The website takes a twin approach to information provision: offering an in-house guide to what constitutes bullying behaviour with appropriate advice and sources of help to targets, and also more general information on what might be encountered in the post-university workplace, including details of research undertaken elsewhere. The topics covered include information on status-based harassment and non-status-based bullying, and on specific attributes of different types of abusive behaviour. There are guidelines for managers, university staff and tutors, and contact details for 26 discrimination advisors who offer confidential discussions, within specific legal guidelines. The university has policies and codes of conduct to promote equal opportunities, social inclusion and political freedom. Tim Field's work in 2000–2001 was used as the basis for the university's definition of corporate bullying which cites the exploitation of both licit and economic inadequacies as a control mechanism for employers.

City University, London, UK, also has a comprehensive section on harassment and dignity at work on its website. It had 23,835 students from 156 countries in 2010. The website offers examples of types of bullying behaviour, guidelines, policy documents, and lists seven trained harassment advisers who are available to both the complainant and the perpetrator of bullying behaviour. Advisers are trained in basic counselling skills and the aim is:

> ... to recruit a cross section of staff, i.e., women, men, Black and Minority Ethnic staff and staff with a disability. No grade will be specified, although experienced people are most likely to be selected. (City University 2010)

Most, if not all, universities and colleges in the UK now have policies on discrimination, bullying and intimidation which are easily accessible for staff and students alike. The Universities and Colleges Employers' Association (UCEA) is the employers' body for universities and colleges of higher education in the United Kingdom, and it provides a framework within which institutions can discuss and seek advice and guidance on salaries, conditions of service, employee relations and other matters connected with employment within the higher education sector. In May 2009 UCEA ran an event for human resources (HR) professionals entitled 'Managing Performance and Respecting Dignity at Work'. The aim of the event was to disseminate information on:

> ... how to implement performance management without infringing principles of dignity at work; and on what to do when bullying claims and other grievances are raised during the performance management processes. (UCEA 2009)

Arts organizations can learn much from policy development, codes of conduct, mentoring, advising and provision of counseling training, as used in the education sector. In the arts, some key agencies also offer training opportunities and other forms of support for targets of bullying. The larger venues and companies are working alongside trades unions, employers' organizations and professional institutes to promote the concept of framing dignity at work within policies covering health and safety, and equal opportunities (this is considered further in Chapter 9). Smaller arts organizations, unsurprisingly, are likely to take some time to instigate changes to instruments of governance.

In the subsidized sector, the arts funding system actively encourages diversity as a positive and desirable organizational aim, which is to be applauded. However, the pursuit of diversity within arts organizations and their audiences is only a small part of a comprehensive package of additional requirements now handed down by funders and, as these additional requirements become increasingly dominant, they are in danger of superseding the core purpose of arts organizations.

Vulnerability and Stress

Within the literature on victims versus targets, some investigation has been made of whether certain employees are predisposed to become targets of bullying and what influences perceptions and experiences of bullying (Aquino et al. 1999; Lewis 1999). In an article for the *British Journal of Guidance and Counselling*, Hoel, Faragher and Cooper consider research into the subjective nature of the response to bullying, and find that:

being exposed to behaviour which may be construed as bullying is in itself not harmful if it is not perceived as such by the recipient. Accordingly, the stronger negative impact is likely to be found among those reporting or labelling themselves as being bullied. (Hoel, Faragher and Cooper 2004: 369)

Tim Field was involved in research into the issue of vulnerability in 2005, and other researchers have noted that the process of dealing with bullying behaviour, particularly where this involves the target in recounting the experience to others, or participating in difficult grievance procedures, may increase the target's vulnerability rather than reduce it. For example, Duncan Lewis poses the question:

Could the experience of evidence gathering, HR investigation and potential litigation give rise to higher levels of stress and shame than the actual bullying experience itself? (Lewis 2004: 287)

It was a concern during the arts research that the process of interviewing self-styled victims of bullying generated increased stress, simply through the rehearsal of the bullying experience. The interview process was designed specifically to minimize distress; however the vulnerability of certain targets was evident, even when some considerable time had elapsed since the bullying. This correlates with data from Hoel, Faragher and Cooper (2004: 380) who found that 'negative effects of bullying linger on well beyond the time of the incident'. There are case studies relating to arts workers that are not recorded here for this reason.

Some researchers into school bullying have studied behaviour among targets and concluded that victim status may determine the frequency with which children are bullied, distinguishing, in the process, between 'passive, submissive' victims and 'provocative' victims (Olweus 1993; Randall 1997). This suggests the potential for some level of participation in bullying by the target/victim and is contrary to the opinion that targets of bullying are entirely blameless, as held by Leymann (1996) and Field (1999).

Those who witness bullying behaviour do not escape unscathed. In a study of a UK trades union, Rayner (1999) reports that only 16 per cent of witnesses claim to be unaffected and Leymann (1987) and Zapf (1999) note the potential role of witnesses in the victimization process, whilst Vartia (2001) records the psychological and behavioural implications for witnesses. Hoel, Faragher and Cooper (2004: 380–381) draw attention to 'negative effects of indirect exposure to bullying' and state that some bystanders exhibit 'fear of becoming the next target or being dragged into existing conflicts' and this may explain the fact that in some of the arts case studies *accessories* to bullying are identified – that is, witnesses who have the power to intervene but choose not to, thereby colluding with the bullying behaviour.

In the early 1990s, personal strategies for improving assertiveness – self-help – were advocated as the way to deal with difficult people (Walmsley 1991; Lundin and Lundin 1995). In the more practice-oriented literature, as reflected in popular writing, the campaign for self-improvement continued (Adams with Crawford 1992; Wheatley 1999; Namie and Namie 1999). Whilst there is undoubtedly potential to help individuals to combat victimhood by improving their internal resources, the quality and depth of research during the last ten years indicates that it is too simplistic to propose self-improvement of targets alone as the solution to dealing with bullying behaviour.

For example, some social theories, such as variations on social constructionism, are driven by a strong sense of social justice and are concerned with liberation from oppression and exploitation. In the field of workplace bullying, the work of Leymann (1996) and Field (1999) tends to be concerned with the stress and trauma experienced by victims and their rehabilitation following torment by a bully. The view is that if our society considers that bullying behaviour is a destructive and unacceptable phenomenon, then this specific social construct exists because we have agreed that it does. In this respect, we are following certain generally accepted social norms, standards or criteria. A social construct is a concept or practice that may appear to be natural and obvious to those who accept it, but – in this philosophy – is an invention or artefact of a particular culture or society. Having endorsed the social construct that bullying is neither satisfactory nor allowable behaviour, it seems an illogical step to decide that it is incumbent on the target of this behaviour to 'fix' it.

In 1994 the Manufacturing, Science and Finance Union (MFSU) in the UK (now Amicus) produced a definition that emphasized the effects of bullying behaviour on the target:

> *Persistent, offensive, abusive, intimidating or insulting behaviour, abuse of power or unfair penal sanctions which makes the recipient feel upset, threatened, humiliated or vulnerable, which undermines their self-confidence and which may cause them to suffer stress. (Amicus–MSF 1994)*

This widely quoted definition was highlighted by Tim Field, whose independent foundation's comprehensive website, BullyOnline, as cited in several chapters, has been the inspiration for the creation of many other similar organizations and sites worldwide. There is an emphasis on the perpetrator having the capacity to control, and on negative behaviour being repeated which evokes a mental and emotional response from the target and has a harmful effect. Arts workers have reported stress and stress-related illnesses that are consistent with the definition. Stress and stress-related illnesses affect performance at work, health, emotional and mental well-being and home life. Recorded effects of bullying include depression, anxiety, sleep disturbances, panic attacks, low self-esteem, protracted stress-related illnesses and loss of confidence, all of which result in reduced efficiency, absenteeism and unsafe work practices. The high frequency and long duration of hostile behaviour results in considerable mental, psychosomatic and social misery (Leymann 1996). Some people harm themselves and even take their own lives as a result of their bullying experiences (Field 1999).

THE THEATRE PROJECT: HIERARCHICAL BULLYING/PEER BULLYING/SERIAL BULLYING

A company with a national and international remit, and established for 22 years, was planning important developments in its capital infrastructure. The organization was mature and settled and members of staff enjoyed a friendly in-house ambience despite the company having grown considerably in size and importance over the years. It had a loyal and long-term core staff team of 20 employees, plus part-time and freelance workers. The Artistic Director,

Michael, founded the organization and was its Chief Executive Officer. His General Manager, John, had worked alongside him for 12 years. They had jointly masterminded the capital development plan.

National and international funding sources had been identified, John had made preliminary funding applications, which were warmly received, and architectural plans had been produced. Key project funders encouraged Michael to create the new post of Director of Fundraising in order to ensure that the balance required for the capital development, plus monies for new commissions and educational work, could be identified to supplement the funding already raised.

The new appointee, Susan, had experience of working in the voluntary sector, although not in an arts organization, and many of the funding regimes were new to her. Beyond his day-to-day work, John took time to ensure that she understood the criteria of those funders who had already offered support.

John had a key role within the organization's social hierarchy, and he acted, to all intents and purposes, as Michael's deputy. They often discussed issues informally together, outside staff meetings or consultant sessions, and sometimes took autonomous decisions. Susan noted this, disliked the fact that she was excluded from these meetings and said so. Michael acknowledged that she had made a valid point, and the informal discussions with John, usually over a cup of coffee in the theatre café, stopped.

Susan then began to pursue John, almost on a daily basis, with repeated requests for information that he had already supplied. Subsequently she would claim to Michael, and anyone else who happened to be within earshot, that John had failed to provide her with the details necessary for her to do her job well and/or that he didn't understand the parameters within which she was working.

Over the next three months it became difficult for members of staff to meet Susan without hearing tales of John's most recent shortcomings. On several occasions Susan telephoned colleagues to complain loudly and abusively about him. Her calls were often made from a busy intercity train. In meetings about the capital development, which were attended by a large number of external consultants, and which John and Susan attended, but Michael didn't, Susan would make loud, insulting 'jokes' about John's appearance and capabilities. John was a quiet, modest man and mostly ignored her remarks, although he found them extremely hurtful and expressed this to colleagues. The external consultants observed Susan's behaviour but took no action. It was not their concern.

By the fourth month, Susan was continually finding fault with some of the junior members of staff, and she could regularly be heard throughout the theatre's offices shouting abuse at them. Her telephone calls to external colleagues continued, irrespective of where she was and in whose company and she began to complain about other staff members as well as about John. In the presence of Michael or any of the board members of the theatre however, Susan was a different person – pleasant, polite and apparently highly efficient.

Privately, one of Michael's external colleagues was told by junior staff that Susan made unreasonable demands of them, regularly asking them to prioritize tasks for her that were outside their remit and that interfered with other work. They said they were too frightened of her to complain. A senior manager discovered that Susan had been withholding important information, which had created major issues for John with potential funders, and confronted her about this, but was told to stop interfering. Eventually, some members of staff jointly approached Michael with their complaints; however, he made it clear that he had major development issues to consider and that he did not want to be troubled by 'personality clashes'.

Eventually, the external associate told Michael of the reports of Susan's behaviour towards the staff and of her loud condemnation of colleagues both within and outside the workplace. Michael was astonished as Susan had never behaved abusively in his presence, but promised to look into it. He met with Susan, and following the meeting he let it be known that she had denied being insulting and making provocative or upsetting remarks. In fact, she stated that she believed John was stirring up trouble for her. No further action was taken.

Susan's behaviour towards John deteriorated even more, except when Michael was present, at which time she was pleasant to everyone. John became increasingly depressed and, eventually, very ill indeed and was away from work for almost a year. During that time Michael employed a personal assistant and became even more remote from the other staff, tied up with the issues inherent in running a major capital project. Two staff members, who had been verbally abused by Susan, left during the year that John was absent. On his return the old pattern of behaviour resumed. Added to the normal insults, Susan developed the habit of feigning concern for John's health in an unpleasant mocking way, constantly asking him if he was all right, and saying publicly that she was worried he might 'drop dead at any moment'.

The capital project was completed and the new building opened. Privately, colleagues told John that during the two years she had been employed, Susan had not, in fact, raised sufficient additional money for the development. During John's absence she had provided the (previously withheld) paperwork, which enabled confirmation of the funding originally identified by John. To save face in public, the senior managers in the organization were covering up a funding deficit, which it would take many years to recoup: there was, in fact, a considerable shortfall.

At the opening of the new theatre, the Chairman of the Board gave extensive thanks naming everyone who had helped, except John, who, despite his 13 years' service, had had a low profile for most of the previous 12 months. He commended Susan, in particular, for her diligence in obtaining the necessary funding. John expressed the opinion that he felt as if he had been 'airbrushed from history'. He left the organization without having another job to go to. He never regained full health. On the strength of her accolades, Susan left to become an officer in a national cultural sector agency.

(*Names and environs have been changed to protect confidentiality.*)

At first sight this is peer bullying as the original target is another manager; however, this perpetrator also bullies junior staff, thus exhibiting the traits of the serial bully. The theatre's Artistic Director (who is also the founder) had a vision encompassing growth and development for this arts organization. Whilst ultimately this vision was delivered, it was at great personal cost to all the participants, especially John, whose relationship with the Artistic Director – that of a close ally who had provided support and encouragement for a considerable number of years – was severed. The stable staff team disintegrated and the economic benefits anticipated as a result of creating the new post did not materialize. Here, as in The Ensemble and The Art Gallery, the bully identifies the power base and focuses on establishing strong links to it: the target is in the way and has to be dislodged.

Crossing into a new area of work is demanding and it can take time to adjust; however, in this case the bully responds with belligerence and antagonism to the person who had assisted her most. She perceives John's relationship with Michael to be a threat to her own position within the organization and takes steps to dismantle it. She upsets and alienates staff who are her juniors – and arguably less able to defend themselves or to object – and she dismisses her peers as if they were being unreasonably intrusive. All of this behaviour is completely outside the established, informal culture of the organization and no one is quite sure how to react. The new manager has difficulty adjusting to the milieu in which she finds herself – perhaps she is insecure about her knowledge and skills level in an unfamiliar environment; the organization has difficulty adjusting to her overbearing management style – for her management is all 'politics and control' rather than 'science' or 'art' (Bratton and Gold 1999: 12–13).

When someone acts as whistleblower, the bully protests her innocence, accuses her principal target of causing trouble, and then retaliates with a heightened campaign, causing two staff to leave during his absence. Meanwhile, the CEO withdraws further from the situation, using a gatekeeper to ensure he is not tainted with the bully's behaviour. By effectively isolating himself from the environment, he seeks to absolve himself from responsibility. The colleagues and associates external to the organization, who witness the bully's words and actions, exhibit the same desire to distance themselves from the behaviour, although they and the CEO are by this time fully aware of what is going on. In this sense, they are all accessories to the bullying, colluding with the behaviour. The very public triumph of the bully in this case must surely have caused some of the remaining staff to question whether their own behaviour ought to change, as in this case bullying evidently paid dividends. Other researchers have noted that people who are not bullies will nevertheless adopt bullying behaviours 'if they see that these behaviours are influential and valued' (Archer 1999: 99)

This manager was loud and ostentatious much of the time; however, bullying between individuals in the workplace is also often a clandestine affair, peppered with quiet allegations and covert threats. The person who suffers most in this case, John, was deeply damaged by the experience and the fact of this damage has been a contributing factor to the debate about whether we are victims or targets, when selected by a bully.

Victimhood

In the field of domestic abuse and violence, dubbed 'bullying at home' by Rathus (1996), increasingly encouragement is given to those who find themselves in abusive relationships to think of themselves as a 'target' rather than as a 'victim'. One website (www.youareatarget.com) for those experiencing abuse within a relationship makes a point of emphasizing its preference. A target is identified by the perpetrator, who deliberately focuses on that individual. Anyone can be chosen as a target and the implication is that the role is not self-selecting. A victim, on the other hand, is a sufferer, a casualty or an injured party. Target has connotations of objectivity, whereas victim suggests someone who succumbs to a situation, perhaps even playing a slightly proactive role by failing to resist.

Is it appropriate to refer to people as victims of workplace bullying, with all that this implies? The term 'victim' is used by several researchers, including William Wilkie who has a background in psychiatry and who focuses on understanding the responses of 'victimised people'. He charts three stages of stress breakdown, beginning with free-floating anxiety, then loss of emotional control and the ability to motivate oneself, sometimes resulting in anger and aggression, and, finally, hypersensitivity and apparent personality change. These processes lead to specific types of behaviour in victimized people:

> [First stage] ... the bullied school child or the victimised worker may have difficulty getting off to sleep, may appear jumpy, unable to relax, and complain of the many body symptoms which accompany anxiety.

> [Second stage] ... the bullied school child may appear irritable and lazy. The victimised adult may not want to go to work, and perhaps on arriving home from work shouts at the family or the dog.

> [Third stage] ... the bullied school child begins to play alone, and the harassed worker looks for any excuse to leave the building ... The bullied school child may suddenly overreact with uncharacteristic violence towards the bully, and this behaviour may be the first that is noticed by the teacher. As a result we sometimes see the victim being wrongly labelled as a troublemaker. (Wilkie 1996: 1–11)

Wilkie believes that the symptoms of third-stage stress breakdown may lead to 'inappropriately aggressive responses' from the workplace victim – the flaring up of the schoolchild in the example above. Whether through anger or another emotional response, often there is a discernible change in the personality of the victim, and what they consider to be most important in the workplace or in life. He thinks it is such changes that propel victims towards leaving their job, often following long-term sick leave. This correlates with John's experience in The Theatre Project: his inability to improve his situation depresses him and he becomes disillusioned with his place of work. It is a mark of his distress that his priorities change and he chooses to leave a stable, long-term employment position in order to escape the abuse.

Arts workers, who discussed their experience of bullying during structured and semi-structured interviews, reported some of the characteristics of all three stages of behaviour exhibited by victimized people. Commonly, instances of persistent anxiety and insomnia were recorded, as was a dread of going to work and the tendency to snap at colleagues when there. Interestingly, some of the research in performing arts workplaces suggested that (like the bullied schoolchild at the third stage) it is the knee-jerk reaction against bullies – usually out of character – that first appears on the radar, rather than the, mostly hidden, bullying behaviour itself. Some of those who reported being targeted had been, or were still, on long-term sick leave.

Depression, sometimes leading to mental and emotional breakdown, featured regularly in accounts of those who claimed that they had been bullied. Research indicates that breakdowns also occur following the maltreatment inflicted on people confined against their will. In 1975, Amnesty International published Biderman's Chart of Coercion, which was developed to document the behaviour that occurs between abuser and victim. The Chart provides a model of the process of abusive brainwashing and was originally created to describe the breakdown of American soldiers due to emotional and physical torture during the Korean War.

Robyn Mann, in considering psychological abuse in the workplace (moral harassment), developed Biderman's stages of coercion to illustrate the actions of the abuser and the responses of the victim (Mann 1996). Some of the responses to these elements, as proposed by Mann, include many of the familiar signs recorded by researchers into workplace bullying, including the effects on victims likened to those suffering post-traumatic stress disorder (PTSD) cited by Randall (1997: 57) and the physical and emotional effects of harassment on the individual reported by Ishmael and Alemoru (1999: 91–92). In addition to those symptoms already discussed, these include (but are not limited to): recurring unpleasant nightmares; flashbacks to the incidents causing the stress; poor concentration; feelings of guilt; palpitations; high blood pressure; embarrassment and pain. Without exception, all the participating arts workers who stated that they had been the target of a workplace bully reported many of these symptoms of emotional and physical stress, and other indicators like them.

Below in Table 5.1 Biderman's stages of oppression are presented in the left-hand column, and are then developed to illustrate the indicators of bullying behaviour.

The evidence suggests that victimhood exists, in the sense that suffering and distress on the part of the person or persons targeted is a consequence of workplace bullying.

Table 5.1   Bullying related to Biderman's Stages of Oppression

Isolation	The bully selects the target and acts to set them apart from colleagues, via unfair criticism, unwanted jokes, complaints, etcetera
Monopolization of perception	The bully works to eliminate the target's focus on anything other than the bully's requirements, via unreasonable demands and misinformation
Induced physical and mental exhaustion	The bully uses tension, fear and controlling tactics to pressurize the target until they are debilitated
Threats	The bully warns of, and sometimes demonstrates, the consequences of non-compliance
Occasional indulgences	The bully uses periodic gestures of kindness or feigned concern to pretend camaraderie, causing confusion in the target
Demonstrating omnipotence	The bully creates dependency in the target, promoting a state of powerlessness
Degradation	The bully stimulates feelings of shame and lack of self-respect in the target, via additional constant fault-finding and unfair criticism
Enforcing trivial demands	The bully humiliates the target, often in front of colleagues

However, Ishmael proposes that there are differing mindsets and behaviours for victims, who 'fail to use personal power and resources' to counter bullying, and targets, who 'have internal resources but struggle to exercise them' (Ishmael with Alemoru 1999: 81–85). If victims lack the ability to deal successfully with the behaviour, and targets have the ability, but cannot use it, then no matter which designation is used, neither category is actually *empowered* to prevent or stop the bullying behaviour.

Field brings another perspective to bear, via the view that the state of being a victim is not permanent:

> ... with insight, knowledge, enlightenment, support and encouragement, plus the desire to learn, grow and evolve, the frame of mind known as 'victim mentality' results primarily from never having learnt or been taught to withstand the unpleasant behaviours of other people. (Field 1996: xix–xx)

Do victims, therefore, suffer because they are incapable of resisting a bully, and is this a transient state resulting from lack of knowledge, experience or skill? If an individual has gained the preferred insights and attained the necessary knowledge, does this mean they will never be a victim, but only ever a target? The problem with these positions is that they focus exclusively on the recipient of the behaviour, and consider the victim/target issue in isolation from the environment in which the bullying is taking place.

From Victim to Target?

At the dawn of research into bullying in the UK, publications of the self-help variety, which sometimes touched upon working with 'difficult' people, implied that it was the response of an individual to negative behaviour that ultimately determined the nature of their experience and, presumably, their designation as target or victim (Walmsley 1991). If this is applied to bullying behaviour it delivers a simple model whereby a bully identifies a subject who, if they have a weak and non-assertive personality, will become

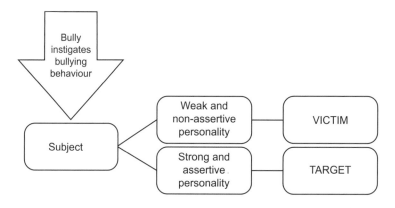

Figure 5.1 Typical self-help explanation of the effects of bullying behaviour (UK, early 1990s)

a victim. If the subject is strong, they are a target, but not a victim, and presumably they will suffer less (Figure 5.1).

If we look to English literature, however, we find examples of those who are a target, but unwilling to become a victim. D. H. Lawrence offers a perspective born of a target's capacity for critical analysis of the perpetrator, rather than their fear of him.

What does he want to bully me into? Does he want me to love him?

… That was it: he blackly insisted that SHE must love HIM … And be bullied into it … he wanted to compel her, he wanted to have power over her. He wanted to make her love him so that he had power over her. He wanted to bully her, physically, sexually, and from the inside.

… Well, she was just as confident that she was not going to be bullied. She would love him … But she was not going to be bullied by him in any way whatsoever … a dark-eyed little master and bully she would never have.

And this was her triumphant conclusion.

… She felt just a tiny bit sorry for him. But she wasn't going to be bullied by him. She wasn't going to give in to him … It must be love on equal terms or nothing. For love on equal terms she was quite ready. She only waited for him to offer it. (Lawrence 1994 [1923]: 138–140)

Is this the quintessential response of a target, rather than a victim? The magnetism and fascination of the enigmatic Alexander is explicit and, Lawrence's spirited language and introspection notwithstanding, in this excerpt Hannele reveals a capacity to observe and analyse that character and his behaviour in an objective and dispassionate way. She concludes that he means to coerce her into loving him, because this will give him power and control; however, she has no intention of succumbing to Alexander's lust for domination, although she does admit that she is prepared to love him anyway, as long as 'equal terms' are observed.

Bullying as a means to gain power and control is clear in the above extract; however Hannele's response has several interesting features: she does not fear Alexander, although he puzzles her and makes her feel uneasy; she has considered his motives, his words and his actions, some of which are irrational, however her response is more akin to a 'no blame' approach (Brown 2004), and although conscious of being a target, she does not present as a victim. It is a moot point whether the effects of bullying would be less marked if all targets, like Hannele, felt 'a tiny bit sorry' for perpetrators. This would be more likely if bullies lost the capacity to instil fear, and if both parties to the behaviour truly were on equal terms. In such a case, where neither of the two parties holds an unfair balance of power, some researchers, for example Zapf and Gross (2001), would consider that the behaviour was not, in fact, bullying at all.

This supposition that weak, inexperienced people become victims, and strong, experienced ones become targets, fails to be supported by the evidence; however, mature, skilled and knowledgeable arts professionals are found among targets of bullying, as is exemplified in The Theatre Project, and also in The Museum (Chapter 3), The Art Gallery (Chapter 1), The Creative Industry (Chapter 6) and The Contemporary Dance Studios (Chapter 3).

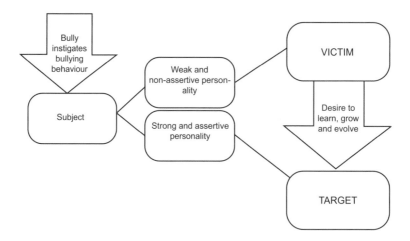

Figure 5.2   Victimhood as a temporary state

If we adopt the 'victimhood is temporary' theory advocated by Field (1996), we arrive at another version of this model whereby the subject becomes either a victim or a target, depending again on their response, with the added opportunity for the victim to achieve target status through personal enlightenment (Figure 5.2). In this interpretation, action to mitigate the distress caused by the bullying is taken only by the individual subjected to it. This does not prevent or stop the bullying behaviour and appears to offer only the subject of the behaviour an opportunity for self-improvement, and not the perpetrator.

These approaches (Figures 5.1 and 5.2) provide relatively superficial views of bullying, given the complexity of the behaviour, and more sophisticated models are needed to reflect the importance of the environment in which bullying is found, how and why it flourishes (Rayner 1999: 34–36, Neilson, Pasternack and Van Nuys 2005) and the progress research has made, particularly in the years since 2000.

Survival

Neither of the preceding models satisfactorily deals with the bigger questions around bullying behaviour; they both rely on the subject of the behaviour to be assertive or even aggressive, or to learn how to be so, as a solution to the problem. In concert with these views, some specialists working with children and young people demonstrate tendencies towards the notion that anyone is a potential target of bullying behaviour, and that the power to remain a target, rather than become a victim, lies with the target.

> *Although children probably have no control over being targets, they have the capacity to choose not to be victims. Victims capitulate to what bullies want. … they give bullies their lunch money, cry in shame when called names, run to adults to get help, or beg for mercy. Children become targets for who they are. They become victims for what they do. Targets have in their power to choose not to become victims. (Baumgartner 2006).*

Ishmael identifies a victim as:

someone who does not use their internal power or identifiable resources to prevent abuse (Ishmael with Alemoru 1999: 81)

and he says that targets:

often have the resources to deal with abusive behaviour, but find it difficult to exercise them because of the external pressures placed on them (Ishmael with Alemoru 1999: 81).

The issue with these assumptions about an individual's capacity to determine their status, as cited by Field (1996), Ishmael (1999) and Baumgartner (2006), is the difficulty of aligning the concept of a target having power and a victim not having power with the fundamental imbalance of power between a perpetrator and a bullied person – whether called target or victim – which characterizes bullying behaviour. This imbalance has been cited by researchers (for example, Turney 2003; Hoel et al. 2003: 413) and is clearly demonstrated in the arts case studies and in research in related areas, such as domestic abuse. (See Chapter 1, Figure 1.3, the power and control wheel modified for workplace bullying).

The assertion that a target has more power than a victim, but not as much as a perpetrator, results in a one-dimensional evaluation of the bullying actor-reactor relationship, which is reminiscent of the self-help models of the early 1990s (see Figure 5.3).

The argument that targets have it in their power to choose not to become victims (Baumgartner 2006) is not well made. Field was actively engaged in considering the implications of vulnerability, and further research is needed on aspects such as susceptibility and capitulation to investigate their role in determining bullying outcomes. After all, if a target has internal resources but is unable to use them (Ishmael with Alemoru 1999) then they are returned to a state of powerlessness. The Ishmael perspective suggests that targets are 'powerless/frustrated' whereas victims are either 'powerless/weak' or 'powerless/ignorant'. Viewing victims as the powerless/weak or powerless/ignorant is supported in *Managing Britannia: Culture and Management in Modern Britain*, where the authors' use of D. H. Lawrence's *Women in Love* as an example infers that the targets of Gerald's bullying (the workforce) become victims because they submit to it willingly – whether from weakness or ignorance is not explored (Protherough and Pick 2002: 176).

There is a parallel view among some researchers into childhood bullying, who suggest that there are two types of victims in relation to the school bully: submissive victims

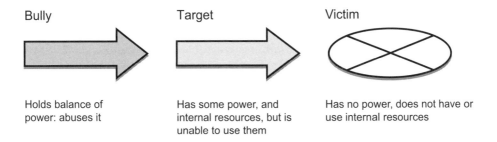

Bully	Target	Victim
Holds balance of power: abuses it	Has some power, and internal resources, but is unable to use them	Has no power, does not have or use internal resources

Figure 5.3   The victim as a failed target

and provocative victims, both of whom give off covert signals which are likely to make them targets (Smith and Sprague 2003). If the 'submissive/provocative' model is applied to adult bullying in the workplace – even if it is accepted that the covert signalling is unwitting on the part of the victims – it introduces into the bullying debate an element causing acute discomfort amongst anti-bullying campaigners, who tend to reject unequivocally the notion of responsibility on the part of the target/victim, and focus instead on achieving justice and on the requirement for bullies, whether individuals, groups or whole organizations, to bear all responsibility for the behaviour.

The difficulty with the conclusions to be drawn from the concepts illustrated by theories built on self-help, victimhood as temporary, and submissive/provocative victims is, however, the inference that bullying occurs in a vacuum, somehow divorced from the workplace in which it is occurring. Also, the onus is on the distressed person, whether designated victim or target, to take action and to change their behaviour, rather than on the perpetrator. This is expressed as active pursuance of self-help, of a desire to learn, grow and evolve, or of working to actively resolve the situation.

THE IMPORTANCE OF THE WORK ENVIRONMENT

In the alternative model below in Figure 5.4, created in response to the findings of the arts research, the environment as well as the behaviour has been incorporated. All subjects of bullies are identified as targets, and the premise is that it is the environment in which bullying happens, as well as the personal response of the target, that determines whether they become victims or survivors: a case of nurture as well as nature, with nurture very probably in the lead.

This model indicates two possible outcomes of workplace bullying in the context of action or inaction by management; however, there is considerable potential for multiple variations, depending on the resources available. Action is achieved when the target's ability to recognize that the behaviour is unacceptable occurs in an environment where management is aware of the issue and can offer support: knowledge, skills and expertise enable management to respond, intervene and identify solutions that will stop the bullying behaviour. Inaction signifies the opposing scenario: the target fails to appreciate what is happening and when, eventually, bullying is recognized as such the target may be powerless to deal with it and the problem is compounded by an environment where bullying is ignored, denied or apparently tolerated by management.

Examples of action are visible in The Contemporary Dance Studios (Chapter 3), The Creative Industry (Chapter 6) and The Playwright (Chapter 9). In the first example, the target removes himself from the bullying relationship and is assisted by a colleague and, although the bully continues to target the replacement advisor, the behaviour is depersonalized and relatively less damaging psychosocially. In the second case, the companies involved in the consortium recognize collectively that the behaviour is undesirable and are mutually supportive, withdrawing from contact with the bully. The same bully does much more damage to staff within her own organization where the supportive environment is not in place and action cannot be taken. In the third example, a prompt response on the part of the organization's board ensured that the bullying behaviour was stopped for good. In all three case studies, the targets are empowered to re-exert control over the situation and rebalance the power. The bullies win in the sense

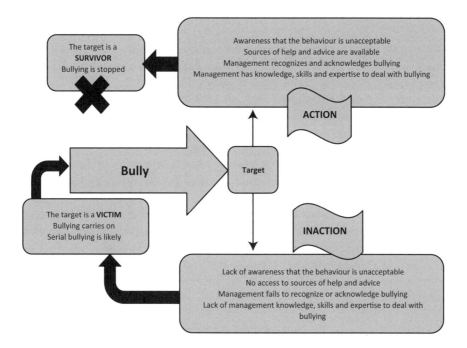

Figure 5.4   Victims and survivors of bullying

that a crisis is precipitated, but also lose because the targets have access to sufficient background help and support, and have become *survivors*.

The arts research, therefore, suggests that the environment in which bullying happens has an important influence on the outcome of the problem for target, perpetrator and the organization as a whole. Some researchers from other employment sectors share this view. Hoel and Salin (2003) categorize the organizational precursors of bullying under four headings:

> *the changing nature of work; how work is organized; organizational culture; and leadership*

> *... workplace bullying might be caused by a combination of these or other forces and ... these vary in different circumstances. (as reported in Lewis 2004: 284)*

Salin (2003) notes that:

> *bullying seems to be prevalent in organizations where employees are dissatisfied with the social climate and the internal communication. (Salin 2003: 36)*

Further, the way in which bullying is handled within an organization or employment sector may contribute to increasing the stress experienced by the target, including shame and embarrassment (Lewis, 2004: 285). One respondent remarked:

> *usually it's the front of house managers who bully because they are 'stressed' and we just cope. (Respondent to the national survey)*

In The Arts Service (Chapter 4), the bullying behaviour occurred at a time when the local authority department was undergoing significant organizational change, including restructuring. A number of researchers have noted the detrimental effect that organizational change of this type has – including the effect of bullying behaviour (Salin 2003; Hoel and Cooper 2000; McCarthy 1996; Sheehan 1996) – and Salin suggests that bullying in these circumstances may be viewed as a 'rational' choice by the perpetrator:

that is a deliberate strategy for improving one's own position. (Salin 2003: 36)

Indeed, in several of the arts case studies we see how the perpetrator manipulates events to their own ends, for example in The Art Gallery (Chapter 1), as part of organizational politics, and such strategies have been noted by other researchers (for example, Neuberger 1999; Niedl 1995; Zapf and Warth 1997). Salin found a clear relationship between bullying and organizational politics in her study of 385 Finnish professional employees holding a university degree in business studies, and notes that organizational politics can have both positive and negative effects and that 'they seem to thrive in competitive and hectic work environments' (Salin 2003: 41).

Indirectly, this also means that bullying is more frequent in these environments, which is supported by previous studies (Einarsen, Raknes and Mathiesen 1994; Vartia 1996; Appelberg, Romanov, Honkasalo and Koskenvuo 1991; O'Moore 2000) (Salin 2003: 42)

The testimony of arts workers is discussed in Chapter 8, and confirms that arts workplaces can indeed be hectic; however, the extent to which they are competitive has yet to be established. Although perceptions are highly subjective, it seems likely that perpetrators of bullying behaviour may deem themselves to be in competition with a colleague, whether or not competition is, in fact, a feature of the working environment. As bullying behaviour may arise for a variety of reasons, and may have more than one cause, the role played by organizational politics deserves further and deeper consideration. In the arts case study The Ensemble (Chapter 6), for example, there is no organizational change as such that would trigger the onset of bullying, except that the creation of a new performance company is, of itself, an immense challenge to all participants in terms of change management.

We have noted that, like those undergoing torture in captivity, some of the bullied targets who responded to the website survey described a descent into ill health and depression. Researchers have recorded depression as a major factor in the deteriorating health of bullied people (Niedl 1996; Vartia 1996; Einarsen and Raknes 1997; Mikkelsen and Einarsen 2002) and Lewis states that depression results from 'attributions of failure that are internal' (Lewis 2002: 143). Empirical research has found links between depression and guilt, as well as between guilt and shame (Harder, Cutler and Rockart 1992). Trumbull (2003) argues that 'shame makes the sufferer want to shrink from others' and the arts case studies reveal how targets of bullying in arts organizations retreat to the periphery of their working environment as, increasingly, they isolate themselves in response to the behaviour they are enduring. Lewis (2004: 293) finds that:

legitimate formal support through personnel departments or trade unions is shunned in favour of support networks amongst colleagues.

In addition there has been an enormous growth of online help and support groups for bullied people – testimony to 'the blend between empathy and encounter' (Lewis (2004: 293) which assists targets in dealing with their negative experiences.

Besides external support networks, another coping mechanism is where targets share experiences with sympathetic colleagues. Where no coping mechanism exists, researchers (Einarsen and Mikkelsen 2003; Hoel, Faragher and Cooper 2004) have noted that severe cases of bullying can, indeed, result in PTSD, as suggested by Randall (1997). It is also the case that stress and depression can cause feelings of helplessness alongside anger (Niedl 1996; Richards and Freeman 2002). Leymann and Gustafsson (1996) and Matthiesen et al. (2003) have noted the lack of support in the workplace for bullied people and the detrimental effect this has, and this is clearly evidenced by the data from the national survey of arts workers and in the arts case studies.

Certainly, the increasing use of multidisciplinary approaches to research into bullying is enabling studies of the subject at a variety of levels. The more popular literature echoes the early self-help publications (such as Walmsley 1991) and remains focused on enabling people to build 'internal' power and self-esteem – to be more confident and assertive – the implication being that they will be better equipped to withstand the bullying that, inevitably it would seem, they will encounter. Some publications present methods for dealing with dysfunctional interpersonal relationships (Lundin and Lundin 1995), all or most of which appear to necessitate change on the part of everyone except the perpetrator of the undesirable behaviour, as observed by Adams with Crawford (1992) and Rayner (1998). Indeed, the arts case studies demonstrate how some bullies are rewarded for their behaviour through accolades or promotion, for example in The Theatre Project, and Salin suggests that 'tough internal competition' which yields rewards and benefits for bullies may contribute to both peer bullying and hierarchical bullying (Salin 2003: 37), as in The Museum (Chapter 3), where two board members bully a high-performing subordinate who is perceived as a threat to their personal power base.

Whilst the self-help model may have its place among literature aimed at the self-improvement market, it reinforces the view that it is the response of the target alone that determines the outcome of bullying behaviour – and the responsibility of the target to prevent themselves from becoming a victim. So, if an individual fails to prevent themselves from becoming a victim, does it necessarily follow that they are also responsible for any changes to their own physical or mental well-being as a result of bullying?

> *a stronger negative [health] impact is likely to be found among those reporting or labelling themselves as being bullied (Hoel, Faragher and Cooper 2004: 369).*

It is difficult to validate the argument that targets of bullying are responsible for their own suffering. How can self-confident, assertive and physically well individuals who happen to be targeted by bullies be answerable for the devastating effect this has on their health and/or on the well-being and motivation of colleagues who witness the behaviour? These adverse health effects commonly include one or more of:

> *insomnia, nervous symptoms, melancholy, apathy, lack of concentration and sociophobia. (Björkqvist, Österman and Lagerspetz 1994: 27)*

Among the precursors of bullying identified by Hoel and Salin (2003), 'organizational culture' features and Lewis (2004) suggests that several work-related factors may combine to cause workplace bullying, whilst Salin (2003) highlights how the levels of dissatisfaction in a workplace have an impact on the prevalence of bullying. The arts working milieu is no different. If the workplace environment lacks the elements of understanding, knowledge and support then the target is both helpless and hapless, and is a casualty of inaction. This is not merely an illustration of the target as submissive victim: a management ignorant of the issue, and how to deal with it appropriately, creates an atmosphere in which the bully triumphs so that bullying is rewarded and most likely continues. In The Ensemble (Chapter 6) and The Art Gallery (Chapter 1) the bullies gain the support of the founder and increase their power and influence; in The Museum (Chapter 3) the pair of bullies discard erstwhile friends and the target, and manipulate the target's successor so that their power base is increased; in The Theatre Project the bully is lauded for work she did not do, and moves on to a more significant role in another arts organization; in The Arts Service (Chapter 4) the bully also moves on, this time within the local authority, having destroyed a department and emotionally abused the individuals working there.

It is not sufficient for a target to have inner resources to deal with the profound damage workplace bullying causes. Many of the targets in the case studies and among the website respondents occupied senior positions in their arts organizations, and were resilient and resourceful individuals who found themselves in a situation where they were prevented from exercising control – not as a result of their personal *(in)ability*, but rather in the context of the environment in which the bullying behaviour happened – an environment that was contaminated by inaction through the ignorance, apathy and inertia of management. The majority of arts workers in theatres and arts centres identified their organization's reactions to complaints as *indifferent* and this is an important, if disturbing, finding.

The Abuse of Power

The practitioners who describe with enthusiasm what it is like to work in the arts (Chapter 8) relate to power as a positive vehicle: it represents passion, energy, talent, capacity, potential, drive. Targets and witnesses of bullying behaviour, on the other hand, tend to relate to power in another, highly negative, sense: it represents authority, force, pressure, compulsion, intimidation, tyranny. Fine lines exist between perceptions and interpretations of behaviour. For example, 'strong management' can become authoritarian and highly directive, then downright dictatorial; 'office politics' can segue into manipulative behaviour and mind games; a 'personality clash' can descend into conflict or bullying. Arguably, the lines may become finer and the effects more highly charged in an emotive environment such as in the performing arts workplace.

It could be claimed that a strictly positivist approach provides researchers with a more objective view: the behaviour exists only insofar as it can be measured – therefore empirical studies can be recognized as being of central importance. However, it is clear that, in the arts, there is a high level of investment in, and attention paid to, feelings and emotions which are often overt among practitioners. For this reason, qualitative as well as quantitative analysis becomes vital: the arts case studies and the personal stories contribute added value to knowledge and understanding of the behaviour, alongside the empirical research. Some researchers are actively engaged in examining parallels with, and connections between, childhood bullying, domestic violence, workplace bullying and even psychopathic behaviour (Chapter 1) and it is the qualitative, perhaps more so than the quantitative, evidence in these scenarios that is likely to yield the most significant outcomes. Beyond the links between bullying and abusive behaviour in non-workplace settings, there are many indications that petty tyranny can and does exist at a number of levels.

Bullying is not a new or unfamiliar phenomenon, and in English literature we have prime examples of bullies among Shakespeare's dramatis personae, particularly Macbeth who is manipulated by his wife; unscrupulous sisters Goneril and Regan in *King Lear*; and the poisonous advisor Iago in *Othello*. Many creative writers have endeavoured to fathom the mental and moral qualities distinctive to those who bully. An example from Tolstoy begins by mirroring a familiar trait reported in many of the arts case studies – the charisma of the bully (in particular, see The Ensemble (Chapter 6), The Theatre Project and The Creative Industry (Chapter 6)).

It would be particularly pleasant to him to dishonour my name and ridicule me, just because I have exerted myself on his behalf, befriended him, and helped him. I know and understand what a spice that would add to the pleasure of deceiving me, if it really were true … (Tolstoy 1806 [2004]: Book Four, Chapter IV)

Pierre, the central character, prompted by an anonymous letter, is half-afraid that Dolokhov, a cold, abnormally violent officer, has been intimate with his wife. The combination of fear and awe that Dolokhov inspires is a powerful mix. Pierre has come to recognize that all his efforts to please the bully have been in vain – and that Dolokhov delights in deception and in doing a disservice. This could be an example of the point at which a target of bullying behaviour begins to realize what is/has been happening to them.

He remembered the expression Dolokhov's face assumed in his moments of cruelty … That expression was often on Dolokhov's face when looking at him. 'Yes, he is a bully,' thought Pierre, 'to kill a man means nothing to him. It must seem to him that everyone is afraid of him, and that must please him. He must think that I, too, am afraid of him – and in fact I am afraid of him,' he thought, and again he felt something terrible and monstrous rising in his soul. (Tolstoy 1806 [2004]: Book Four, Chapter IV)

Both targets and witnesses of bullying behaviour describe graphic facial expressions and gestures as characteristic of some types of bullying. Dolokhov's series of pointless, crude and sometimes unthinking assaults on other people recounted in the novel is reminiscent of the senseless actions by bullies that have been reported. Taken individually, they could be dismissed as one-off incidents, which are merely unpleasant and regrettable; taken together, they reveal an underlying pattern of behaviour that is unbalanced, if not psychopathic. In the above excerpt, Pierre recognizes that the sight of him produces this same expression on the bully's face, and some targets have stated that the way a bully looks at them makes them afraid, and also afraid to look afraid. It may be that the knowledge that some form of punishment is inevitable creates for targets an emotional response that is also 'terrible and monstrous', for example:

- the unhappiness caused when a major, national employer makes it clear that the choice to opt out from certain terms and conditions is not a real choice – and that there are lots of potential employees out there willing to accept what is offered, and few jobs;
- the wretched feelings engendered when an artistic director in an important arts organization makes shared leadership so unworkable that they force a colleague to leave, and then assume all the executive power for themselves;
- the frustration and distress generated when a funding agency officer attends an arts organization's board meeting and overtly threatens the loss of grant-aid if the organization does not do what the funder wishes, rather than what the governing body and staff have chosen as the best practice course of action;
- the hopelessness and despondency produced when a local government department commissions a sub-contractor to undertake an undesirable task – such as identifying which local venue should be closed down to save money – and then ignores the advice that closing down a venue is not necessary if alternative steps are taken, because that does not suit the political purpose.

One contributor, who wished to remain anonymous, has commented:

I'm certainly in a better emotional and personal place now than back then … and more importantly I'm enjoying the work I'm doing which is such a bonus. Only when you discover that work and pleasure can be one and the same thing do you realize what a horrible experience working within a bullying environment can be. And I know you understand this from first-hand experience.

6 *Management Interventions*

There are reports and academic studies exploring workplace bullying from a variety of different angles. Many publications include advice to employers on practical steps to take to help to eradicate, or to mitigate the effects of, bullying (for example, Reynolds 1994; Giacalone and Greenberg 1997; TUC 1999). Lewis (2004: 282) notes that bullying is a phenomenon:

> ... *rapidly on the increase ... increasing numbers of employees being exposed to bullying behaviours.*

And he urges (2004: 296):

> *those charged with dealing with the aftermath of an event to consider the importance of the shame construct.*

By this Lewis means the elements of embarrassment and shame on the part of the target that can accompany a bullying experience.

Rayner (1999) warns of the need for researchers to understand the contextual framework of the issue before recommending intervention or prevention strategies and, alongside this, Hoel, Faragher and Cooper (2004: 370) note that:

> ... *levels of bullying appear to vary considerably between organizational sectors ... organizational context may affect not only levels of bullying, but also its effect on recipients.*

A variety of terms are used to describe a range of abusive behaviours and these behaviours may originate from a number of different sources. For example, the behaviours can be described as personal in origin (Einarsen et al. 2003) or organizationally derived (Lewis 2002; Salin 2003). Further, Lewis (2004: 283) argues that the range of behaviours is so 'highly subjective' as to be 'open to multiple explications'. Hoel, Faragher and Cooper (2004: 369) assert that it is:

> ... *the subjective experience of being bullied which may manifest itself in mental and physical health problems.*

So, understanding the creative environment and the context in which bullying occurs in arts organizations may help us to gain a better understanding of the behaviour. Bearing in mind the point Hoel, Faragher and Cooper (2004) make about the importance of context when considering interventions, understanding the setting in which bullying occurs may also enable us to deal more effectively with the consequences. In The Museum (Chapter 3), for example, James endured a great deal of mental stress over a period of many months. Particularly after breaking down and crying in front of his own staff, his personal suffering was so intense as to affect his mental, as well as his physical, health.

Research into workplace bullying is new to the arts, and alongside the quantitative evidence there are interesting insights to be gained from the anecdotal evidence of theatrical and literary storytellers (for example, Ronnie Barker, David Hemmings and John Upton). Within their contributions, such artists often provide details of the experiences of stage and screen actors, directors, writers and other artists, and offer descriptions of the wide variety of personality types they have encountered throughout their careers and of strategies they have employed to deal with difficult individuals as well as unhelpful managements.

The next case study is an example of the activities of the same person in two different contexts: hostile behaviour to subordinates within an organization and intimidating behaviour to colleagues in external organizations: horizontal bullying. This is similar to the behaviour described in The Theatre Project (Chapter 5) and is particularly interesting because the bully in this case had previously witnessed bullying by a colleague in another company, but had taken no action. This recalls the observation of Archer (1999) that witnesses of tyrannical behaviour in paramilitary organizations may adopt bullying behaviour themselves, if it is seen to be successful (see Chapter 1).

THE CREATIVE INDUSTRY: PEER BULLYING/CORPORATE BULLYING/SERIAL BULLYING

Several small companies, and some individuals, from a variety of creative disciplines rented space in a Centre for Creative Enterprises. Hayden was one of two directors in a small interior design company. Her role was to develop the business for the firm, which she tackled with enthusiasm and a great deal of personal magnetism. Hayden perceived that lottery funding was bringing finance into new areas, including community and arts buildings. However, the company did not have experience in these areas, so she identified potential partners from within the other creative enterprises in the centre in fields complementary to interior design and who had a background and/or contacts in the appropriate sectors. This included a furniture-maker, a company of textile artists and a collective of six artists working in ceramic and glass. Talking persuasively to these three organizations, Hayden's charm and zeal convinced them to join forces as a team in pursuit of new work in community and arts centres.

Alek, Manuela and Daniel represented the other companies and the team bid successfully for several projects. Hayden's organization learned much about working in the voluntary and arts sectors from the others and its reputation grew. As a result, Hayden, who was the company's public face, was offered a position on an important national advisory panel, which she accepted. Having done so, Hayden's demeanour changed and the team spirit that had prevailed during previous projects disappeared.

She positioned herself publicly as leader of the consortium, despite the fact that this had never been discussed with her colleagues and her company was by no means the largest in the group. At the start of new projects she visited each of the companies individually, issuing the vague, imperious instruction that they upgrade the quality of their work. As she was entirely non-specific, however, this caused confusion; each company thought it was being singled out as no one company knew that the others were being treated in a similar fashion, and Alek, Manuela and Daniel felt personally insulted and became anxious about how they should respond.

Internally, the harmonious atmosphere of the interior design company began to diminish. Hayden's behaviour had become intolerably officious – she was constantly and literally looking over everyone's shoulder and was rude and intimidating to the administrative staff and the professional designers. Reception and administration staff became ill, and an increasing number took sick leave more and more frequently. One designer in the firm confessed that he was afraid to speak up because Hayden's co-director in the company was also her husband. Another designer left the practice rather than tolerate her behaviour any longer.

Externally, Hayden began to scrutinize and to question the information provided for projects by the other members of the consortium, even though the details were outside her sphere of knowledge. Sometimes she did this in meetings with clients, intimating that it was necessary for her to keep an eye on the other members of the team to ensure their work was of sufficient quality. Sometimes she harried Alek, Manuela and Daniel by phone, and sometimes the whole team collectively by email. As a result of her deficiency in appropriate knowledge – she was not a furniture-maker, a textile artist or a glass specialist – the questioning in which she engaged continued to cause misunderstanding and anxiety on the part of project clients, as well as among the members of the team.

Colleagues from the other companies began to experience a sense of dread when faced with the prospect of communicating with Hayden. When they discovered, over a period of time, that they were all being targeted, Alek, Manuela and Daniel began to minimize their contact with the interior design company, each selecting other designers to work with instead.

Eventually, when approached by Hayden to bid for new projects, the other members of the consortium became unavailable. They continue to work with each other; however none of them work with her or her company any longer. Hayden sought out new colleagues in other companies, but in each case has had difficulties sustaining professional relationships beyond a short period of time.

(Names and environs have been changed to protect confidentiality.)

Hayden was an ambitious woman – for herself and for her company. She saw an opportunity to access new sources of funding and business and pursued these vigorously. Her personal charm enabled her to attract the interest of colleagues from other companies. In effect they were making the most of the centre's internal economy; however, in the process Hayden seems to have developed a misplaced sense of her own importance. Perhaps the success enjoyed by the consortium and her company put pressure on her to achieve more. Perhaps being invited to join a national advisory panel, which may have been a daunting prospect, triggered her bullying behaviour. Whatever the reason, Hayden became conceitedly assertive and dogmatic in her opinions, engaging in peer bullying of colleagues, and also, as a company director, managerial and corporate bullying of members of staff.

Adopting tactics which sit comfortably under the banner 'divide and rule', it appears that the bully has no clear idea of what she is trying to achieve: her visits to team members are not designed to boost morale and appear to have no purpose related to better team performance. They are not consistent with constructive leadership (Rayner 1999). Once her colleagues share information about their individual experiences, they come to understand that they are being subjected to bullying behaviour and they are empowered by mutual recognition and support to take action, which they do. Their ability to distance themselves from the perpetrator's behaviour, both physically and emotionally, enhances their chances of successfully dealing with the behaviour in this case.

Hayden's company initially gained from the alliance, and once she was secure in the knowledge that she and the company were being lauded, the trademark charisma of the bully was replaced by behaviour displaying arrogance and egotism. The egotism may have been there from the outset: perhaps the bully was seeking to enhance her status or to be recognized as an important person, hence the change in her demeanour in her own place of work.

Within the design company the bully's behaviour disturbs the equilibrium of the workplace to the extent that staff members are seen to increasingly absent themselves from work and, in one case, to leave. It must be construed that this was not an aim but a by-product – this is the bully's own company, after all. It seems likely, therefore, that Hayden's increased self-regard resulted in a view that other people within her compass were insignificant; therefore they were legitimate targets for criticism, deserved or otherwise.

Dieter Zapf, of the Department of Work and Organizational Psychology, Frankfurt University, acknowledges that there may be instances where an organization is the cause of bullying but this may manifest itself through a specific individual (Zapf 1999). This is evident in the case study The Arts Service (Chapter 4) where an entire department is dismantled, apparently single-handedly, during a restructuring process. However, this does not seem to be the case here, as the bully's behaviour presented itself in two different settings, both within and without her workplace, and had two sets of negative effects.

As with Susan, the bullying manager in The Theatre Project (Chapter 5), communication and miscommunication is an issue here. Just as Susan withholds information, causing difficulties for a colleague and ensuring her own personal gain, Hayden uses miscommunication that confuses and instigates anxiety among her fellow workers. Zapf describes conscious miscommunication as a mobbing strategy, and Susan's lies as well as Hayden's unintelligible reprimands seem to support this. There are many negative consequences of the bullying exhibited here: the personal distress of the staff in the interior design company, resulting in illness, absenteeism and eventual loss of expertise; the bewilderment and anxiety of Hayden's professional colleagues from the other industries, resulting in their embarrassment at her unethical behaviour; and eventually the loss of business partners for the bully's own company.

We have seen that external colleagues were able to detach themselves successfully from the perpetrator, their business affairs not being inextricably linked. They were also able to confer, to recognize that they had all been targeted and to offer mutual support. The company employees, on the other hand, were economically dependent on their workplace. They may have been able to confer about the harassment; however, in this case, because of the personal link between the co-directors, they felt they could not report the behaviour. In the workplace, the process by which employees can make complaints about bullying behaviour is crucial to resolving the problem – and in this case the employees' routes to escape were sick leave/absenteeism and leaving their job. This is a common feature of workplace bullying. In The Theatre Project (Chapter 5), for example, the CEO disbelieved the complaints made by his staff; in The Museum (Chapter 3), the board members disbelieved the CEO; in The Arts Service (Chapter 4), Jenny's attempts to make a complaint under the local authority's disciplinary and grievance procedure were thwarted by the representatives of the human resources department.

Social Interaction

Bullying is a function, albeit a particularly negative one, of how people act on and influence one another. An extension of role theory, impression management is both a theory and process: the theory argues that people are constantly engaged in controlling how others perceive them; the process refers to the conscious, or unconscious, effort to influence the perceptions of other people in order to achieve a particular goal. The latter can take the form of regulating and controlling information in social interaction, for example Chapter 2 outlines how Erving Goffman cast the idea in a dramaturgical framework.

Self-presentation is the process of trying to influence the perception of a personal image and it is interesting that bullies are often accused of manipulating others' perceptions of them – presenting one set of values and behaviours to those presumed to have the most power, for example, and another to the target(s) of bullying behaviour. Or, in The Creative Industry, initially presenting a charming persona until such time as the bully's key aims have been achieved, after which the mask slips.

As bullies are aware of how they are being perceived by their audience, role theory would argue that they manage their interpersonal behaviour strategically so as to design and to shape, or influence, impressions formed by others. Some sociologists approach the issue as integrationists – combining micro- and macro-level theories to provide a comprehensive understanding of human social behaviour. For example, Ritzer and Goodman (2004: 357) propose four highly interdependent elements in their sociological model:

1. a macro-objective component (for example, society, law, bureaucracy);
2. a micro-objective component (for example, patterns of behaviour and human interaction);
3. a macro-subjective component (for example, culture, norms, values);
4. a micro-subjective component (for example, perceptions, beliefs).

This model is of particular use in understanding society because it uses two axes: one ranging from objective (society) to subjective (culture and cultural interpretation); the other ranging from the macro-level (norms) to the micro-level (individual level beliefs). Integration helps to explain social phenomena because it shows how the different components of social life work together to influence society and behaviour. In the same way, the use of combined methodologies in the arts research allowed for the analysis of statistical as well as narrative evidence, valuing both sets of information and resulting in a more complete picture of the issue of bullying.

Critical theory is social theory oriented toward evaluating and changing society as a whole, in contrast to traditional theory which is oriented only to understanding or explaining it. Core concepts are:

1. that critical social theory should be directed at society in its entirety, taking account of how it came to be configured at a specific point in time; and
2. that critical theory should improve understanding of society by integrating all the major social sciences, including economics, sociology, history, political science, anthropology and psychology.

In line with critical theory, workplace bullying studies have taken place within a range of disciplines in the behavioural sciences, including psychology, psychiatry, sociology and social anthropology. Liefooghe and Mackenzie Davey (2003: 200) say:

> Critical theory research has explicit value commitments, and pays direct attention to moral and ethical issues. It is often suspicious of unconflicted accounts. The discourse also holds that people can and should act – an additional activist tone, found clearly in the work of Habermas (1975, 1987, amongst others). Thus while, like postmodernism it seeks to interrogate unitarist analyses, unlike postmodernism, it values some accounts above others.

Research into workplace bullying in any discipline needs to consider moral and ethical issues, at least to a certain extent, in order to establish the nature of what is being studied. Similarly, qualitative examination of the subject needs to go beyond a purely positivist approach in assessing and evaluating the behaviour, and to acknowledge the roles played by context and social interaction.

Dealing with Complaints of Bullying: The Pilot Study

None of the arts workers in the pilot study thought that management had dealt satisfactorily with complaints about bullying. Only 11.2 per cent of these arts workers knew of a written policy to deal with the types of bullying behaviour named in the Dignity at Work Bill – compared with 23.1 per cent of arts managers, who believed that bullying was covered within existing policies. The majority of the website respondents, at 55.6 per cent, believed that arts organizations were not persuaded there was a problem with bullying and/or had not given any direct consideration to policy. A further 22.2 per cent reported that policies were in place; 16.7 per cent stated that management had not considered policy but would not condone bullying behaviour; and 5.5 per cent said that, in the absence of a policy, management would consider a complaint.

Conversely, 30.8 per cent of the managers who responded at the same time reported that management had handled complaints well, and denied any negative results. In the national survey, 6 per cent of participants thought management performance was satisfactory and complaints had been handled well, whilst 37.5 per cent thought the opposite was the case. In fact, for how management handled complaints, the results from managers aware of bullying behaviour and the bullied group are virtually inversely proportional: 57.1 per cent of the aware managers thought management performed well, compared to 4.5 per cent of the bullied group; 53.5 per cent of the bullied group thought management performed badly, compared to 0 per cent of the managers.

This trend continues in the perceptions about the extent to which management recognizes corporate responsibility in relation to bullying. There is little evidence to indicate whether the existence of a policy has an impact on the incidence of bullying behaviour, although interview and text contributions indicate perceptions that policies exist but are not adhered to, and that some workers are too intimidated to take action (Chapter 4). It may be, for example, that in The Creative Industry an anti-bullying, harassment or other suitable policy existed, but that workers felt powerless to take advantage of it because of the personal link between the two company directors.

There was no perception among managers that bullying behaviour was becoming increasingly common: all of them perceived that the frequency of bullying had reduced or remained unchanged during the last twelve months or five years. Two managers had intervened and/or assisted someone who had a complaint of bullying. One of these stated that, in another incident, she '… was accused of bullying myself!'

In the national survey 3.6 per cent of respondents had been the subject of a complaint about bullying by a colleague: two-thirds of these were part of the bullied group. As the manager in the pilot study had assisted a colleague who was targeted, it may be that the complaint against her had been made by the bully, reinforcing the evidence that perpetrators often accuse the person they have been targeting, as in the minimizing, denying and blaming part of the Power and Control Wheel (See Chapter 1, Figure 1.3 and Table 1: The power and control wheel elements adapted for workplace bullying).

Whilst some managers had intervened in cases of bullying, either on behalf of complainants or on behalf of management, none had gained experience of both sides of the complaints procedure and none had been the target of a workplace bully. One manager had noted bullying behaviour towards staff by a board member in a theatre, and commented: 'yet theatres rarely have procedures to cover such situations. We do now!'

The viewpoints of arts workers and arts managers about how complaints are handled are not, in fact, mutually exclusive: despite the fact that an increased percentage of managers are aware of bullying in the national study, many people governing arts organizations and managing them at senior level do appear to be in denial about its existence in the arts workplace. Equally, there is little evidence to suggest that boards of governors or senior management teams would condone such behaviour – if they were aware of its existence and prevalence. Acknowledging that there is a problem, and raising awareness should be the arts world's first step towards resolving the issue of bullying.

Dealing with Complaints of Bullying: The National Survey

Again, participants were asked to consider whether their employers had handled complaints of bullying satisfactorily (Table 6.1). A few did not respond and 24.9 per cent did not know. At 4.8 per cent, a small number thought management had handled complaints well, that is to the satisfaction of all parties; however 39.8 per cent did not agree and 28.1 per cent stated that there were variations in how complaints were handled. The majority of those who thought complaints were handled badly, at 55.6 per cent, were men. This view was taken by 22.2 per cent of managers themselves and perceptions

Table 6.1   How management handles complaints of bullying

	Survey group %	Bullied group %	Non-bullied group %
Non-response	2.4%	2%	2.7%
Yes (well)	4.8%	3%	6%
No (badly)	39.8%	56.6%	28.7%
It varies – sometimes settled satisfactorily by management, sometimes not	28.1%	27.3%	28.6%
Don't know	24.9%	11.1%	34%
Total	**100%**	**100%**	**100%**

Note: values are in-columns percentages pertaining to the survey group (249 observations) and the two subgroups, the 'bullied group' (99 observations) and the non-bullied group (150 observations).

that their organization had not handled complaints of bullying well were prevalent in arts centres, normally operating on a regional or local basis, as well as in the larger-scale venues with a national remit.

A much higher proportion of the bullied group, at 56.6 per cent, thought management had handled complaints badly than did the non-bullied group at 28.7 per cent, and more of the non-bullied group did not know – 34.0 per cent compared to 11.1 per cent of the bullied group.

Respondents were asked to consider whether complaints of bullying had been handled to the satisfaction of the person making the complaint (Table 6.2). Again, a few did not respond and 27.7 per cent did not know; 7.2 per cent thought those who had complained of bullying had been satisfied with how their complaint was handled; 35.3 per cent did not agree; and 27.4 per cent stated that there were variations in how satisfied complainants had been. Again, a much higher proportion of the bullied group, at 50.5 per cent, thought their organization had not handled complaints to the satisfaction of the complainant than did the non-bullied group at 25.3 per cent, and more of the non-bullied group did not know – 38.7 per cent compared to 11.1 per cent of the bullied group.

Table 6.2   Satisfaction of complainants of bullying

	Survey group %	Bullied group %	Non-bullied group %
Non-response	2.4%	0%	4%
Yes (complaints handled well)	7.2%	6.1%	8%
No (complaints handled badly)	35.3%	50.5%	25.3%
It varies – sometimes settled satisfactorily for complainant, sometimes not	27.4%	32.3%	24%
Don't know	27.7%	11.1%	38.7%
Total	**100%**	**100%**	**100%**

Note: values are in-columns percentages pertaining to the survey group (249 observations) and the two subgroups, the 'bullied group' (99 observations) and the non-bullied group (150 observations).

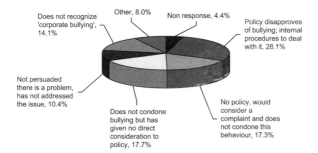

Percentages established on 249 observations

Figure 6.1   Organizational attitudes to bullying

On this occasion, a higher percentage of the bullied group felt the outcome varied for complainants than had thought their employer's handling of bullying behaviour varied.

Opinions on organizational attitudes to bullying were canvassed (Figure 6.1) and overall 28.1 per cent thought that their organization had a policy disapproving of bullying and internal rules and procedures to deal with it. Certainly, some organizations are likely to include mechanisms for dealing with negative behaviours within disciplinary and grievance procedures and/or health and safety policies. Fewer people among the bullied group (25.3 per cent) than the non-bullied group held this view, perhaps illustrating the subtle nature of some types of bullying behaviour and/or the inefficacy of existing policies to deal adequately with these behaviours.

As Table 6.3 shows, whilst acknowledging that management would not condone bullying behaviour, 26.3 per cent of administration/clerical staff and 33.3 per cent of other staff said their organization was not convinced there was a problem with bullying and had not addressed the issue (column D); 25 per cent of the box office and front-of--house staff, and 20 per cent of the cleaning staff, said their organization was not always aware that terms and conditions could be detrimental to employees (column E); 25.9 per cent of management staff said their organization did not condone bullying, but had not given any direct consideration to policy (column C).

Table 6.3   Perceptions of organizational attitudes to bullying, by area of work

Areas of Work	A	B	C	D	E	Other (including non-responses)	Total per area of work
Admin/clerical	26.3%	21.1%	10.5%	26.3%	10.5%	5.3%	100%
Box Office	31.3%	12.5%	0%	6.3%	25%	24.9%	100%
Cleaning	0%	20%	40%	0%	20%	20%	100%
Front-of-house	28.1%	18.8%	21.9%	3.1%	25%	3.1%	100%
Management	29.6%	14.8%	25.9%	3.7%	18.5%	7.5%	100%
Production	39.3%	10.7%	17.9%	7.1%	14.3%	10.7%	100%
Technical	33.3%	23.3%	18.9%	10%	10.1%	4.4%	100%
Other	9.6%	9.5%	19%	33.3%	9.5%	19.1%	100%

Note: values are in-rows percentages pertaining to the survey group (238 observations).

Key for interpretation (Tables 6.3 and 6.4)
A: The organization has a policy, which disapproves of bullying, and internal rules and procedures to deal with it.
B: There is no policy on bullying; however, the organization would give consideration to a complaint and does not condone this type of behaviour.
C: The organization does not condone bullying, but has not given any direct consideration to policy.
D: The organization is not persuaded that there is a problem with bullying and has not addressed the issue.
E: The organization does not recognize that some terms and conditions are detrimental to employees and are equivalent to corporate bullying.

The attitudes of the bullied group and the non-bullied group differed (Table 6.4). A higher percentage of the non-bullied group were in organizations that had anti-bullying policies and procedures (row A); 21.3 per cent of non-bullied people believed that although there is no policy on bullying, their organization would give consideration to a complaint and does not condone this type of behaviour, compared to 11.1 per cent of the bullied group (row B). In the bullied group, 15.2 per cent state that their organization is not persuaded that there is a problem with bullying and has not addressed the issue, compared to 7.3 per cent of the non-bullied group (row D); 17.2 per cent of the bullied group also stated that their organization does not recognize that some terms and conditions are detrimental to employees and are equivalent to corporate bullying, compared to 12 per cent of the non-bullied group (row E).

Table 6.4   Organizational attitudes to bullying, by subsamples

	Bullied group %	Non-bullied group %
Non-response	4%	4.7%
A	25.3%	30%
B	11.1%	21.3%
C	15.1%	19.4%
D	15.2%	7.3%
E	17.2%	12%
Other	12.1%	5.3%
Total	**100%**	**100%**

Note: values are in-columns percentages pertaining to the two subgroups, the 'bullied group' (99 observations) and the non-bullied group (150 observations).

In Tables 6.3 and 6.4, among those who responded 'Other' were arts workers who contributed their own comments, which clarified their perceptions of organizational attitudes, and some of these comments are recorded in Table 6.5; others relating to policy are cited in Chapter 3.

Views among the eight people from the non-bullied group tended to be vague, expressing uncertainty about policy. Among the 12 from the bullied group, attitudes were more forthright. Overall, the view was that policy is not implemented, and that management is disinterested and inactive about dealing with bullying behaviour.

**Table 6.5   Selected additional comments on organizational attitudes, by
subgroups**

Bullied group (12 people commented)
Don't know (2)
Varies at different management levels
Bullying is part and parcel of daily life without recourse to higher management
The bullies are two senior managers
Denial/inactivity
Not interested
If it suits them they turn a blind eye
They realize there is a problem but do nothing about it
The organization is currently investigating the bullying. In the past it has not dealt with the bullying satisfactorily and has not supported the bullied to any degree, but as far as I know they don't condone it.
Non-bullied group (8 people commented in all)
Don't know (3)
Bullying is ignored – it's bad PR
Deal well with staff bullying – reluctant to address management bullying

How are Managers Managing?

The majority of the arts managers in the pilot study were in senior posts – often as CEO of their organization. In the context of managing people, judging by the reported level of appropriate qualifications and/or the types of training they had undertaken, they lacked adequate education or skills for their considerable human resources or personnel responsibilities.

In the national survey, more than a third of employees (37.3 per cent) had not undertaken any job-related training within the last three years, including 25.2 per cent of line managers and 35 per cent of those who supervised other line managers. A similar result was recorded within the bullied group at 36.4 per cent (-0.9 per cent variance on the norm), however there were more marked variations in the bullied group's experiences of training provision:

- more of them had not asked for, or been offered, training – 37.4 per cent (+4.5 per cent);
- more had requested training but no further action had been taken – 28.3 per cent (+1.0 per cent);
- future training was planned for fewer of those than had requested it – 30.3 per cent (-4.2 per cent).

We do not know for certain whether a lack of training may contribute to bullying in the arts – however, it seems highly likely that poorly or inadequately skilled managers will be ill-equipped to deal with the problem in the workplace, and that targets of bullying may be aware of being undertrained, but unaided in their attempts to remedy this.

According to the responses, managements that were indifferent to complaints about working hours, pay and bullying predominated in all types of venue, as well as in all geographical locations. Where no anti-bullying policies were in place, 32.6 per cent of non-bullied people said their organization would give consideration to a complaint and does not condone bullying behaviour, and 24.3 per cent of the bullied group said their organization does not recognize that some terms and conditions are detrimental to employees and are equivalent to corporate bullying.

In the pilot study, most managers had acquired informal, hands-on training in managing people through their workplace. Some were particularly sensitive to answering questions about the topic, and one manager indicated an underlying belief that the fact of being employed in the arts in various capacities over a period of time was, *per se*, sufficient to equip him to manage people effectively. Notwithstanding this viewpoint, it is difficult to imagine that simply being employed is sufficient to equip arts managers – or indeed any managers – to deal effectively with complex, contentious or difficult personnel problems or situations, such as complaints of bullying.

Increasingly, workplace bullying has come within the remit of organizational health and safety, equal opportunities and diversity policies. All of these are concerned with securing the welfare of the workforce, but how well equipped are senior managers and boards of governors in the arts to deal with negative social behaviours, including bullying?

In the pilot study with managers, there was no attempt to distinguish between personnel management and human resources management (HRM), rather the focus was on how managers acquired their skills and it was expected that many would have gained some knowledge and experience through the workplace rather than through access to formal or accredited training opportunities. However, it had not been expected that for 42 per cent of managers this would be the *only* way by which they had learned about managing people. The survey group comprised senior arts professionals whose organizations employed circa 800 people and the level of training they had acquired to assist them in dealing with staff welfare issues, other than through doing their job, seemed inadequate.

For example, one respondent had had no training, either formal or informal, and no experience, yet this senior manager was the CEO of an organization employing more than 100 staff. He was working directly to the board and personally supervising staff including other line managers. He was aware of bullying behaviour in the workplace, in relation to a specific employee, but believed that bullying had become less frequent during the last twelve months and the last five years. His experience was informal only; however, he believed that bullying had been dealt with satisfactorily on the part of both management and complainant, and he was sure that management did not condone bullying behaviour, despite not having a policy. In many ways, this example typifies the overall impression gained from the pilot study of arts managers in regard to workplace bullying, and it is unsurprising that the arts workers in the study felt management was not persuaded that there was a problem and had not addressed the issue.

Despite having significant line management responsibilities, managers had received little education or training in personnel or human resources issues. This is important in light of organizational responsibility for employees' welfare at work. Lewis and Rayner (2003) explore the impact of HRM on the bullying phenomenon, in the context of organizational culture and the decline of trades unions, and the researchers recommend a 'careful review' of the reach and impact of HRM (Lewis and Rayner 2003: 380). This is a position to be strongly supported from the perspective of encouraging best practice; however, in the case of the arts organizations in the pilot study, the prevalence of informal hands-on training in the workplace as the sole learning mechanism may be taken as an indicator of the absence of HRM ideology or functions. The respondents represented themselves as those 'with most responsibility for personnel matters' and, as indicated previously, one manager summarised his experience of managing people as:

Forty years as actor/stage manager, director, artistic director at 3 theatres.

The successful career path is not disputed; however, there is an underlying assumption in this argument that the fact of being employed in the arts in various capacities, by definition, equips an individual to manage people effectively. The arts research does not test this as a specific issue; however, it is likely to be as untrue in the arts as it would be in any other profession – 40 years in industry, business or education does not necessarily result in a skilled manager of people. There is, of course, a view taken by some arts professionals that may have a bearing – that 'the arts are different'.

Tolerating Bullying

In the pilot study, the majority of arts managers failed to recognize bullying behaviour as a feature of the workplace: existing policies did not name bullying explicitly, or they named it only after a site-specific bullying incident had both occurred and been registered by those with governance capacity. This corresponds with the issue of permissibility (Rayner 1999), when employees perceive that management tolerates bullying unless the opposite is demonstrated. The assertion by managers that the handling of workplace complaints was considered satisfactory by all parties, whatever the outcome, displays a degree of naivety not commensurate with the individual and collective maturity and professional experience of the survey group.

As might be expected, the managers appear to be strongly aligned with organizational culture and policy; however, the absence of accredited training in personnel or HRM issues means there is no evidence as to whether they are equipped as individuals to deal effectively with contentious or difficult issues, such as objections to working hours or complaints of bullying. Ostrich syndrome emerged as a feature of arts managers' attitudes in this difficult subject area as they failed to admit to the existence of bullying in the arts. One respondent who had previously declared no knowledge of bullying behaviour within her/his organization nonetheless admitted it had occurred 'in another organization only. Also arts. Repeated unfair criticism.'

This may be symptomatic of the understandable desire among senior arts managers to avoid admission of culpability on their own or their organization's part. Interestingly, it also provides another perspective on attribution theory, whereby, like targets of bullying over time, the arts managers 'consistently attribute reasons for negative events externally to themselves' (Rayner 1999: 29).

Among those expressing dissatisfaction with the way in which management dealt with bullying incidents, 87.5 per cent of arts workers in the pilot study described themselves as victims of a workplace bully. In the national survey, however, only 56.6 per cent of the bullied group expressed the same level of dissatisfaction. This needs to be considered in the context of the assertion that bullied people report negative behaviour more than non-bullied people (Rayner 1999). Possibly, respondents in the pilot study equated personal discontent with the perceived failure of management to deal satisfactorily with complaints of bullying in general. Nonetheless, the remaining 13.5 per cent, who were not complainants, were similarly critical of procedures to deal with bullying behaviour, and in the national survey 29.3 per cent of non-bullied people felt that management had performed badly in this respect.

The participants who felt that their organization was not persuaded that there was a problem with bullying described graphically the consequences of not having written policies nor effective methods and/or personnel to specifically deal with difficult behaviours:

> As far as I am aware we don't have a policy on bullying. We do have a mission statement which states that the company ethos is one of mutual respect and trust, but this is contradicted by the behaviour of the management. It is a very small organization (8 employees) and the Executive Director is the bully. Recent attempts to address the issue through meetings with the trustees have culminated in the ED convincing the trustees that there is no problem.

We have seen that the majority of respondents in arts organizations felt management did not handle complaints of bullying behaviour well and, given the lack of training in dealing with personnel or human resources issues among managers participating in the pilot study, perhaps this is not surprising. If HRM ideologies are failing to be effective, with line managers who cannot or do not access relevant training at an adequate level, the workers' lack of representation signalled by Lewis and Rayner (2003) can only deteriorate further, compounding workplace issues that are already difficult. This loss of voice – the absence of a genuine opportunity to express their opinion and to make a complaint about the bullying – is what afflicted the employees in The Creative Industry.

One important action management could take would be not to dismiss out of hand complaints of bullying. The arts research has shown that this indifference to complaints implies permissibility, which is positively correlated with bullying. Instead, management should focus on introducing accredited methods of investigating the issue in an effort to resolve it – for example, properly conducted forensic interviews, as used during the arts research, are legally sound, in part because they ensure the interviewer's objectivity, employ non-leading techniques and emphasize careful documentation of the interview.

Developing a policy to deal with bullying at work has climbed the agenda for arts managers, alongside developing policies for discrimination or abuse on the grounds of race, gender, age, disability and faith. Increasingly, there is information and guidance for human resources and personnel officers and others (for example, the Chartered Management Institute's *Bullying in the Workplace: Guidance for Managers*, 2005) and the reasons for policy development have been outlined by researchers and others seeking effective ways of dealing with the behaviour:

> All sensible employers have a policy on harassment and discrimination. A policy protects both employees and the employer. The motivation is twofold: to provide an atmosphere in which employees can fulfil the duties and obligations of their contract free from harassment, discrimination, victimisation and scapegoating, and to comply with UK and European law,

specifically, the Sex Discrimination Act (1975), the Race Relations Act (1976), and the Disability Discrimination Act (1996). (Bullyonline.com 2005)

In the absence of an effective policy, arts workers found they were isolated and at a loss as to sources of help. This was particularly true of smaller arts organizations and/or those where a designated human resources professional was not available. Although even when such a professional is in place, as in The Arts Service (Chapter 4), poor implementation negates the point of having a policy. The effect of workplace bullying can be all the more severe when the CEO is the perpetrator, and also the only conduit to higher authority:

The organization has no policies that I am aware of to deal with the above [examples of bullying behaviour]. Moreover, it does not have a personnel officer, nor a nominated officer to whom a member of staff can turn if they are experiencing ANY sort of difficulty within the workplace. The Board only ever get the version of events as presented by the Chief Executive. I am quite sure that the Board would not condone bullying if they perceived that it was happening. A feature of many bullies is that they have a very plausible manner, such that their superiors cannot believe them capable of unpleasant behaviour. This leaves the employees in impossible situations; it appears that THEY are the problem. (Respondent in the pilot survey)

Researchers in the field have made a number of recommendations that are important and useful to the performing arts sector. Among these is the introduction of effective, safe and fair policies on bullying behaviour:

No organization is immune from bullying though the scale and intensity of the problem vary greatly between organizations. This suggests that all organizations should have in place policies and procedures which can deal with problems when they occur, and which may act as a deterrent to bullying in the first place. (Hoel and Cooper 2000)

Salin (2003: 42) warns of the bullying that results from the ever-increasing struggle for efficiency, work intensification, and reliance on performance-related reward systems, and managers, in general, agree. In The Arts Service (Chapter 4), this 'target culture' was instrumental in the demolition of a department, and this is a phenomenon that is further discussed in Chapter 8. In the 2005 Chartered Management Institute's study of workplace bullying among managers (Chartered Management Institute 2005b), conducted by Woodman and Cook, 76 per cent of the managers, in organizations where an anti-bullying policy was in place, felt that their organization was quite or very effective at deterring bullying, compared to 43 per cent of those in organizations that had no policy and no plans to develop one. Similarly, more than three-quarters of managers in organizations with a formal policy on bullying felt that their organization responded effectively to specific incidents, compared to less than half of those in organizations without a formal policy. Hoel and Cooper recommend that an effective anti-bullying policy should provide targets of bullying with a safe reporting procedure:

... protecting them from possible retribution, whilst at the same time ensuring a fair hearing of the case. Severe or repeated breach of policy should be met with sanctions. However, in order to ensure their effectiveness, a monitoring system needs to be put in place. (Hoel and Cooper 2000)

The sanctions noted by Woodman and Cook (2005) included both informal and formal processes, that is, opportunities for employees to discuss bullying with management, as well as access to disciplinary procedures. Other elements included clear definitions of bullying behaviour, guidelines on acceptable conduct, awareness training, defined responsibilities for trades union/employee representatives and for managers. To support targets of bullying behaviour, recommendations were to include a contact point for advice, internal confidential counseling and access to external counseling and mediation.

Some participants in the pilot research also found policy development to be effective:

> *I have been involved in a couple of [bullying] incidents which happened some years ago whilst working for other organizations. The [current] Trust has a policy called Challenging Harassment which covers all of the above. (Respondent to the pilot survey)*

The development of effective policy in the performing arts will depend heavily on the provision of appropriate training and the ability of arts managers both to recognize their responsibilities and to sharpen their skills in the context of managing people and staff welfare. The research indicated that arts managers in the pilot study had had little relevant training in human resources issues, and also that both the managers and their organizations tended to be dismissive about the need for such training. The training requirement goes beyond merely raising awareness of bullying as an issue: arts managers have an opportunity to work proactively on the issue of workplace bullying, embracing best practice rather than responding belatedly to a requirement to catch up with policy development in other sectors. First, arts organizations must acknowledge their accountability for employee conduct and adequately equip their managers to deal with the attendant responsibilities.

It cannot be assumed that an ability to manage people well is acquired as a routine consequence of working in the arts. In fact, it is more likely that what is achieved, as an employee progresses from one management post to another, often more senior, role, is custom and practice in managing people 'after a fashion'. There is no evidence to suggest that knowledge, expertise or skills in the effective management of people are gained in this way, and little indication that arts organizations are involved in the active promotion of continuing professional development in the field of human resources. In the national survey, information from those who managed other people revealed that 34 out of 135 line managers (25.2 per cent) and 50 out of 143 supervisors of other line managers (34.9 per cent) had not received any work-related training in the last three years. Five out of the nine people working directly to the board of their organizations (55.6 per cent) had not received training either.

Turney (2003: 99–107) presents two case studies illustrating that learning through doing the job can result in apprentices or trainees experiencing 'learned helplessness', whereby they passively accept inappropriate criticism from authoritarian mentors in hierarchical organizations. It is possible that on the job training can also result in arts managers acquiring the capacity for learned dominance, particularly if this is deemed, by them and their organizations, to be appropriate to a managerial/leadership role. Lack of accredited education and training opportunities may contribute to a misinterpretation of management and leadership as control. This may be an important contributory factor to the high incidence of bullying behaviour in the labour-intensive performing arts. It is not without significance that the emergence of the highly successful and valuable Clore Leadership Programme followed the final report of a task force set up by the Clore Duffield Foundation in 2002 to consider ways to improve cultural leadership in the UK.

The task force identified a number of recent studies testifying to a crisis in cultural leadership – a crisis confirmed by its own consultation. (Task Force Final Report 2002)

Similarly, research into an optimum leadership style for the commercial world has led to the identification of transformational leadership as an aspirational model (Alimo-Metcalfe and Alban-Metcalfe 2005). Unlike charismatic leadership, which centres on being inspired by a compelling personality, transformational leadership aims to transform participants into leaders, supporting them to assist and encourage each other, to work in harmony and to be aware of, and work towards, what will help the organization as a whole.

Support at Work

This case study examines peer bullying in a performing arts organization with, technically, a cooperative structure – all the musicians are on an equal footing. The formation of a cooperative company is a model that is often favoured by new or young artistic companies, sometimes set up to tour or to work in educational or community settings.

On the surface, the members of the ensemble appear as equal parties in this encounter. To an extent this was true at the beginning, although Claire as instigator can be seen to hold the balance of power initially – it was through her influence, and the support of the other members, that early attempts by Derek to dislodge Richard were resisted. Richard is popular and competent, traits often associated with targets of bullying. Derek's behaviour as perpetrator indicates that he feels displaced by Richard – the aggressive projection of a perpetrator's feelings of inadequacy on to his target is widely acknowledged (for example, Field 1999). Perhaps Derek feels inadequate because he is the oldest member of the group, yet finds himself in a new, young company with people several years his junior.

However, following the first failed attempt to oust the target, Derek adopts another tack and begins to exhibit the charisma associated with bullies, by focusing his attention

---

THE ENSEMBLE: PEER BULLYING

A new ensemble was set up by Claire, a young accomplished performer, to provide music workshops and performances in schools, both in inner-city and rural settings. She recruited five others to form a cooperative organization – three males and two females with backgrounds in performing, conducting and writing music. All were young, in their twenties, and three were in their first jobs after college or university. From the outset the company worked collaboratively on devising material, writing and arranging new music, although individual strengths soon began to appear, so that after the first three or four months Jackie had taken on most of the administration and organization of the performances and workshops, and Richard moved more and more into conducting, and took the lead in directing the work of the others. Claire, Mary and Paul were quite happy with this arrangement; however, Derek, the oldest member of the company by two or three years, soon began to resent Richard's position and sometimes became petulant and argumentative during rehearsals.

Derek began to cast aspersions on Richard, making 'joking' remarks to the others about his appearance and how he spoke, as well as his musical tastes and skills. Soon, Richard's partner also featured in Derek's taunts and increasingly malicious rumours. At Derek's instigation, the ensemble held a meeting to discuss the 'creative work' during which Derek found fault with Richard on a number of counts, questioning his loyalty to the company as well as his musical ability. Richard calmly rebutted Derek's accusations and other company members agreed. Richard was popular with Claire, Jackie, Paul and Mary, all of whom worked well together. Claire, as founder and key contact for the company's funding agencies, announced that there was no case for Richard to answer and that the matter was closed.

Following this discussion, Derek's behaviour during rehearsals changed. He was extremely pleasant to everyone, including Richard, and made a particular point of singling out Claire's performances and her workshop ideas for praise whenever possible. When alone with Richard, however, this demeanour was not always sustained. Derek and Claire became more and more friendly, and he, as a more experienced player, regularly made suggestions about the development of the group, to which Claire listened.

The first Christmas concert was an important debut for the company, scheduled to take place in a city-centre concert hall and due to be covered by the local media. During rehearsals, Derek's pattern of behaviour from the early months returned. He was rude to Richard, creating a tense and uncomfortable atmosphere which Richard found it difficult to allay. The morale of the ensemble deteriorated considerably, and Richard felt increasingly ostracized by Derek's behaviour.

Following the concert, which was successful despite the hostile ambience during rehearsals, Claire convened another company meeting to discuss the 'creative work'. Once again, Derek found fault with Richard on a number of counts, questioning his commitment to the company's shared ideology as well as his playing skills. Richard remained calm in the face of this tirade. Jackie attempted to be supportive on his behalf. Paul and Mary, apparently nervous of the situation, contributed little. Finally, Claire declared her concern for the future of the ensemble which couldn't continue to function with a severe lack of trust among its members.

Richard left the company almost immediately and was replaced by a friend of Claire's – a younger and less-experienced player. In the wake of this, Derek's partnership with Claire strengthened and he acquired new status and influence. The other musicians became wary of incurring criticism, which Derek was quick to offer, and shortly afterwards Jackie left too, as did Paul and Mary. John and Claire recruited new people to replace the musicians who had departed.

(Names and environs have been changed to protect confidentiality)

on Claire who is the perceived power base. The perpetrator's behaviour has a rather sinister nature, reflecting the Jekyll and Hyde transformations often cited by witnesses and targets of bullying. The effects on the target are also familiar from the literature:

Richard's isolation from his colleagues intensifies alongside the bullying behaviour (Amnesty International 1975) and his ability to counteract Derek's accusations lessens. When Richard has become more vulnerable, and the whole company is under pressure, the bully recreates the unpleasant rehearsal scenarios, implying it is the target's incompetence that is causing disruption and distress. The result is that the bully succeeds, and the target is demoralized and leaves the organization, which is fragmented and disintegrates (Hirgoyen 2000). The target's replacement is a less experienced performer perceived, by the bully, not to be a threat. The other company members who witnessed the bullying were onlookers rather than accomplices, but felt its ripple effect all the same and left their jobs (Rayner 1999).

What can arts workers do in a situation such as this? Where does an employee go for advice and assistance when a bully effectively ensures that they are ousted from an organization and where no process is in place whereby management can assist, or no effective management is in place? Alongside a track record in ensuring that employees have rights regarding terms and conditions, such as hours of work and rates of pay, in the UK, trades unions have a history of supporting workers when problems are encountered in the workplace.

Other professional agencies and institutions are becoming active in terms of providing support (see Chapter 9), and increasingly around the globe legislation is being put in place to deal with bullying behaviour (see Chapter 7). There are other independent agencies and organizations working to support targets of bullying and to help employers find ways of tackling the behaviour in their workplaces. Many of these are voluntarily run and they provide informal advice and support for individuals bullied at work. There are so many groups now that new fora for exchanging information are being set up regularly so information and resources can be shared, one example of which is the UK Support Group Network. The website explains:

> The Support Group Network is an umbrella organization linking workplace bullying support groups around the world. It was set up in 2003 with the primary aim of ensuring effective help for victims of workplace bullying and abuse. (UK Support Group Network 2010)

Bullying Help and Support Groups

Some help and support organizations work within specific professions. In the selection in the Appendix, for example, the first four groups focus on resources and/or advocacy for particular communities of interest – the police, church ministers, IT workers and Scottish teachers. Other groups are geographically based, and many of these promote regular face-to-face networking opportunities for people who have experienced bullying. There are a large number of such groups in various parts of the UK.

Given that the Appendix provides a few websites from a few other countries, it cannot be denied that workplace bullying is, unfortunately, a global problem. As at November 2010, there has been no other research into workplace bullying at national level specifically within the cultural sector; however, given that bullying is such a significant feature of the contemporary arts workplace – albeit for all the wrong, distressing reasons – it is to be hoped that new research in the UK and elsewhere will contribute to our knowledge about bullying in the arts. Perhaps, then, we can move towards identifying truly effective systems for managing the problem and gain insights into how it may be eradicated altogether.

7 *Bullying and the Law: A Global Issue*

In 1999, Zapf identified two distinct foci when he compared the literature about bullying in England to that in Scandinavia and Germany: the research in Britain focused on the attacker as a single individual (Adams with Crawford 1992; Field 1996; Rayner 1997) whereas the Scandinavian and German research concentrated on the victim attacked by one or more people (Zapf 1999: 76). By 2003, the research foci in Scandinavia, Germany and England had merged into a 'European' research tradition, and an 'American' research tradition had been added. Commenting on this concept of two traditions within academic research in the Preface to *Bullying and Emotional Abuse in the Workplace: International Perspectives in Research and Practice*, Einarsen et al. (2003) cited the European model as one representing mobbing/bullying and which remained focused on the perpetrator, whilst the American one denoted emotional abuse/mistreatment and was focused on the victim or target.

However, this may be a simplification. When bullying becomes an issue it is often because information and data on bullying experiences is first gathered about, and usually by, targets of bullying. Next the focus turns to redress, perpetrators and finally prevention. Inevitably, data-gathering about perpetrators is considerably more difficult and still relatively rare. Much more research is needed in this area if we are to move towards a more comprehensive understanding of the motivation for bullying behaviour in individuals and the climate in which it flourishes and grows.

The established pattern in Europe, America and the Antipodes is that support groups (for targets) tend to be set up first. This is beginning to happen in China and Japan. In 2006 the extent of school bullying in Japan, resulting in a spate of suicides among young children, was reported by the BBC (BBC 2006a) and hit the headlines worldwide. In September 2009, *The Telegraph* reported an unusual event in southern China:

> *A community of dwarves has set up its own village to escape discrimination from normal sized people. (The Telegraph 2009)*

These people were tired of 'being pushed around and exploited by big people' and, despite the Western view that treating humans this way is distasteful, some felt the creation of a bizarre type of theme park:

> *… was the dwarves' best chance of employment given the surplus of labour in China. (The Telegraph 2009)*

There has been intensive online debate about this issue.

As networking expands, many of the anti-bullying support groups lobby effectively for the amendment of existing legislation or the introduction of new laws, usually with the twin aims of protecting the targets of workplace bullying and, in so doing, making organizations and management more accountable for the behaviour of bullies among their workforce. In tandem with this, unfair working terms and conditions imposed by corporations are increasingly being targeted. Research in Europe began earlier than in America, and as data on the effects of bullying behaviour has accumulated and the literature has grown, so researchers worldwide have become increasingly interested in the organizational causes of bullying behaviour (for example, Salin 2003) and in the psychological profile of perpetrators. Thus we can see that researchers in Australia, New Zealand and European countries have demonstrated that they are just as concerned with targets (Turney 2003; Amicus/MSF 1994; Field 1999) as with perpetrators. Bullying help and support groups are found everywhere, and some of those in Europe, Canada, the USA and Australia are listed in Appendix 1.

In analysing approaches to the study of workplace bullying, researchers discuss the perspectives adopted by a range of interest groups, including academics, campaigning individuals, lobbying organizations and professionals dealing with bullying repercussions through medical, legal and management professions and consultancies. The use of multimethod approaches is posited to achieve a many-layered framework for research, reflecting personal, sociocultural and organizational attitudes and behaviours (for example, Liefooghe and Olafsson 1999). Similarly in the arts research a combination of quantitative and qualitative analyses proved effective: survey results supplemented by interviews and case studies offer more fully rounded information that goes beyond data-handling.

It has been suggested that a need exists for more empirical studies on the nature and causes of bullying (Einarsen 1999: 26) and for more research into specific employment sectors. Certainly, the way in which some behaviours are interpreted does seem to depend, to an extent, on the sector in which employees are working. For example, in New Zealand's Employment Court Cases, cited later in this chapter, one of the working environments in which bullying was not found, was in a busy hotel kitchen, because that environment was deemed to be a tough climate (*Nagai v Carlton Hotel (Auckland) Limited*, unreported, Scott J, 19 October 2004). Salin points out the danger of such environments as places in which employees and managers can:

become socialised into treating bullying as a normal feature of working life. (Salin 2003: 36)

The UK further and higher education sectors were chosen by Duncan Lewis for his research into the impact of shame among bullied university and college lecturers, partly because of the significant changes taking place in the way education is delivered in the UK and because of the shifting focus in the way public sector organizations are managed (Lewis 2004: 282). The methodology for bullying studies is considered by Rayner, Sheehan and Barker (1999) in the context of the benefits and limitations of incidence studies and clinical studies, and this is further explored in relation to research in the arts in Chapter 2.

Since 1999 many UK trades unions and their umbrella organizations have supported research into workplace bullying and have advocated the development of policy and procedures, including training for managers on how to deal with perpetrators and assistance programmes for employees (TUC 1999; UNISON 2003; BECTU 2005). They have also focused on corporate bullying with a view to protecting workers' rights and improving employment terms and conditions. Studies have explored the role of trades unions and the responsibility of employers to protect workers (Ishmael with Alemoru 1999; Namie and Namie 2000) and it is significant that 84.3 per cent of participants in the national survey of performing arts organizations called on BECTU to take immediate and determined action on the issue, which the union has done.

Many researchers have noted the shortcomings of the judicial systems in terms of dealing satisfactorily with bullying behaviour, and some have provided signposts as to how legal impediments can be overcome. (Chadwick 1997; Costigan 1998; Leather et al. 1999; Schell and Lanteigne 2000; Namie and Namie 2000). Workplace bullying is a global phenomenon and there is a worldwide commonality of interest. Nevertheless, concern with and levels of access to legal redress differ inter-nation and indeed inter-continent, and in some cases appear to be aligned with specific cultural and social mores.

The Cost of Workplace Bullying

Empirical evidence has been gathered on the financial costs of bullying behaviour that stem from related health problems. Leymann (1990) suggested that the costs of employees taking sick leave, including estimates for loss of productivity and the need for professional intervention (health workers and human resources officers, etcetera), could be between US$30,000 and US$100,000 per employee, or between £20,000 and £60,000. However, in 2007, Tamara Parris, Senior Consultant and Partner at Parris, Wolfe and Associates in Canada, estimated that a specific bullying event:

> based only on a 6-month period of the several years' experience, cost approximately [C]$300,000 [£197,000]. (Parris 2010)

This was calculated using a model devised by Dr Dan Dana of the Mediation Training Institute International (MTI), an organization that was founded in 1985 in the United States and is now working globally. It is based on a case study entitled Cost of Conflict, and calculates elements including:

- distracted team/employee time;
- opportunity cost of distracted, unproductive time;
- impact of diminished decision-making;
- terminated/resigned employees;
- employee restructuring;
- intellectual and property theft/damage;
- diminished motivation;
- unproductive work time;
- employee health costs.

It was estimated that, in total, bullying costs more than US$180 million over a two-year period in lost time and productivity.

In the UK, research commissioned by the Dignity at Work Partnership calculated that, taking into account absenteeism, turnover and productivity costs:

> *... the total cost of bullying for organizations in the UK in 2007 can be estimated at approximately £13.75 billion. (Giga, Hoel and Lewis 2008)*

Costs are substantial in terms of productivity alone, given the findings that 25 per cent of bullied employees leave their jobs as a result of bullying and that witnesses of bullying also leave their jobs (Rayner 1999). It should be noted that high staff-turnover can be an indicator of workplace bullying and other factors that cause distress, and that such situations should alert employers to problem areas. For example, in the arts case studies, staff turnover and absenteeism noticeably increased as a result of bullying in The Art Gallery (Chapter 1), The Theatre Project (Chapter 5) and The Creative Industry (Chapter 6), and in several of the organizations featured in brief contributions to the pilot studies.

In the UK there has been an increasing number of legal actions where bullying has been identified as the main source of complaint. In April 2010, the conciliation service ACAS said that complaints about workplace bullying had risen as a result of the recession. Often, outward signs of conflict in a workplace, including bullying, were hidden because they did not result in workers going on strike or to an employment tribunal. Further, ACAS found there were serious implications for the health and well-being of staff, including stress. So, in addition to fiscal considerations, the cost of bullying can be measured in terms of the health of affected individuals, the performance and morale of organizations, and the public profile of an entire sector (TUC 1999).

As awareness has grown, bullying has become an increasingly onerous job-related issue (Einarsen and Skogstad 1996; Rayner 1997). It is also clear that it is prevalent across a range of organizational groups and industrial sectors (Hoel, Cooper and Faragher 2001; Hubert and Van Veldhoven 2001). Some managers have argued that the arts are sufficiently different from other employment sectors to merit being treated in a different way. However, the author has found no evidence to suggest that this is, in fact, the case, except in the sense that management culture allied with the traditional terms and conditions in creative organizations may serve to intensify problems such as bullying, making these more frequent and more virulent in arts settings. In Chapter 8 Tom Starland from Carolina Arts comments with genuine passion on why, in some respects, working in the arts is different (Starland 2002) and in April 2010 he added a qualification to his earlier remarks:

> *working in the arts is more interesting than most jobs, but it is still a job and should operate like any other job. (Personal email to the author)*

In international studies, researchers are comparing and contrasting the approaches used to address the problem of workplace bullying (Zapf and Einarsen 2001; Zapf and Gross 2001; Rayner, Sheehan and Barker 1999). A guide to the level of awareness across the world is the progress of measures to prevent and to legislate for workplace bullying, many of which were begun in the late 1990s.

We must look to Scandinavia for the world's first law on bullying, as distinct from laws related to discrimination. On 21 September 1993, Sweden adopted the Victimization at Work Ordinance (Swedish Work Environment Authority 1993), which covered both one-on-one bullying by individuals and corporate bullying by employers. This provided legislation to combat actions destined to give offence or which resulted in ostracization of people, including supervision with harmful intent and groundless administrative penal sanctions. The onus is on the employer to plan and organize work so as to prevent bullying, to make clear that bullying is not accepted, to provide early detection of signs of victimization, to rectify unsatisfactory working conditions which are the basis for bullying, to undertake special investigations to ascertain if causes of bullying are related to the way in which work is organized and to have special routines for offering help and support to employees who are subjected to victimization.

Employers must be prepared to deal with the psychological, social and organizational aspects of the working environment, to the same extent as questions of a physical or technical nature (Victimization at Work (AFS: 1993: 17 1993))

The Swedish Work Environment Authority was formed in 2001 through the amalgamation of the 10 districts of the Labour Inspectorate, and the National Board of Occupational Safety and Health. The Authority's paramount objective is to reduce the risks of ill health and accidents in the workplace and to improve the work environment as a whole, that is, including the physical, mental, social and organizational aspects. If bullying unequivocally comes within the compass of workplace health and safety (Turney 2003), increasingly employees in the UK are likely to want policy and legislation to develop along the lines of the Scandinavian model, although the arts research indicates that some managers in the cultural sector might seek to reject the obligation that such a framework places upon employers.

Under the provisions of the 2004 Working Conditions Act and the Equal Treatment Act, Dutch employers are obliged to provide a workplace where employees can do their jobs without being exposed to violence, harassment and/or discrimination. This includes sexual harassment and psychological aggression, and the legislation includes mobbing/ bullying and racism. It extends the rights of employees to be protected from undesirable behaviour perpetrated by clients, patients and the public (Hubert and Van Veldhoven 2001). An updated Working Conditions Act came into effect in 2008.

The European Foundation for the Improvement of Living and Working Conditions reports that, in 2004, an evaluation was carried out to investigate how employers were implementing the provisions of the Working Conditions Act governing violence in the workplace (Van Dam and Engelen 2004). Compared with other evaluations in 1995 and 2000, the 2004 evaluation revealed that employers were more likely to have a specific policy on workplace violence and were more inclined to take preventive measures. During the research by Van Dam and Engelen (2004) almost 75 per cent of the employers who were interviewed reported that they had a written policy on workplace violence, compared with 57 per cent of employers in the pilot study in 2000/01. Over half of the employers in the Van Dam and Engelen study had appointed a counselor, compared with 34 per cent in the arts pilot study 2000/01).

According to the European Foundation, employers also reported that they received fewer complaints about aggression and violence than previously, which surprised experts who had expected the number of complaints to rise due to an increased awareness of bullying among employees, a greater participation rate by women, and a more diverse workforce. Until 2004, in the Netherlands the terms 'mobbing' and 'bullying' tended to be used to refer to harassment by colleagues and the term 'intimidation' most frequently indicated threats of physical violence. A new indicator of harassment, 'bullying' was introduced in the 2004 TNO Working Conditions Survey (Van Dam and Engelen 2004).

Although the original concept of intimidation was correlated to the new indicator of bullying, the distribution pattern of this new indicator was quite different. 'Bullying' (by customers) was mentioned by 7.3 per cent, while 10.1 per cent referred to being bullied by colleagues in the past year. On the other hand, most claims of intimidation related to intimidation by customers, indicating that the two concepts are related but different.

Leymann's view was that the term bullying was inappropriate for adult harassment or mobbing because it had connotations of physical menace (Leymann 1996). However, it is evident that in The Netherlands 'intimidation' has this implication, and interesting that the Dutch research suggests that more physical threats, and less psychological harassment, emanate from customers than from colleagues.

Wim van Veelen, the Health and Safety Policy Advisor to the Netherlands Confederation of Dutch Trade Unions, FNV, writing about why the 2004 Act was reviewed, contradicted the 2004 evaluation by the European Foundation for the Improvement of Living and Working Conditions, stating:

> Risks like harassment, bullying and violence are rising in the Netherlands, and among the highest in Europe. Stress and pressure at work from reorganizations are also important causative factors in occupational diseases. (Van Veelen 2007: 5)

Van Veelen reports that among the main conclusions of an Alert report from the Netherlands Center for Occupational Diseases in 2005 was a special alert about the rise in violence and intimidation at work. Ultimately, Van Veelen believes that the new system can be seen:

> ... as an intermediate step on the way to a uniform, Europe-wide system of regulation. (Van Veelen 2007: 6)

The arts research did not include a comparative study of bullying by customers and colleagues, and the bullying incidents reported indicate that these related to colleagues; however, box office and front-of-house staff, comprising employees with the highest levels of customer contact, did report levels of bullying behaviour at slightly higher rates – 24 per cent and 21 per cent respectively – than backstage and other staff. In reference to the public sector, Hubert and Van Veldhoven (2001: 415–424) note:

> It is not the targets or the relationships with clients, but the interpersonal relationships with colleagues and the boss that play an important role in the evaluation and judgement of one's work and one's possibility for promotion.

The health service also reports bullying by clientele as well as by other workers. In May 2006, an article in The Daily Mail announced that NHS staff had been 'bullied by patients and colleagues'. It may be, however, that the UK experience of workplace bullying in the arts more closely mirrors that of employees in education and public administration.

A Global Issue

FRANCE

In France, the courts recognized moral harassment, though not by name, long before legislation was implemented. The 2002 law *Loi de modernisation sociale* is based on the conclusions of the April 2001 report of the Economic and Social Council (which became the Economic, Social and Environmental Council of France in 2008) – a consultative public body that conducted public hearings on bullying (mobbing). The 2002 law defines mobbing (bullying) as:

> *the perverse implementation of power … a means of subjugation and persecution of the other, questioning his fundamental rights as the respect which is due him or her …*

Consequences, as defined, can

> *… be detrimental to the good functioning of the company: disorganization of production, both quantitative and qualitative, and financial effects. (Workplace Bullying Institute)*

Since the publication of the law on 17 January 2002, the French anti-bullying campaign website, Harecèlement Moral Stop, reports that case law defining bullying has expanded considerably and many cases are listed on the campaign website. There was a further amendment to the law on 4 January 2003 in order to clarify the necessity for employers to prove that the actions the complainant names as evidence of harassment do not, in themselves, constitute harassment: the onus is on the employer to demonstrate that such actions were taken on an objective basis, and were unconnected with harassment.

France has a duality of jurisdictions: there is one for civil servants (one in four of the working population) with peer civil servant administrative judges, although these individuals are not, in fact, trained as judges. The second system of judiciary judges, who are trained by the National School of Magistracy, is for all other workers. The new law treats public sector employees differently to private sector employees, and France was found to have breached the European Convention of Human Rights (ECHR) primarily because of the inequities across the systems.

The fact that the ECHR criticized France for the differential treatment of its employees suggests that the response of some UK arts managers during the research would be similarly dismissed. The arts managers in the pilot study sought to justify the assertion that the cultural sector is 'different' to other employment sectors and that normal workplace terms and conditions should not apply. Conversely, UK working practices and regulations, backed by legislation, are centred on ensuring parity – equal opportunities policies seek to negate discrimination on the basis of, for example, race, colour, ethnic origin, creed, belief, gender, marital status, sexual orientation, disability, size, age – making it difficult to morally justify the claim that working in the arts is 'different'.

CANADA

Occupational Health and Safety Act (Ontario)

In October 2004, in the Canadian province of Ontario, a Private Members' Bill (Bill 126) was introduced in the Legislative Assembly of Ontario. The intention of the Bill was to amend the Occupational Health and Safety Act so as to protect workers from harassment in the workplace. The Occupational Health and Safety Amendment Act (Harassment) 2004 defines harassment as including 'sexual harassment and harassment because of race, ancestry, place of origin, colour, ethnic origin, citizenship, creed, sexual orientation, age, record of offences, marital status, same-sex partnership status, family status or disability'. The Act requires employers to ensure that every worker is protected from workplace-related harassment, and to prepare appropriate policy and guidelines. It also requires that harassment prevention training be provided for workers, including those who exercise managerial functions. Workplace-related harassment is defined (in section 49.1) to mean:

> *(a) harassment by a worker's employer or supervisor or by another worker, whether or not the harassment occurs at the workplace, or*

> *(b) harassment that has the effect of interfering with the performance or safety of any worker at the workplace or that creates an intimidating, hostile or offensive work environment for any worker.*

In 2009, Bill 168 was introduced in the Ontario Legislature to amend the Occupational Health and Safety Act to address issues of workplace harassment and violence. Its intention was to strengthen the existing Occupational Health and Safety Act and to add more workplace safety elements. Bill 168 was passed in December 2009 and came into force on 1 June 2010 as the Occupational Health and Safety Amendment Act (Violence and Harassment in the Workplace) 2009.

The Ontario description of harassment is wide-ranging and incorporates status-based constituents in addition to conventional discriminatory factors. The requirement to provide training for workers, including managers and supervisors, in managing harassment is significant, especially when compared with the findings of the UK performing arts research– which identified a low level of training in human resources skills in arts managers generally. The emphasis in the Ontario Health and Safety Amendment Act is on behaviour, not location. The UK arts case histories describe instances of bullying behaviour that occurred outside employment premises, particularly infringing on employees' non-work time. Examples of behaviour that intrudes into non-work time include persistent telephone calls to a worker's home at unsocial hours; a requirement to attend out-of-hours gatherings unconnected with an employee's duties; relentless email demands for information during a worker's holiday period. In the Occupational Health and Safety Amendment Act (Harassment) 2004 definition of work-related harassment, the requirement to avoid social degradation of the workplace is also implied (Hirigoyen 2000).

Protection from Harassment Act (Quebec)

In the Canadian province of Quebec, The Protection from Harassment Act was introduced in 1997 and was followed by new legislation in June 2004 to protect employees from *le harcèlement psychologique*. According to the Commission des normes du travail, the 2004 legislation states that:

> *For the purposes of this Act, 'psychological harassment' means any vexatious behaviour in the form of repeated and hostile or unwanted conduct, verbal comments, actions or gestures, that affects an employee's dignity or psychological or physical integrity and that results in a harmful work environment for the employee. A single serious incidence of such behaviour that has a lasting harmful effect on an employee may also constitute psychological harassment.*

The Act ensures that employees at every level have recourse to the legislation in the event of psychological harassment, although how this may be taken forward varies according to whether the employee comes from the public or private sector and according to whether or not the employee is a member of a union. The Commission des normes du travail now includes helpful advice and information on its website.

In the first three years after the Act in Quebec was passed, that is 2004–2007, the Commission reported having received 6,850 complaints under the law prohibiting bullying in the workplace. Among its findings the Commission noted that 95 per cent of complaints alleged repetitive harassment, and that 97 per cent of complaints were settled in the early stages of the process and were not referred to the Commission.

The potential for one single bullying incident to do harm is highlighted in the Act, if that incident has a harmful lasting effect. This is an interesting development, especially in light of the position of Leymann (1996), who stipulated that mobbing had a minimum duration of once per week for six months. In a definition of workplace bullying, Einarsen and Skogstad (1996: 191) state that they 'will not refer to a one-off incident as bullying'. Hoel, Cooper and Faragher (2001) further explore the duration of bullying and measure the frequency reported in terms of occasionally (very rarely; now and then; several times a month) and regularly (several times a week; almost daily).

During the performing arts research, short-term or one-off bullying behaviour was not reported by those respondents who claimed they had been targeted, although the case histories note that the perpetrator of negative behaviour often commits occasional hostile or aggressive acts directed at others in the presence of the principal target (that is, the person reporting the behaviour). The Quebec Act identifies the reaction of the target and the duration of the harmful effect as the qualifying factors. It also gives the targeted employee the right not to work if harassment is likely to continue, clearly establishing the protection of the target, rather than the regulation of the bullying behaviour, as the primary aim of the legislation. In the interpretation of the Protection from Harassment Act, however, the legislators impose an objective process to analyse whether or not harassment has taken place, and also to protect the rights of the employer. In section 81.18 they use the criterion of a:

> *... reasonable person ... a person with ordinary intelligence and judgment ... to see how this person would have reacted ... finding himself in a situation similar to the one related by the employee. Would this person conclude that this was a harassment situation? ... The effect of*

the application of such standards must not be to deny the normal exercise by the employer of the management of his human resources. It is important to distinguish the actions taken by the employer as part of the normal and legitimate exercise of his management right, even if they involve unpleasant consequences or events, from those taken in a manner that is arbitrary, abusive, discriminatory or outside the normal conditions of employment.

The Protection from Harassment Act, manifests an approach that strives for an equitable balance between employers' and employees' rights. For some artists, arts managers and workers, the notion of the 'reasonable person' and the 'normal conditions of employment' appears problematic. Chapter 9 examines the hypotheses surrounding artistic temperament, wherein some argue that artists are, by nature, not always reasonable when working – indeed, the myth persists that the greater the artist, the less reasonable or sane or ordinary they are likely to be. Similarly, we have seen that some arts managers have argued that terms and conditions for those working in the arts are, and should be, necessarily 'different' too.

UNITED STATES OF AMERICA

Via one of its related websites, the Workplace Bullying Institute (WBI) provides information on active and past legislative projects in USA and Canada. The WBI began to encourage the enactment of anti-bullying laws for the workplace, state by state, in 2001. Suffolk University Professor of Law David Yamada drafted the text of the Healthy Workplace Bill to include workplace bullying and this has been used as a template for anti-bullying bills across the United States. The original bill grew out of his seminal legal treatise on workplace bullying and the need for status-blind harassment laws.

The Healthy Workplace Bill was drafted with the twin aims of (a) providing legal redress for employees who have been harmed, psychologically, physically or economically by being deliberately subjected to abusive work environments – that is, workplaces where an employee is subjected to abusive conduct severe enough to cause physical or psychological harm, and (b) providing a legal incentive for employers to prevent and respond to the mistreatment of employees at work. Since 2003, 20 states have introduced a Healthy Workplace Bill and there are 14 Bills active in 10 states as at April 2011. In May 2010 the New York Senate passed the Bill; however, it was then put on hold in The NY Assembly Labor Committee and will not have another chance to proceed until later in 2011.

In calling for an anti-bullying law to be introduced, WBI makes the point that current laws are 'status-based' in that the target of bullying must be a member of a protected status group – that is, a group based on gender, race, ethnicity, religion, etcetera – in order for the harassment to be illegal; harassment requires discriminatory mistreatment. However the WBI points out that:

[Non status-based] bullying is four times more prevalent than illegal harassment. (WBI Zogby International Survey 2007).

Some commentators on international perceptions of bullying have noted that the American perspective is primarily focused on the victim and determined through concepts of emotional assault and mistreatment (Einarsen et al. 2003). Certainly, the American and

Canadian literature is less developed than that issuing from Europe and from Australia (Keashly and Jagatic 2003). However, as the earliest examination of bullying emanated from Scandinavia, the research tradition is much older in Europe than in the United States and Canada, and an examination of the advancement of anti-bullying support organizations and lobbying campaigns in Chapter 6 indicates an evolutionary process – a time-based linear development, demonstrating that the European and North American research traditions may be viewed as sequential rather than bifurcated.

AUSTRALIA

The Australian Council of Trade Unions (ACTU) has embarked on regular campaigns to raise awareness amongst the community, workers, unions, employers, health professionals, occupational health and safety (OHS) authorities and governments about the fact that bullying is a serious health and safety hazard. In a speech to health and safety representatives to launch the ACTU Work Strain Causes Real Pain campaign in 2004, Erich Janssen, ACTU Occupational Health and Safety Commissioner, remarked:

> In an Australian study conducted last year … they found that 85 per cent of the 325 human resources practitioners that were surveyed, had experienced bullying, or seen others bullied at work. (ATCU 2004)

This high incidence of workplace bullying may be expected among those whose remit includes dealing with problem areas in interpersonal and intra-organizational relationships. Links between bullying and human resources management (HRM) in the UK are explored by Lewis and Rayner (2003) whose thesis is:

> … that 'the' philosophy and components of HRM may create an environment in which bullying can remain unchallenged, allowed to thrive or actually encouraged in an indirect way. (Lewis and Rayner 2003: 370)

The arts research presents a parallel proposition: like the ideology of HRM, the arts are people-centric. Ostensibly, both exist because people are valued: HRM is concerned with maximizing the potential of people at work, the arts with maximizing human creative skill and imagination. It may be, however, that whilst both are focused on the ideology of improving the human condition, neither in fact advances the welfare of their primary resource – employees.

In 2008 the Australian Legislative Assembly passed a new Work Safety Act, which wholly replaced the former Occupational Health and Safety at Work (OHS) Act of 1989. The Act came into force on 1 October 2009. Legislators believed that there was 'an urgent need' to replace the original Act's OHS legislation to address contemporary changes to work and employment arrangements and to address emerging risks:

> … such as occupational violence, bullying, stress and fatigue. (Work Safety Act 2008)

The Act includes an explicit reference to the well-being and psychological needs of workers, and places more responsibility on employers to minimize risks in the workplace, as far as reasonably practicable, and to consult more with the workforce about health and safety issues.

NEW ZEALAND

In New Zealand, in July 2009, the Department of Labour (*Te Tari Mahi*) produced a report, Themes in Employment Law, containing written guidance on workplace bullying. The introduction to the report stresses the serious impact bullying can have on the workplace and sets out the implications for employers and employees. Some cases at the Employment Court or the Employment Relations Authority are cited in the report as examples of the circumstances in which bullying can and does happen. Two examples are denoted as vertical bullying, one of which was upward bullying by an employee. Some complaints of bullying were upheld, but not all – some were concluded to be examples of 'firm management'.

In New Zealand, the legal recourse available to complainants of bullying includes a personal grievance claim under the Employment Relations Act 2000 (ERA) or a breach of contract claim under common law. The Health and Safety Employment Act 1992 (HSE) requires employers to take reasonable steps to protect employees from harm – and bullying can potentially cause both physical and psychological harm – and if the employer fails to do so, they risk a Department of Labour prosecution.

In three cases in New Zealand, employers experienced a situation where employees who had bullied, and against whom disciplinary action had been taken, then brought a personal grievance complaint against the employer. Two of these cases were dismissed because the employer was found to have acted in accordance with correct procedures; however, in one case the employer's actions were not upheld, although compensation payable was limited due to the complainant's contributory behaviour. Overall, when workplace bullying is proven, then, both common law and statutory obligations apply.

Writing in the *New Zealand Medical Journal* in 2004, Dr Steven Kelly, Surgical Registrar at Christchurch Hospital, describes workplace bullying as the silent epidemic. Citing toxic work environments as a result of economic and commercial pressures, coupled with management as control (for example, in Bratton and Gold 1999: 11–13), he notes that the New Zealand Resident Doctors' Association (NZRDA):

> ... *has recently reported an 'avalanche' of complaints about resident medical officers being subjected to workplace bullying and harassment. The reason for this dramatic increase is not clear, but it may indicate a long-term problem that is only now becoming apparent because individuals are prepared to speak about it. (Kelly 2004: 1)*

This is confirmed by the increasing prevalence of court cases described by the Department of Labour (*Te Tari Mahi*), such as those cited in the July 2009 report. Bullying has been found in instances involving overt and aggressive behaviour; insidious and covert behaviour; imposition of unjust financial penalties; physical threats; and overly familiar, manipulative behaviour. However, in law, bullying has not been found in instances where the behaviour (in one example, a busy hotel kitchen, as noted above in this chapter) was considered to be appropriate to the nature of the workplace environment; where the attitude of the alleged bully was deemed to be matter of fact; where infantile behaviour was the norm; or where the applicant was described as overly sensitive (two cases).

The New Zealand Employment Court has not yet specifically defined workplace bullying, and New Zealand researchers such as Andrea Needham, an experienced Human Resources consultant and author, and Hadyn Olsen, Director of WAVE (Workplaces Against Violence in Employment), are among those working to raise awareness of the issue. A report in the *New Zealand Herald* in April 2010 confirmed Olsen's view that workplace bullying:

> ... was a huge stress factor for many people – the majority of whom chose not to make a complaint or bring up the issue, out of fear of being bullied further. (Tapaleao 2010)

In the same article, Tim Bentley, associate head of Massey University's School of Management, who undertook a study of bullying behaviour, said bullying in the workplace was:

> high generally, but 'notably higher' in the health and education sectors.

Olsen pinpointed a lack of management development programmes to assist with understanding bullying as a key issue in New Zealand:

> 'Part of the reason that workplace bullying is huge [in New Zealand] is that we don't invest in management development and especially in terms of dealing with conflict,' Mr Olsen said. Bullying thrives with management that doesn't know how to manage. (Tapaleao 2010)

The New Zealand experience has been paralleling developments in the UK. In 1999, the subject was still relatively new – Adams with Crawford (1992) being the acknowledged UK trailblazers with the publication of *Bullying at Work: How to Confront and Overcome It*. Research into bullying in the health services, for example, was carried out by Einarsen and Skogstad (1996) and Lyn Quine (1999). Steven Kelly concludes that:

> ... the medical profession is a caring profession, and although we care very well for our patients, it appears that we need to do more to care for each other. (Kelly 2004: 3)

Similarly, arts companies worldwide consider themselves to be fully professional and highly principled organizations. Scale notwithstanding, they are usually passionate about the artistic quality of their work, and committed to achieving optimum standards of excellence on behalf of their beneficiaries. As in the medical profession in New Zealand and the UK, it seems that whilst undoubtedly caring for their artistic creations and audiences, arts workers also need to do more to care for each other. Despite outward differences, it is likely that similar management cultures exist in the two sectors, or at the very least equivalent work-related pressures and stressors.

UNITED KINGDOM

In the UK, following the lack of parliamentary time in 1997, the Dignity at Work Bill was introduced in the House of Lords on 3 December 2001 and, by May 2002, had had its third unopposed reading in the House of Lords, which encouraged many to expect it to become law during the next parliament. The Bill, had it become law, would have applied to Wales, Scotland and England, but not to Northern Ireland. Section 2.5(1) of the Bill provided for the presentation of a bullying case at employment tribunal, if reported within three months of the first incident of bullying. It also offered employers a defence mechanism:

An employer shall not be liable ... where the following circumstances apply:

(a) at the time of the act or acts complained of, the employer has in force a Dignity at Work Policy [outlined in the document] and has taken all reasonable steps to implement and enforce the Policy, including the appointment of a competent person to assist the employer in undertaking the measures he needs to take to comply with the requirements of this Act and the Dignity at Work Policy;

(b) the act or acts complained of are repudiated by the competent person as soon as reasonably practicable, and in any event within three working days after they are notified to him by the employee or his representative; and

(c) as soon as is reasonably practicable, the employer takes all steps as are reasonably necessary to remedy any loss, damage or other detriment suffered by the complainant as a result of the act or acts of which he complains.

The Bill was designed to encourage employers to put into effect a dignity at work policy, and by 2010 many UK organizations had done so, despite the fact that the Bill was never passed, and thus never became law. Generally, it was thought that had the Bill passed, the resulting Act would enhance and clarify legislation employed in cases of bullying. In terms of making a complaint within three months of the first incident, however, research in arts organizations and in other employment sectors suggests that targets can take some time to recognize that they are being bullied.

Currently, some UK workplace bullying cases have been brought under a variety of other laws, including those governing heath and safety at work, sex discrimination, race relations, disability, public order and employment rights. Increasingly, complainants and their legal advisors have looked towards the Protection from Harassment Act 1997, which was heavily used when it first came into force to deal with domestic violence, including stalking, offences. It was regarded as innovative legislation, involving public intervention in matters that previously were left to private resolution. However, Von Heussen (2000) noted that a statute of this type could be problematic, because this involves:

... creating a new civil tort, two new criminal offences, and unprecedented procedures to address a newly perceived problem which has psychological and social dimensions and implications. (Von Heussen 2000)

Generally, we think of stalking as a male on female sexual pursuit but, as with bullying, the perpetrator can be a female stalking a male, the behaviour can be a same-sex pursuit or may occur regardless of gender and sexual issues. It is generally acknowledged that legal sanctions can make a long-term difference where previously behaviour was legally neutral. Von Heussen felt that early evidence suggested that this would be the case with the Protection from Harassment Act, if it received vigorous enforcement. Preliminary analysis indicates the necessity of careful attention to the psychological dimensions of stalking and harassment cases (Von Heussen, 2000).

In the case of *Majrowski v Guy's and St Thomas's NHS Trust* [2006] UKHL 34, The House of Lords confirmed that under the Protection from Harassment Act 1997 an employer can be vicariously liable for harassment by one of its employees. The capacity for culpability on the part of employers, even when they are not directly involved in bullying or harassment incidents, and particularly when these happen without the employer's knowledge, provides a compelling reason for ensuring that best management and leadership practice is implemented in the workplace. The Crown Prosecution Service publishes regular legal guidance on the Act.

Sociopsychological dimensions are prevalent in the arts research, and undoubtedly the legal sanctions referred to by Von Heussen have encouraged many organizations to introduce anti-bullying policies and procedures. Such policies and procedures were very rare during the pilot study in the cultural sector.

Although the Dignity at Work Bill never became law, the problem of bullying/harassment has been addressed in the UK. As harassment is covered by various pieces of legislation in other parts of Europe, it is not surprising that the most recent UK legislation uses similar terminology. The Equality Act became law on 1 October 2010. In addition to discrimination based on one or more protected characteristics (age, race, religion, et cetera), there are important changes and new regulations about bullying which employers need to consider.

In relation to harassment, employees can now complain about behaviour they find offensive, even if it is not directed at them – see The Arts Service (Chapter 4); employers are potentially liable for harassment of employees by third parties (that is, non-employees) – see The Creative Industry (Chapter 6); those who make complaints under the provisions of the act are protected if they are victimized – see the section on whistleblowing, below.

As can be seen from the above modest selection of legislation in various parts of the world, stratagems to introduce suitable anti-bullying legislation are ongoing worldwide. Despite the efforts of activists and trades unions, the UK has only begun to sign up to the global legal movement, nevertheless the introduction of the Equality Act 2010 is to be welcomed as an important first step.

Whistleblowing

Employers have a duty of care for the welfare of their employees, and this includes responsibility for their health and safety in the workplace. Once an employee has approached their line manager, safety representative or trades union representative, about a risk to their own well-being, or the welfare of others, and is not satisfied that their complaint has been dealt with adequately, then the law provides them with protection if they 'blow the whistle' on their employer. This is in marked contrast to the experiences of the employee in The Arts Service (Chapter 4) who failed to make a successful complaint about how her immediate line manager was being treated, and the knock-on effect this had on her and other staff. So, particularly in relation to the relatively new Equality Act 2010, it is worth being familiar with the law.

The Public Interest Disclosure Act 1998 protects workers who blow the whistle about malpractice – as does the Equality Act 2010 (in that it protects those who are victimized for making complaints). The 1998 Act applies where an employee has a reasonable belief that their disclosure tends to show one or more of the following offences or failures to observe a law, agreement or code of conduct:

- a criminal offence;
- a breach of a legal obligation;
- a miscarriage of justice;
- a danger to the health and safety of any individual;
- damage to the environment; or
- a deliberate covering up of information tending to show any of the above.

Whilst workplace bullying is not a criminal offence *per se*, the Protection from Harassment Act 1997 is clear that aspects of bullying can be addressed by existing criminal legislation and this has been strengthened by the introduction of the Equality Act 2010. The employer's legal obligation to protect staff is self-evidently breached by workplace bullying; if bullying involves unfair punishment then a miscarriage of justice may be taking place. The arts case studies indicate how bullying puts health and safety at risk and creates a toxic work environment; in The Arts Service (Chapter 4) the HR professionals deliberately attempt to mask any evidence of wrongful behaviour.

The UK's Health and Safety Executive (HSE) strongly supports measures that protect whistleblowers from any form of negative counteraction or victimization. HSE has a complaints-handling system and aims to ensure that concerns about health and safety are dealt with effectively and efficiently. The Executive states that their members of staff do all that they can to preserve the confidentiality of workers who raise concerns about health and safety, whenever confidentiality is requested (See also Public Concern at Work and other agencies supporting whistleblowers, in Chapter 6).

Cyber-bullying

Cyber bullying has long been more closely associated with the intentional bullying of children online by their peers and is often more associated with teenagers. However, adults and the workplace are not immune to cyber bullying and it can manifest itself in many different forms. (Reproduced courtesy of www.SafeWorkers.co.uk)

Cyber-bullying is particularly of our time and is variously characterized as flame mail; electronic bullying; mobile phone bullying; internet bullying; offensive blogging; and other similar terms. It has been the subject of a number of studies of social control through email, for example Romm and Pliskin (1999). Their research builds on earlier work (for example Kling 1991) on power and politics in information technology (IT), extending it to email and, more specifically, to the use of email for petty tyranny. Romm and Pliskin's work includes a case study in which the Chair of a university department used email to manipulate, control and coerce employees. The authors link the events in the case study with four of the five effects on subordinates of tyrannical behaviour by managers (Ashforth 1994, as reported in Romm and Pliskin 1999). These consequences are:

- low leadership-endorsement;
- fostering of employees' stress and reactance;
- creation of employee helplessness and work alienation (not cited in the case study but considered to be latent);
- undermining of employees' self-esteem and consequent decrease in their performance;
- undermining of social unit cohesiveness (Romm and Pliskin).

All of these symptoms are recognizable as effects of other types of bullying behaviour – in effect this is still power and control, albeit remotely – particularly in an organizational or group context, indicating that email is not necessarily an impersonal or detached medium, but one that provides perpetrators with an additional harassment tool. The study concludes that there are specific email features that make it amenable to manipulation for devious purposes. These features are described in Romm and Pliskin (1997) as:

- speed;
- multiple addressability;
- recordability;
- processing;
- routing.

The thrust of Romm and Pliskin's argument is that email delivers instantaneous communication and can be utilized between one or more individuals, and also amongst large groups of people. This immediacy can have a significant manipulative impact. The ability to send information quickly and simultaneously to a large group of people puts the originator in a powerful position. In terms of storage, the capacity to reserve messages for transmission at a later point in time, for example when this may be politically expedient, serves to increase the creator's control and power. Editing capabilities deliver the ability to modify the constituent parts and sequence of messages before transmitting the messages to others – neutral messages can thus be transformed into potentially incendiary ones. Finally, email boasts the property whereby the sender can select addressees, including undetectable ones; this is particularly significant when used in conjunction with the editing options whereby messages can be modified and, ultimately, misrepresented. Undetectable addresses can be achieved by, for example, using blind carbon copy (bcc), or similar, facilities.

Email should be considered a technology with strong political potency. Markus (1994) took the view that negative use could be an unintentional side effect; however, Romm and Pliskin (1999) note the opportunities for deliberate exploitation. The discussion about whether negative use may be unintentional or deliberate is on a parallel with the debate surrounding intent in bullying – as in Vartia-Väänänen (2003), Field (1996) and Randall (1997). Lack of expertise with technology could lead to unwitting bullying. Skilful use of technology, including voice messaging, abusive or derogatory websites, email and text messaging, undoubtedly provides a new set of opportunities for individuals to exploit others, should they so wish, by manipulating people, circumstances, events and political situations for advantage.

There are many examples of how educational and other establishments include guidelines on cyber-bullying in advice given to tackle both school and workplace bullying. In the UK, the government's website explores cyber-bullying and offers an introductory guide within the section aimed at young people, warning about bullying by mobile phone, email, instant messaging and chat rooms, social networking sites, interactive gaming, sending viruses and abusing personal information.

In Massachusetts, USA, the Massachusetts Aggression Reduction Centre (MARC) is housed at Bridgewater State College. Its goal is:

> *to bring low- or no-cost services to K-12 education, law enforcement, and other professional caregivers for children in the Commonwealth of Massachusetts. Our services include school programs, conferences, workshops, consultation, and research, in the area of bullying prevention, cyberbullying education and prevention, and violence prevention. (Bridgewater State College 2009)*

MARC was founded and is directed by Dr Elizabeth Englander, a Professor of Psychology at the college, and an expert in the field. MARC also benefits from the services of other academics and faculty members, graduate students, undergraduate students and support staff. Educators and professionals have access to a range of innovative services, for example MARC publicizes conferences and those scheduled for 2010 included: Cyberbullying: Train the Trainer – four conferences between February and April in different parts of the state; Girls & Cyberbullying; and Bullying: Train the Trainer. In June 2010, MARC organized, with the support of the Massachusetts Department of Elementary and Secondary Education (DESE) and the Massachusetts School of Professional Psychology (MSPP), a conference called Preparing For the New Bullying Law: A Day for Administrators. Two dates for this conference were sold out in different parts of the state and a third date was added to meet demand.

MARC provides resources for educators and parents, including speakers for school parent evenings, and among the leaflets it makes available are Tips for Texting (a guide for parents) and GLBT Bullying ... Some Facts (about bullying connected to gay, lesbian, bisexual and transgender issues). The Centre also has a strong track record of research, and makes available publications and research papers that are downloadable from its website. For example, relatively recently Elizabeth Englander has published statistics on bullying and cyber-bullying (2008–09) and Peter Rafalli (2010) has written an article on cyber-bullying.

In the UK, Teachernet online publications, aimed at teaching staff in schools, sets out the legal position regarding cyber-bullying in schools – including where this is bullying of school staff. Further information is available on the Teachernet and Digizen websites. All UK state schools are required to have anti-bullying policies under the School Standards and Framework Act 1998 and independent schools have similar obligations under the Education (Independent Schools Standards) Regulations 2003. Policies and processes for dealing with cyber-bullying against teachers, as well as pupils, are covered by these regulations.

Although cyber-bullying is not a specific criminal offence in the UK, laws such as the Equality Act 2010, the Protection from Harassment Act 1997 and the Crime and Disorder Act 1998, which apply to harassment or threatening behaviour, are likely to apply to cyber-bullying. Where bullying by mobile phone is concerned, the Telecoms Act 1984 makes it a criminal offence to make anonymous or abusive calls and, if a person is harassed persistently on their mobile, the person harassing may be committing an offence under the 1997 Harassment Act. In addition, section 127 of the Communications Act 2003 makes it a criminal offence to send:

> *by means of a public electronic communications network, a message or other matter that is grossly offensive or of an indecent, obscene or menacing character*

The UK government issued two guidance documents on anti-bullying on 15 April 2009. The guidance advises on how to deal with bullying outside school, and different versions of the guidelines are available for local authorities, youth workers, college staff, play workers, transport providers and children's homes. This specific guidance relates to workers with children and young people, however they are also frequently relevant to adult cyberbullying.

An increased amount of research into cyber-bullying is taking place, and information and resources are becoming more widely available from a number of sources, including the Anti-Bullying Alliance which has a range of research reports available to download from its website. The ways in which educational establishments are tackling the phenomenon – particularly those with cross-sectoral partnerships such as MARC – should be closely followed by arts and other employers, because as communications technology develops and changes, and as the structure of our working lives adapts to 24/7 virtual living and working environments, so workplace bullying by electronic means is becoming increasingly prevalent.

The impact of developments in technology on employment and work environments has been immense and arts workplaces have benefited like many others, exchanging manual and electrical systems for computer-controlled lighting boards, and obsolete rigs and apparatus for sophisticated electronic sound and stage equipment. Box office systems are computerized, and software programmes enable marketing data to be readily gathered alongside the automation of ticketing procedures. Directors, administrators and managers access communications and information technology on a daily basis, using it to carry out basic administrative tasks as well as to undertake specialist artistic, financial, marketing, management and risk assessment functions. Communication by email, and by video conferencing, has reduced substantially the requirement for meetings, for correspondence on paper and the extended use of the telephone.

Workplaces, like schools, frequently have policies in place to limit access to inappropriate material from external sources, including the internet, and apposite security measures to implement them. This is also the case with many parental-controlled home computers. Often policies and procedures relate to workplace-specific use of voice mail, email and the internet, as assigned to an employee's computer or telephone extension, reminding employees that these are solely for the purpose of conducting company business. These procedures can be used to remind workers that the company owns their emails, and that emails that 'discriminate', on the basis of classifications such as gender, race, etcetera, or that otherwise harass or offend employees, can be dealt with under the Equality Act 2010. The effectiveness of these policies and the relatively new law has yet to be proven.

Technology has delivered a vast amount of freedom. We live in an era with an almost global unregulated internet; however, the potential for the 'communications utopia' to be reversed is very real. In the future, more stringent ways may have to be found to monitor inappropriate communication between adults by email, mobile phone, instant messaging, chatrooms, message boards, social network sites and virtual worlds. This may go beyond the intra-organizational and we may find measures have to be introduced to monitor interagency communications more closely. When we consider the negative possibilities of using tools such as phone cameras, webcams, film and video – it is clear that bullies can and do turn technological tools to their advantage when necessary. Cyber-bullying in the arts workplace features in two of the case studies, The Contemporary Dance Studios (Chapter 3) and The Creative Industry (Chapter 6). In both cases the bullies made dishonourable use of email to threaten and abuse. If we believe the arts to be the articulation or application of human creative skill and imagination then self-expression by arts workers should be a positive exemplification of this. We are much better served when artists and arts workers turn their attention to the exposure of abusive conduct, as in the film *Bully* (dir. Larry Clark 2001), than we are when they engage in shameful negative behaviours.

CHAPTER

8 *Are The Arts 'Different'?*

A study conducted in 2003 by the University of Warwick's Institute for Employment Research for Arts Council England, Artists in Figures, painted a picture of a vibrant and economically active cultural sector: employment in the arts and culture had increased by over 150,000 in the 10 years to September 2003. At the end of 2000, 760,000 people were employed in cultural occupations in the UK, compared with 610,000 in 1993. Since 1993, unemployment within the pool of cultural labour had declined from 9.5 per cent to just 2.5 per cent. The survey also stated that individuals in cultural employment often sacrificed potential earnings and job security to follow their chosen career.

It seems that people in cultural occupations are three times more likely to be self-employed than those in non-cultural occupations – 39 per cent compared with 12 per cent. Among the self-employed, people in cultural occupations are twice as likely to have a second job than people in non-cultural occupations – 10 per cent compared with 5 per cent. While those in cultural employment receive above overall average earnings – that is national and all-sectors – their earnings are generally substantially less than similarly qualified professionals working in other fields. The Warwick University study shows the earnings of those working in arts and culture have declined relative to overall average earnings. In 1991 average earnings in cultural occupations were 22 per cent higher that the national, all-sectors average, but this declined to 14 per cent by 2000 and the decline is most marked in London. For example, in Inner London in 1991 earnings in cultural occupations were 21 per cent higher than the average, falling to just 6 per cent in 2000. People directly employed in cultural occupations were half as likely to claim state benefits than those in other areas of employment – 4 per cent against 8 per cent. This may suggest that pay levels are therefore not as low in the arts as in other employment sectors, or it may reflect the fact that in the national survey 28.5 per cent of workers were part-time, casual or freelance employees, and that some arts workers had more than one job. The report also found that the proportion of people working beyond statutory retirement age in cultural occupations was twice that of those in non-cultural occupations.

In February 2010, Creative & Cultural Skills, the sector skills council for the creative and cultural industries in the UK, published a report, *Performing Arts Blueprint*, highlighting skills shortages, skills gaps and poor investment in training in the performing arts. The research shows that 53 per cent of the UK's performing arts businesses are experiencing problems with recruitment because candidates lack experience; 21 per cent say that potential employees do not have the correct specialist skills for the job, and more than one third of current employees lack the skills performing arts companies need. Despite this, investment in training in the performing arts has not increased – skills shortages mean that 50 per cent of performing arts organizations have increased the workload of existing employees:

The effects of skills shortages and skills gaps are different. The impact of a skills shortage is an increased workload for everyone else in the business, and missed opportunities to take on new business, causing business to be turned away … Skills gaps, on the other hand, can lead to existing business being lost through poor delivery or impossible pressure on the workforce. (Creative and Cultural Skills 2010: 21)

The Nature of the Arts Workplace

The performing arts are labour intensive and essentially collaborative in nature, requiring individuals to work together in creative partnerships. Missouri State University (formerly Southwest Missouri State University), for example, in its introduction to its performing arts courses, particularly elaborates on the importance of people to, and within, performing arts organizations, stating that it:

… understands the essentially public nature of the performing arts and the ramifications of such a nature: that performing artists, as vehicles of human expression, must actively participate in the community and not be isolated from it; that the performing arts fulfill a variety of needs which range from enlightenment to entertainment to economic development; that the performing arts are inextricably linked to the visual and language arts; and that the performing arts must consistently seek to develop breadth of expression in deference to the diversity of the public they serve. Inasmuch as the performing arts are of, by, about and for the people, the university's commitment to the performing arts is a statement of oneness with its community. (Missouri State University 2010)

Commonly, people working at technical, administrative and executive levels in performing arts organizations deal with a range of pressures which can include strict deadlines, long hours for the level of remuneration, and colleagues, line managers and leaders with variable egos and temperaments. Working hours tend to be seasonal, flexible and unsociable. Large numbers of people who work in the cultural sector work in other sectors as well (whether by choice or need) and the pay for very few people is very high, but for the most part the pay tends to be below comparable jobs in other industries. For example, Performing Arts Blueprint reports that '73 per cent of the performing arts workforce earns less than £20,000 per year' (Creative and Cultural Skills 2010: 15) and that '93 per cent are either part-time or self-employed' (Creative and Cultural Skills 2010: 17).

Whilst some arts jobs may be seasonal, temporary or part time, and some hours are long and rates of pay are low, undoubtedly in other professions working hours are long and unsociable too, as with junior doctors, and/or seasonal, as in tourism, catering and hotel work. Those working in sport and for the fire brigade often work in other professions as well. There are many freelance, part-time, casual and short-term workers in a range of sectors, including education, retail, agriculture and manufacturing.

The notion of 'the arts as vocation' was postulated by Peter Hewitt (as quoted by Davies and Lindley 2003) and is echoed by many arts managers. This is interpreted in a number of ways – not all of them, unfortunately, useful or beneficial for arts workers. For example, it is asserted that those working in a performing arts environment do not have the expectation of a 'normal' nine-to-five working day, of a well-remunerated position or of working with conventional colleagues: those who choose to work in theatres and arts centres, rather than in offices, factories or shops, are 'different'. In the pilot study, one manager commented on working longer than average hours:

> *Management has a recognition that, up to a point, it goes with the territory – if you want nine to five, work for the council.*

The issue of whether particularly young, often graduate, arts workers manage to get paid at all has also been raised recently. In February 2010, Lyn Gardner's Theatre Blog in *The Guardian* noted that internships – unpaid or expenses-only work experience placements – 'can be an invaluable way for those wanting to work in theatre to get a toe-hold in the profession'. However she also says:

> *Unpaid work has become the accepted route into the creative professions … the greatest subsidiser of the arts is not the government, but the artists and other arts professionals and volunteers who are prepared to sacrifice income for the chance to do something they love and believe in. (Gardner 2010)*

There is something hypocritical in our attitudes here. Too often interns are not just unpaid, but, according to Gardner, undervalued and over-exploited. She paints a picture of them often undertaking all the worthless and thankless tasks:

> *sometimes working the same hours as those in salaried employment; on occasion even replacing someone whose job has been cut. (Gardner 2010)*

We who work in the arts subscribe to notions of inclusion, embrace diversity and pride ourselves on our integrity, and we would, and do, disapprove of and criticize exploitation when it happens in other professions – so do we turn a blind eye when it happens on our own doorstep? Do we excuse this by claiming that the arts are 'different'?

The perception that arts organizations work outside the rules and limitations of the ordinary milieu (as represented by the public and private sectors) appears to be widespread. So is it the same outside of the UK? Are the arts 'different' everywhere else too? Dr Brian Kennedy, Director of the National Gallery of Australia from 1997 to 2004, in a 2001 speech to the Canberra Business Council, entitled 'The Arts! Who gives a Rat's?', made much of the arts as 'a special kind of business'. He emphasized the difference between the language of business and the language of the arts, stressing that the arts are different from entertainment, although 'they can be entertaining':

> *When we buy a product in a shop, we know what to expect. With an artistic event, a work of art, an artistic performance, we are paying for an experience, the effect of which is not quantifiable and may vary from person to person. The arts, thus, produce a special kind of product, an experience. (Kennedy 2001)*

So, then, Kennedy believed that in Australia the arts were special and different. This might lead us to suppose that the same could be said of the people who manage and deliver them. In 2002, American filmmaker David Mullen thought that the arts were different too, but not in a good way. In his online blog he complained that anyone with an artistic thought, armed with a paintbrush or a pen or a camera, can rightly call themselves a painter, a writer, a photographer – not everyone can call themselves a surgeon, an airline pilot, a plumber. Of his own profession he said:

> *Filmmaking does not have to be a profession; certainly there are days when my bank account is so low that I wonder if this is more of a hobby than a job!*

In July 2002 the editor and publisher of *Carolina Arts* (USA), Tom Starland, wrote candidly about what he had learned in 15 years:

> *The arts are a business, an industry – full of politics. Some people act like the arts are different than the rest of the world. As long as money is involved – it's all the same. You produce a product or service. You hope people will feel what you offer is worth the price you want. And, you're in competition with a lot of other producers, so you need to promote, market, and profit. A lot of artists and art groups never understand this concept and they suffer for it. (Starland 2002)*

Based on Starland's view that the arts are not different – they are full of politics like everything else – we might assume that the people involved in the arts must be no different to the people involved in other sectors or professions. Except that later in the same article Tom Starland presents for consideration another aspect of working in the arts:

> *We who are in the arts should pinch ourselves every morning we wake. We're living a charmed life. Think about it – you or I could be working in a major corporate conglomerate. We could be ditch diggers or working for the IRS [Internal Revenue Service]. Working in the arts isn't easy, but it sure beats a lot of other things we could be doing to make a living. I hope everybody knows how lucky we are. (Starland 2002)*

Now, the arts are special and different again because they are better than a lot of other things. Perhaps working in the arts is regarded as different from an individual perspective, even if the arts industry behaves like any other. Or does it? At Lancaster University in the UK, PALATINE, the Higher Education Academy Subject Centre for Dance, Drama and Music, received dedicated funding in 2003–2004 from the Higher Education Funding Council for England (HEFCE) for a research project entitled CAREER which was designed to address the issues surrounding graduate employability.

In a subsequent article on the scheme, as part of the CAREER project, Ralph Brown produced a guide to recent literature relating to enhancing graduate employability in the performing arts, in which he indicates that the arts and creative industries are not like other industries. He states that the CAREER project was particularly focused on:

> *... the distinctive features of the labour market in the performing arts and creative industries. In the world of the Arts, the job market is very competitive and employment prospects for graduates are relatively uncertain. Career paths in this field are also very different from traditional career models in other industries. (R. S. Brown 2007)*

Brown asserts that despite the fact that performing arts courses have been listed at the lowest end of university league tables for graduate employment:

> ... courses in dance, drama and music are generally providing excellent preparation for the demands of the creative industries. (R. S. Brown 2007)

The cultural sector as a whole is increasingly dominated by part-time, self-employed and freelance working. In the UK music industry, the Musicians' Union, which has more than 30,000 members, confirms that approximately 90 per cent of people have freelance or self-employed status. Performers in dance can face the greatest difficulties. A dancer's working life often begins at an early age and performing careers are short (about 10 years on average). Employment is sporadic and often short term, with many dancers also working in non-dance areas to support themselves, especially in the period immediately after graduation. They then face the prospect of embarking on a second career, which is often not dance-related.

> ... the dance world of work is complex. It is multi-faceted with a framework of interconnected employment sectors characterised by complexity, creativity and dynamism. It is a socio-economic network. (Burns 2007: 8)

In spite of the fragmented nature of the performing arts sector, people still think in terms of having a career, although career paths in this field do not have much in common with traditional career models in other industries, according to Wetfeet, a 'recruitment solutions provider':

> Those who do well in the performing arts are creative, expressive individuals who are passionate about their craft. Patience, perseverance, and stamina – in addition to talent, practice, and a thick skin – are crucial to success; performing artists must get accustomed to rejection. Actors and professional dancers may perform the same roles for months, sometimes years. Film actors must sometimes shoot the same scene over and over again. And regardless of how a performer is feeling – whether he or she is exhausted or in a bad mood – the show must go on. (Wetfeet 2006)

The concept that the arts are 'different' persists today. The following contributions are from three performing arts practitioners; each was asked to describe the nature of the performing arts workplace and how they believe it differs from other workplaces. There is a clear correlation between their input and that of other arts managers consulted.

ARTISTIC DIRECTOR, THEATRE

In no particular order, what I notice is:

(1) There can be a sense that normal rules do not apply, probably engendered by the sense that it is hard to get work in the arts, and that we are *very* lucky to be doing something we love, so a sense of perspective in terms of work-life balance, health and safety, pay for work

doesn't seem to apply; after all who needs a life-work balance when your work is what you live for, not in a workaholic sense, but in the sense that Theatre is the place where I am most myself?

(2) Correspondingly in rehearsal, normal rules also do not apply when it comes to not bringing emotions and personal stuff to the professional table; it's often all there, without much sense of the checks that 'professional decorum' would normally impose.

(3) The range of material we are asked to cover in any given day – I think we are true Renaissance people – to be able to teach mask technique and non-verbal status body language one minute, then script edit, then instruct a lighting designer and deliver a £450k touring budget, arts council grant, or plan a volunteer development programme, and deal with a staff bullying claim the next – but then I guess that might be true of anyone heading up an SME [small- or medium-sized enterprise], I just wouldn't know.

(4) There is a lot more burdensome bureaucracy of reporting and back-covering in the arts, I think – all that time spent reporting to various funders on the steps taken to ensure the protection of vulnerable adults, equality of opportunity, targeting social need, etcetera. – it feels as though the main business of the business, that is, Artistic Excellence or even just running a good commercially successful venue, doesn't count. What counts is the by-product of meeting other people's targets. Maybe I seem a bit cynical, although I try not to be, but I'd say that if I work 47 weeks of the year about five of those are spent on achieving Artistic Excellence, which is the actual *raison d'être* of what I do. I think if I actually sat down and looked at this ratio over the last ten years I might leave the Arts! Maybe I'd do better working in some other field and doing Arts as a hobby!

(5) The pay is lower – when I look at what my skills would buy outside the arts …

(6) The furniture is usually a lot nicer in other walks of life.

(7) People are more fascinated by what we do if we're in the arts, but correspondingly they can make a lot of assumptions about how skilled, hard working, mentally disciplined we are. I've had cracks about what time I must get up in the morning, etcetera.

This arts employee eloquently expresses the concept that the arts are 'different', as voiced by other theatre professionals. She communicates that the arts are exciting and special – indeed, so special as to negate the need for the rewards associated with a 'normal' work environment – for example, a reasonable balance between time at home and at work, a decent income, the duty of care employers owe to employees and that employees owe to themselves. The view of professionalism in the context of preparing theatrical productions is an interesting one: the implication is that all performers exploit their emotional life experiences and bring these to their art form – unlike those in any other profession. Patently, performers are proficient and intelligent professionals who learn, improve and refine a set of skills appropriate to their art form. They apply themselves to the development of a range of performance techniques, and the extent of self-discipline and expertise required to achieve excellence transcends the device of connecting with their psyche. Also, individuals in non-arts professions have little choice but to bring their emotional experiences with them to their particular professional table, albeit not always overtly. Were this not the case, there would be no charismatic captains of industry capable of inspired leadership, no workers in the caring professions and ethnographers would not need to consider their own 'interpretive lenses' (Hall 2001) when undertaking research.

Skills in workload organization and the requirement for multitasking are certainly features of working at management level in the arts and of many other SMEs. The frustration created by the experience of 'burdensome bureaucracy' is recognized by Protherough and Pick (2002: vii) who dub it 'managerialism'. Undoubtedly, within the arts establishment of funders and policymakers, who set targets, invent criteria and require accountability from those they support, there has been a shift to quantitative rather than qualitative evaluation and assessment methodology. Ironically, the very ingredient that has attracted this creative artistic director to the arts – the opportunity to achieve artistic excellence – is the one element within her workload that is being relegated to a 'by-product of other people's targets', in danger of being lost altogether, perhaps, by the requirement to deliver the end products of managerialism. It could be argued that it is within her power to change her situation; however, that might be possible only by changing her profession.

The recognition that rates of pay and physical working environments of the arts are less attractive than elsewhere, taken alongside other people's perceptions of those who work in the arts, implies that the arts remains the poor relation of the commercial world of business and industry. The private sector is represented as having better terms and conditions and highly skilled, hardworking and practical employees, not the 'unfocused, fanciful types' in the arts. It is ironic that this concept should persist, even today.

At the time this first contribution was made, the artistic director was dealing with upward bullying in the workplace – she had become the target of an employee – and she handled the situation well. However, the organization's governing body imposed more and more rules which radically changed how the arts organization functioned, and reduced the scope of her ability to make creative choices. She became increasingly unhappy – and finally left. Reviewing her situation some time later, she felt she had gained new perspective and insight into her situation:

> Looking back, I really feel that I was perhaps subject to bullying by the institution. The choices I've made now to deal with that core problem are:
>
> Accept a huge pay cut from £43k to about £10k p.a. – leaving and setting up a new company, and also taking on freelance directing work, in order not to have to deal with the managerialism. I'm able to use my own and my board's judgement on management issues and act within the norms of the law and the agreements set out in my industry by the unions, rather than being governed by the conflicting demands of an establishment.
>
> Do project-based work so that bullying individuals can be weeded out and not re-employed on future projects (being mindful of the fact that I only get paid when I have a project on the go, so I feel morally OK about this climate of uncertainty because I work to the same

conditions as the people I employ). This might sound a bit mad, but I think people drawn to the theatre are either highly functional or grossly under-functional, with not much in the middle. It's great not to be stuck with the latter once they show themselves.

Spreading my funding sources globally, not just within the region or the UK, so that no one funder can hold our projects entirely to hostage.

Actively lobbying government and funders to address problems – the monopoly that funders have can turn them into bullies – working hard to set up and then maintain the Theatre Association so that we have protection.

Working outside the arts as a consultant on the high rate of pay that my skills can (thankfully) command there, thereby freeing me to make artistic excellence rather than a survival wage the top criteria in my artistic choices.

Always ensuring that I have a management partner (a line producer) working with me on any project so that we are protected on HR issues the same way two signatories are protected on an account.

Following my experience, I don't think an artistic director can cover a CEO's role as well in a building where there is an in-house producing programme that would take her into rehearsal. Limited resources or not – those are two jobs. I'd never accept that type of a job again.

The difference is night and day. Now that I've found the company's direction and created balance and control in my life I'm SO happy, and feel very creative! I think addressing these questions ... was definitely part of that process.

This artistic director took a step back and looked long and hard at the terms and conditions of her employment and at the quantity and quality of her creative work, and found them wanting. She interprets her situation as one in which she was forced to deliver formulaic work required by the establishment, which she now describes as burdensome bureaucracy. Deciding to set up her own company, and engage in freelance and consultancy work, has had economic consequences for her; however, there is no doubting the sense of freedom to be creative this has given her. Having dealt with bullying by a colleague, she ensures that she can choose co-workers on her own terms. She is actively engaged with the arts constituency in a multiplicity of roles and is the successful founder of a new arts organization.

The view that theatre workers are 'either highly functional or grossly under-functional, with not much in the middle', may appear to be an extreme one; however, those whom the Artistic Director (Theatre) describes as being highly functional are the ones she wants to work with, and there is no doubt that dysfunction, in one respect or another, is at the core of negative behaviours like bullying.

ARTISTIC DIRECTOR, DANCE

Why is it [working in the arts] different?

I was teaching a new group of students yesterday and the course leader and I spoke about the nature of the dance sector. I guess in everything we do we are striving for excellence.

The reason why we are carrying out the work is often driven by a passion for the arts, an ambition to succeed in this competitive industry but [an arts organization's] existence is one with huge financial pressures … Many of the ideas are driven by pressure to deliver the highest quality with little or no reward.

There are many unwritten rules [in the performing arts workplace] … there are many different ways to get our dance students to do things.

Compared to others – that is, other employment sectors – there is a different drive to make money.

Having worked in both the commercial and arts sectors I have found that the main difference is the motivation behind the work we are doing. The arts workplace is generally more rewarding, perhaps because we feel we are doing something that makes us feel good or makes others feel good. In contrast, in other workplaces it tends to be motivated by financial reward and career opportunities.

Arts projects are often run for relatively short periods of time, fuelled by creative energy and rewarded by the results of the work. Because of this timeframe it provides little security long term and no clear career path, but provides the freedom and opportunity to experience different projects and feeds the creativity and ambition of artistic individuals.

The workplace for the artistic team is often on the move and workers can get on top of one another, sharing rooms on tour, spending social time together, as well as rehearsing and performing daily.

There are positive outcomes of this environment: feeling like you are a part of a family who can provide emotional support and social time; encouraging a greater understanding and connection between team members during rehearsals and in performance. This close relationship can often cause unnecessary tensions and conflicts, which can affect the performance of the artist. If you are lucky you have a permanent base where rehearsals and administration staff are based; [however] the 'workplace' for the artistic team is often on the move.

Other differences apparent are in the personality of the artistic directors who can often be very demanding and expect the highest standards at all times. The arts workplace can be emotionally and physically exhausting and there are huge pressures to deliver the highest quality service.

This Artistic Director teaches dance as well as running an independent touring company – multitasking which is necessary to her exit strategy from the profession. Again, the concept of striving for excellence and being driven by a passion for the arts is highlighted, juxtaposed with the paucity of financial reward, thus reinforcing the total commitment and dedication of the artist: art for art's sake. Whilst the sincerity of the expression is not in any doubt, the belief that this marks the arts out as different to other professions is surely misplaced? Who, except the very jaded, in *any* business, would declare that they did *not* strive for excellence, or they were *not* committed or dedicated to their chosen profession? Unenthusiastic or demotivated workers are found in most employment sectors, and are not exclusive to non-arts fields. Perhaps the issue of fiscal return is the real one that resonates here – business and industry being unashamedly interested in profit, which is perceived by many artists and arts organizations to sit uncomfortably alongside artistic integrity.

The physical environment of the workplace referred to by the Artistic Director, (Theatre) features again here. In this case, the transient nature of touring is symptomatic of impermanence, and an acknowledged stressor among musicians, dancers and other performing artists (Giga, Hoel and Cooper 2003: 3).

The final comment refers to the need for dancers and dance teachers to inspire others, to harness creativity and constantly to invent new ways of working. Again, whilst these are laudable, if demanding, features, the capacity for imaginative and original ways of thinking, acting and working cannot be said to be exclusively confined to arts workplaces.

FOUNDER AND PARTNER, TOURING THEATRE COMPANY

Definition of the arts workplace?

Probably the main difference is the way energy is directed towards an end product, which is a goal with an almost grail-like aura.

Most other businesses can direct energies in a less frenetic and more controlled way (otherwise they'd be failing as businesses). It would seem to replicate the energy surges of the hunter-gatherer – lots of effort to make the kill at almost any cost, then a good rest afterwards with a project complete.

[This] seems to sum up the way we would view it – except when you're touring three different shows, and a venue wants posters for next July *now* … hmmm.

Working in the arts as against other sectors feels like wading through treacle at times. When we compare notes with people who work in other sectors, they are astounded by the inefficiency (laziness) of the arts (almost complete inability to respond to emails or phone messages). This stifles the whole sales process, usually multiplying the workload by a factor of 20 (completely unacceptable by the standards of all other sectors). There are golden exceptions to this, but they are few.

The only reward is the actual practice of the art itself and the response to it.

> As founder, there is both responsibility and ownership ... this leads to tenacity in the circumstances described above when dealing with people who wouldn't be able to hold down a post in other sectors through their poor performance.
>
> This is not relevant internally in our own small organization, but there can be intimidation by larger organizations and the definite feeling that the small do not matter one bit.

This contribution is from a founder partner in a theatre company based in London, which tours nationally and internationally, who is a musician and actor/writer. His company devises and performs original work for all ages, engages in role-play and improvization in business settings, and also works in conventional theatre productions and film.

This is another multitalented individual and, for him, the emotional experience of striving for excellence is described as 'energy', and the objective – the artistic product – is transmuted to the stuff of mediaeval legend. Theatre focuses on the artistic product, whilst drama focuses on the process, so the core of his activity as a theatre practitioner and writer/musician is arriving at a product – apparently, no matter what the (personal) cost. The artistic process, or how his energies are directed, he describes as 'frenetic' compared to how he believes non-arts businesses operate. In fact, it seems highly likely that many people outside the arts work in a way that sometimes is characterized by feverish activity, confusion and hurry – not just the dealers on the floor of any stock exchange, for example. It is certainly not the case that all commercial businesses are in strict control all the time of how they direct their energies.

The notion that arts organizations are less in control of their energies than others is undermined by the requirement they have to manage multiple priorities. This company is touring three productions in repertoire – performing a children's show, an adult cabaret and a musical in different venues, frequently on consecutive nights in different parts of the UK and on tour abroad. Organizing the distribution of publicity material months in advance is a minor part of the logistical operation this represents. Perhaps some creative individuals and companies do exist in a world of organized chaos; however, perhaps they are more disciplined than they think, or want to admit. Whether or not this is the case, in recent years arts organizations have had to conform to new ways of working; they have had to become overtly organized.

Despite the reference to 'laziness' on the part of arts organizations, it seems more likely that arts organizations, particularly the smaller ones, are carrying such considerable workloads that some tasks do, from time to time, become delayed or remain incomplete. The Artistic Director (Dance) made reference to the difficulties of touring – having to both work and socialize with a group of people causes tension from time to time. The Artistic Director (Theatre) recognized that she had to deal with dysfunctional people, and the third respondent, too, notes that he has had to persist in working with inefficient or ineffective colleagues because of his sense of responsibility and ownership as a founder.

What is at the core of an arts organization's work today? Is it *art* or something else entirely? Certainly, it once was the case that art was at the centre; performing arts workers believed in and subscribed to it when they entered the profession – whether as actors, backstage staff, composers, dancers, designers, directors, education workers, front-of-house staff, librettists, musicians, stage managers, technicians, writers, etcetera. The focus was on the work, and the quality of the work was key. That was also the criteria used by funders to support the subsidized arts sector. Arts councils and other agencies sustained and rewarded excellence in terms of talent, skill, expertise and artistry.

In the UK in the late 1970s, the idea that arts organizations needed to become more businesslike took hold; companies and individual artists needed to demonstrate that they were operating within a strategic framework. Since then, other aspects of how arts organizations function have come under scrutiny so that, beyond the assessment of the quality of artistic work, funders today seek to measure how arts organizations handle issues such as educational work, marketing and audience development, financial systems, fundraising and sponsorship, disability, diversity and social inclusion. This is all very well – indeed funders should be approaching the task of spending, particularly public, funds with *care, diligence and skill* – as long as the core purpose of arts organizations, the art, remains centre stage. Unfortunately, the constantly expanding task of gathering extensive data has created intolerable pressure on arts organizations, particularly on their managers. In the last decade alone, it can be seen that this pressure to deliver both statistical and qualitative information, and to meet targets, appears to be playing a major part in the rapid upsurge of bullying behaviour in the arts workplace, as, like the Artistic Director (Theatre), managers struggle with increasing levels of burdensome bureaucracy in their working lives.

The Target Culture

In the words of Dr Brian Kennedy, former Director of the National Gallery of Australia:

> *We live in the Great Age of the Beancounter. (Kennedy 2001)*

The growth and spread of workplace bullying mirrors the growth and spread of managerialism as mapped in *Managing Britannia* by Protherough and Pick (2002). They use the term to refer to a phenomenon they first noticed in the 1980s whereby management had become synonymous with a target-setting process wholly based on quantifiable data:

> *... dealing largely in symbols and abstractions. British culture was itself turned into an "industry" and rendered down to columns of statistics. (Protherough and Pick 2002: vii–viii)*

The Artistic Director (Theatre) outlines some of the effects of managerialism in an arts context, noting the changes that have been introduced so that the arts establishment's requirement is now that managers produce 'scientific' appraisals in which everything possible has been tallied, measured and calculated, and in which milestones have been surpassed, targets exceeded and goals unfailingly achieved. The effect of this being, according to the account given, that creative individuals working in arts management perceive that they have become a bevy of bean counters. This echoes research findings that note in the contemporary working environment:

> *the ever-increasing struggle for efficiency, work intensification, and reliance on performance-related reward systems, which may lead to an increase in bullying and violating and abusive*

conduct by managers and co-workers. (McCarthy 1996; Sheehan 1996; Wright and Smye 1997; Lee 2000) (as reported in Salin 2003: 42)

Reflecting this, in terms of the education sectors, Lewis states:

Trade unions and academic staff operating in these education sectors have subsequently argued that this is an environment where bullying has become a synonym for tough managerial styles. (Lewis 2004: 282)

In 1991, a BBC Radio Four programme about 'bad bosses' attracted widespread interest; in 1992, Andrea Adams and Neil Crawford published *Bullying at Work: How to Confront and Overcome It* and, following this, the first research (for example, by Oxford University in 1998) into workplace bullying in the UK was carried out in organizations with a clearly defined chain of command where discipline was a prime factor – the army, police and prisons. The BullyOnline website then reported that there had been an increasing number of complaints of bullying behaviour from the voluntary sector. In 1999, research in the National Health Service – also a hierarchical bureaucracy – revealed bullying behaviour was increasing (Quine 1999). By 2002, bullying behaviour was being reported in education establishments (Lewis 2002), followed later by the Church of England (Bates 2004). In 2007 the findings from the first research into bullying in the arts were presented in the author's PhD thesis. Management issues in education, religion and the arts were scrutinized in *Managing Britannia* in 2002, before the research findings on bullying were known.

Protherough and Pick cite the existence of managerialism in the vocational sectors as being the result of the transfer of theories of scientific management (Taylorism – holding that the manager's function was to discover 'scientifically' the most efficient use of workers, thereby increasing productivity) from traditional (manufacturing) industries and institutions to the new vocational 'industries' – the arts, education, health, religion. They state the need for management to be context-specific:

the modern world believes as fervently in the transferability of management as it believes that management skills are separate and identifiable realities. Managers of supermarket chains can nowadays expect to be head-hunted for posts in national museums; managers of finance companies or high-profile television performers can expect to be offered high-level managerial positions in our universities. (Protherough and Pick 2002: 13)

This is reflected in the arts case studies: in The Art Gallery (Chapter 1) and The Museum (Chapter 3), the bullies were board members from outside the arts profession who had been imported from financial and project management sectors respectively. In The Theatre Project (Chapter 5), the bully was a manager with experience of working in a charity, but in a non-arts sector. In The Creative Industry (Chapter 6), the consultant who harangued her colleagues knew nothing of their areas of expertise and in The Arts Service (Chapter 4), the incoming manager was from a separate local authority department and had no previous experience of arts philosophy or ethos. Perhaps the validity of transferability of management, in the arts as elsewhere, needs to be questioned? Perhaps non-familiarity with new management responsibilities fuels the feelings of inadequacy and insecurity noted as part of the bully's psychological make-up.

Protherough and Pick (2002) lament the passing of public institutions including the Arts Council of Great Britain, the regional Arts Boards, the Crafts Council, the Museums and Galleries Commission and the Office of Arts and Libraries to make way for the creation of the UK's first version of a 'Ministry of Culture', known as the Department of National Heritage, in 1992. The impact this had on the arts infrastructure was significant – beyond providing financial support, the new body would have 'responsibility' for the arts, whereas its predecessor (the Office of Arts and Libraries) had always been careful to say that accountability rested with artists and the Arts Council. The economic importance of the arts industry was suddenly a consideration, and new bureaucratic steps were introduced for the creation of industries, where none had been before. These steps included the collection of data to identify strategic importance; highlight potential development areas; reorganize the arts industry under state-controlled management; redefine aims, purposes and functions within managerial language; and target setting and monitoring. This correlates with the information provided by arts practitioners. By 2006, these functions are familiar to arts managers, many of whom are charged with their implementation on behalf of arts organizations today.

The language in the text of *Managing Britannia* is rife with references to control and dictatorship, and warlike images pepper the pages. It is asserted that artists and politicians had never imagined that a government ministry for culture would be introduced in the UK:

> *The monolithic brutality of Stalin's USSR, Mussolini's Italy and the Third Reich – all of which featured a Ministry of Culture – were, it was thought, too indelibly imprinted upon the British mind for this country ever to embark on that course. (Protherough and Pick 2002: 103)*

Given the position of managers within this framework, the advent of workplace bullying in the arts, then, may be an inevitable result of intimidating governmental tactics employed across the whole of the arts constituency. Colleagues have indicated that changes began whilst Margaret Thatcher was Prime Minister (1979–1990), and have accused her of 'dismantling society – there are only individuals now' (anon). Certainly, since Tony Blair took office in 1997, the government's thirst for statistical information and reports on the arts, through its Department of Culture, Media and Sport, has created increased pressure on arts management at every level. Arts management might have learned to ape the regime imposed by government, just as Archer (1999: 94–106)) noted that in organizations with a military structure, the behaviour of the tyrannical manager could be overtly encouraged and even imitated by others, particularly if it was perceived as 'strong management, which gets things done'.

The Artistic Director (Dance) described herself and her colleagues as people who can often be very demanding and expect the highest standards at all times. The arts workplace can be emotionally and physically exhausting and there are huge pressures to deliver the highest quality service. A chain reaction of bullying is much more likely to occur in a pressured and demanding environment than in a relaxed and imperturbable one.

The transference of management tactics and *modus operandi* from industry to the vocational sector has resulted in a number of changes to working practices, one of which was the introduction of Total Quality Management (TQM) to the arts and also to education. Protherough and Pick cite an instance where one academic questioned the success of the work of the Quality Assurance Agency (QAA) for Higher Education, established in 1997, saying:

> The QAA's work is not about improving teaching: it is about controlling teachers. (Charlton 2000) (as reported in Protherough and Pick 2002: 91)

In the same way, it may be seen in the case study The Art Gallery (Chapter 1) that the owner's aspirations in setting up a watchdog on the board had little to do with improving the quality of the gallery's work and everything to do with controlling the managers. In this instance the watchdog was both a bully and the tool of an owner who was, effectively, bullying at a remove. In The Museum (Chapter 3), the bullying Chair's intentions were far removed from improving the quality of the creative experience for the museum's patrons and focused entirely on controlling the curator to gain personal power. In The Contemporary Dance Studios (Chapter 3) and The Arts Service (Chapter 4), the founders and the incoming manager respectively were not interested in ensuring the merit, and protecting the value, of the services to be rendered to the beneficiaries: such considerations were secondary to the desire for domination.

It is a feature of the arts case studies that bullies win. In the wake of bullying, it is the targets and witnesses who tend to leave the organization while management discreetly buries the experience. The authors of *Managing Britannia* note a similar pattern with managerialists – those who embrace the managerial ideology – and the authors suggest that managerialists perpetuate their own myth. It may be the same with workplace bullies in the arts: perhaps they admire and pay court to each other for being 'strong' managers? Where problems are perceived, bullies invariably attribute these to poor performance from the workforce, and by their behaviour can be seen to be subscribing to Douglas McGregor's Theory X – people dislike and will avoid work and need to be directed, including being threatened with punishment if necessary – rather than Theory Y – people are self-motivated, creative and responsible and do not need to be controlled or punished to produce good work.

Managerialism seems to be founded on the notion of a relationship with employees comprising: low trust + high control = managerialism. This is not far removed from bullying, and we might represent that equation as: (perpetrator inadequacy x perceived threat) = mistrust; mistrust + desire for control = bullying behaviour.

In the pilot studies, it was apparent that managers had virtually no training (formal or informal) in managing people. It seems that even where management education is gained formally and at degree level, it is possible that managers are given training that is ultimately irrelevant to them:

> dissatisfaction with most of what passes for management education has led a number of scholars ... to unite in expressing grave concern about its ineffectiveness ... there is too little attention to teaching students how to learn and think, and too much indoctrination and examining out-of-date business anecdotes ... some now argue that the attempts to establish management as a separate field have been misguided. (Protherough and Pick 2002: 75)

In terms of training opportunities and qualifications, in 2010 the *Performing Arts Blueprint* is again reporting a disparity between:

what is available through the formal education sector and what the performing arts industry actually needs (Creative and Cultural Skills 2010: 19)

and noting that lack of specialist technical skills is a major problem. In addition, in the smaller arts businesses:

[m]any employees take on management- and business-related responsibilities which are not in their areas of expertise. As such, administration skills suffer from as much of a skills gap as technical skills. (Creative and Cultural Skills 2010: 21)

Management and administration skills include managing people, to a greater or lesser degree depending on the circumstances. The lack of experience and the gap in skills reported in *Performing Arts Blueprint* correlates highly with the examples in the case studies and the findings of the national survey. The report also notes the problems this creates in terms of effective management and leadership, saying this is still 'assumed' in the performing arts, as was the case during the pilot study of arts managers.

Bullies, like managerialists, fail to understand as well as to value people. In considering the lessons learned from the case studies, we can see that arts managerial-bullies subscribe to the myths outlined by McKeown and Whiteley (2002) in their plea for organizations to reconsider their operational ethos and 'unshrink' themselves. In the left-hand column in Table 8.1 their common myths are set out and set against these are illustrations of how these are exemplified in the arts case studies and in social theory.

The key message about managerialism from Protherough and Pick (2002: 196) is that:

in the health, education, social services and the arts modern management was not working.

They assert that belief in managerialism is so widespread that failures are always explained in terms of outside influences, rather than any fault in the initial belief. In Chapter 6, a perspective on attribution theory, as reported in Rayner (1999: 29), was considered

Table 8.1   Case studies related to common myths about the workplace

Common Myths	Arts Research Examples
You are what you do	Being Chair is the most important job: The Museum
Work comes first	CEO sacrifices personal and professional integrity: The Theatre Project
The boss is superhuman	Domineering consultant: The Creative Industry
The plan must be secret	Withholding information: The Theatre Project and The Creative Industry
People obey orders	The Art Gallery and McGregor's Theory X
Organizations are machines	New manager: The Arts Service
All change is good	Restructuring for its own sake: The Arts Service

Source: McKeown and Whiteley 2002.

in which, like targets of bullying over time, the arts managers who were in denial about workplace bullying 'consistently attribute reasons for negative events externally to themselves'. Here, attribution theory applies to perpetrators of bullying behaviour – where 'outside' simply means outside of the perpetrator, and often connected with the target. Hence bullies often counter-accuse targets of bullying, as with the Director of Fundraising in The Theatre Project (Chapter 5), the founders in The Contemporary Dance Studios (Chapter 3) and the pair bullies in The Museum (Chapter 3).

Protherough and Pick (2002: 205) offer a description of the differences between the characteristics of modern managerialists and what they term 'proper, old-fashioned management' which is likely to be:

> ... gentle, amateur, scholarly, patriotic, modest, unambitious, dutiful, charitable or sportsmanlike ...

and those of the modern manageralist, who is likely to be:

> ... ambitious, entrepreneurial, hard-nosed, interventionist, focused, driven, work-centred ... committed to modern managerialism.

Whilst these do not reflect exactly the attributes of a target and a bully respectively, there are some similarities. Rayner (1999: 29) has noted that studies of schools demonstrate that targets of bullying do tend to be 'generally quieter' people. They may be deemed to be amateur in the sense that they enjoy their work and are greatly interested in it, for reasons beyond its financial return, and not in the sense that they lack skill. As quieter people, they may lack ambition in the sense that they are not thrusting – although in the context of the arts they may still be driven by passion for what they do. Perpetrators of bullying behaviour, on the other hand, relentlessly pursue power and examples of all the attributes of the modern managerialist may be found in the wider psychological profile of the arts bully assembled during the research.

Ultimately, managerialism is about control, and control is the object of the bully: so managerialism and bullying are both forms of tyranny. Managerialism is so-called management by bullying. In the last 12 years among employers, trades unions and employees there has been increased:

- identification and recognition of bullying behaviour as undesirable;
- awareness of the negative impact on the health and happiness of victims;
- acceptance that it is a problem affecting a large section of the workforce;
- provision for practical and personal support to targets;
- instances of legal redress being sought;
- attention paid to the economic impact of bullying.

However, despite this the behaviour continues, criticism of the perpetrator remains the exception rather than the rule and, as with 'fat cat' managerialism, as outlined in *Managing Britannia*, bullying is, in fact, often rewarded. Einarsen states that:

> the prejudices against the victim produced by the bullying seem to cause the organization to treat the victim as the problem. (Einarsen 1999: 19)

In so doing, management is condoning bullying behaviour and becoming an accessory after the fact.

The rise in awareness of bullying behaviour generally is consistent with a move towards Protherough and Pick's description of managerialism in the UK, and the high incidence in performing arts organizations may reflect particular tensions within a sector whose managers patently are not comfortable with the concept of arts organizations as machines or with expressing creative work in terms of quantifiable outputs. This puts pressure on the arts infrastructure generally and in particular puts pressure on:

- individuals to perform well, sometimes in difficult circumstances;
- supervisors to be exemplary role models, extracting maximum results from those they line manage.

And due to competition for resources, pressure is put on:

- departments to pull their weight internally;
- organizations to compete with same-sector rivals;
- individual sectors to lobby for resources nationally;
- nations to compete, for example within Europe;
- continents to vie for global positioning.

The Employee Relations Team at the London School of Economics (LSE) published a paper entitled Guidance on Managing Pressure at Work which cites the following examples of what can cause excessive pressure:

- prolonged conflict with others, harassment or bullying;
- under- or over-promotion and overloading or little to do;
- torn loyalties between work and home;
- a high degree of uncertainty about jobs and career prospects;
- uncomfortable working conditions and inflexible/over-demanding work schedules. (London School of Economics 2010)

In the section Guidelines for Managers, actions and steps that can be taken to reduce stress include:

- demonstrating a co-operative rather than adversarial manner, and engendering team spirit;
- taking action to tackle the causes of stress, including stopping any bullying, harassment or prejudiced behaviour;
- adjusting workloads, if necessary;
- being aware of the pressures outside work;
- advising staff that they can be referred to a St Philips Medical Centre Doctor or can make their own appointment for a session of counselling;
- seeking advice from Human Resources on how to manage staff suffering from excessive or prolonged stress. (London School of Economics 2010)

These steps are important, signifying as they do the need for: positive leadership; a focus on teamwork; awareness of, and action on, bullying and other stressors; and clarity of information and advice. It is also evident that if managerialism is at the root of workplace bullying in arts organizations, then the pressures experienced by performing arts organizations are also experienced in other employment sectors. In that sense, the arts are not different.

Peter Stark has over 35 years' direct experience of leadership and management in the cultural sector and of the interaction of that sector with issues of economic and social regeneration. He is an internationally acknowledged expert in cultural policy development, in cultural management training and in the conceptualization, design and realization of cultural precincts and projects – principally in the context of urban renewal. He comments on his profession thus:

> *Is there a connection to the similarities – and fundamental differences – I've observed to management at the sharp end of the health service or during armed conflict? In these two areas managers deal – literally – with matters of life and death. You don't get the appropriate ration of drugs/bullets and someone will die.*

> *In parts of the arts we can and do attach similar weight to 'the show must go on/go up on time'. Artists invest everything of themselves in their work – we respond or try to – and can get caught between that need for empathy with the artist and our duty of care to those we manage.*

> *My definition of what was needed in an arts administrator (from 1973) probably falls into the trap of 'over-emotionalising' the trade, but I still like it:*

> *What we need is capable masochists, without the desire for martyrdom, with a flair for the arts they administer and the ability to cope with an occasionally schizophrenic existence. (Personal email to the author 2010)*

From the perspective of handling negative workplace behaviours, perhaps our understanding of arts management and administration needs to recognize the importance of valuing positive leadership and best practice in management. Perhaps what we need now are: accomplished and motivated people, without a desire for dominance, with a flair for the arts they manage, and the ability to deal with stimulating and challenging work experiences.

9 *Creativity, Genius and Artistic Temperament*

People who are part of the artistic infrastructure report that they value creativity, *per se*, and most arts managers, and many arts workers, like to think of themselves as taking a particularly imaginative and inventive approach to resolving the many and various organizational and operational issues they encounter commonly. This view is aligned with a widespread belief that the arts are different. Some of these potential differences are examined in Chapter 8, and experience indicates that the cultural sector certainly views itself as set apart, in one way or another. It is understandable that the central role of creativity in the arts – imbued as this is with passion, energy, imaginativeness and inspiration – should be considered by practitioners to be worlds away from the central issues on the factory floor, in the office or the shop. To transpose this difference as an all-encompassing singular truth to every aspect of the arts, however, including working terms and conditions, is unrealistic and unsupportable.

In fact, creativity is not the sole preserve of the artist, and the attributes of passion, energy and commitment, imaginative invention and inspired lateral thinking are just as much a part of the arts administrator's or manager's skills. In addition, in current hard-pressed times, resourcefulness is born of necessity both in the cultural sector and also elsewhere.

Only Connect

Even at the level of small arts companies, there are many difficulties inherent in shared management, and delivering it successfully is a genuine achievement on the part of the two principals involved. Derek Chong has commented on bifurcated management structures and on how finding the right person for senior posts is increasingly onerous:

> ... *given the combination of skills desired by arts organizations. For example, it is a rare prize to find a major dancer with professional management training ... An aesthetic leader with management skills is a coveted individual. Adopting a bifurcated management structure, with dual executive positions, is one alternative solution. (Chong 2002: 67, 70)*

Here is the very honest, warts and all, story of an arts organization that has grown and flourished over a substantial period of time. This is not a major national or international company, but a small- to medium-sized one operating principally (to date) in the UK. This is a contribution from a founder, reproduced almost verbatim.

Click Wheel grew from my creating a hugely successful piece of work for young people, specifically schools, on the theme of sexual health, and realizing that:

- it had the capacity to expand beyond the health authority for whom it was created;
- the health authority was not theatre literate and didn't understand how best to plan and run an effective tour;
- they were over-bureaucratic, decisions took too long and were often made for the wrong reasons (the need for long chains of command, lack of willingness to take responsibility and fear of the creative process itself).

At that time Yuriko was working, very unhappily, in sales, and was depressed about her job prospects. She needed a job that more fully utilized her formidable skills.

So I suggested to her that we had a piece of product here that had potential for a business. She was unconvinced at first, so I obtained a list of sexual health contacts within health authorities. We both then sat together at her kitchen table and 'cold called' down the list. It was a tough job and it quickly became clear that I was the best person to make these calls as I best understood the product and how it would fit into their specific health strategy. After about 40 calls we had a short list of names of people who were interested in discussing the idea and we held face-to-face meetings with them.

This formed our first year of touring: it was clear from the outset that Yuriko had the administrative time and skills, and the ability to deal with financial systems, and she took on these roles with a passion and energy. I became the creative ambassador and engine for ideas. Areas of grey we thrashed out between us!

I think in the early days we both laboured under the misapprehension that it was *our* company. As Artistic Director, I felt it was my creative vision that had led to the idea happening in the first place, and, as Administrative Director, Yuriko put in long hours structuring the administrative systems, making sure we had a manageable cash flow, and introducing a clear constitution and contracts. This created clashes about ownership – was the company mine or hers? We avoided this discussion for many years, although as the person dealing with wages she did have an advantage in that I had no clue specifically as to how and where money was being spent. I realized that 'he who holds the cheque book calls the tune'. I was never a signer of the cheques and didn't see income and expenditure accounts; although, of course Yuriko was handling these with absolute integrity, this did still inevitably lead to resentments!

Clearly, this had to change, which it did when we opted to relocate to a very disadvantaged community in a rural area. The nature of our work altered and, due to her personal circumstances, Yuriko relied more heavily on me to lead in terms of what the direction of the company should be. In fact, she was very against the move – she neither liked nor trusted the organization that had proposed the move, instinctively feeling that they were only interested in using the company for their own ends – that is, obtaining capital funding for their own purposes. In retrospect, I acknowledge that she was right about this; however, at the time I felt strongly that we desperately needed a base within a community in order to give the company a stronger identity and for it to grow as an organization: we were at a stage where it needed to change its structure, as well as the nature of what it did.

So it's fair to say that in the first eight to ten years' of Click Wheel's existence there was a tension between the creative and administrative directors, which I think both of us were acutely aware of, even though these issues were rarely discussed head on! This was possibly to the detriment and smooth running of the organization. There was a point when Yuriko's husband had a stroke and I was running the whole show for a time, when I began asking awkward questions about structure and organization, which Yuriko saw as overstepping the mark – and these tensions then boiled over and very nearly destroyed our working relationship and indeed the company itself. Fortunately, I stepped back from the brink, realizing that it would jeopardize all we had built. Similarly, when Gary joined the company (new staff coming in always changes the balance of power) he attempted to exploit the areas of weakness within the organization and to effectively set us against each other. In fact, this conveniently had precisely the opposite effect: it made us talk more together, iron out our unspoken resentments and difficulties, respect what we each brought to the company and learn to trust each other again. It also made us sit down and hammer out our shared vision for the future.

Over the years Yuriko and I have learned the hard way that, where staff are concerned, assumption is the mother of all mess ups. Choosing the right people for our organization is the most important decision that we make and effective communication is the key to recruiting and retaining talented people.

It's also worth saying that in the very early days Yuriko and I took on the role of good cop/ bad cop with me always playing good cop. She became the person within the organization who wielded the big stick and did all the nasty jobs – I was able to be Mr Nice Guy, which was great for me but not much fun for her. Once again after our heart-to-heart about how and whether to continue with the company, I feel that this all changed and I took greater responsibility for making and executing the tough decisions. I now feel that both of us share the burden of the difficult roles within the organization, while still recognizing that each of us has areas of strength and has to be allowed to do what they do best!

We have never to my knowledge had a situation where one of us has attempted to wrest control from the other. It has always been a very strong and clear working relationship, although of course there have been times when one of us has been disillusioned and wanted to throw in the towel – generally the other has stepped in and provided support and encouragement, energy and ideas to get us back on course.

Over the years we have been, at different times, overly autocratic and also too laid back; we have micromanaged staff members and also been far too hands off. There is a balance, which has to be negotiated, and it has to be done fairly and transparently. And what is agreed with staff members must be well documented – for the benefit of both parties. Many of the systems we now have in place may only prove their worth in the breach rather than the observance, but the time and energy we put into our staff also reaps rich rewards.

Now the company is changing again: the next phase will be to hand it over, gradually, to others who will care for it and ensure that it continues to thrive. The arrival of Shyla and Gina will, I hope, mean that we are able to give more responsibility to new company members. Yuriko and I recognize that if the company is to outlast our energy, interest and ability to run it effectively, then we need new people close to the heart of the company who will carry it forward. It has always from the outset grown organically – we have made mistakes about personnel (the biggest mistake you can make in my book) and have suffered because of those errors, both in extra hours put in and loss of sleep, but we do now feel (I think) that there are other members within the company who we can trust and to whom we will hand over greater creative *and* organizational responsibility over the coming months and years – that is, once we are clearly established on a firm financial footing. It goes without saying that we love the little child we have nurtured together – and that we have spent a great deal of our own time for very little reward in order to see it survive.

Having a board of trusted members running the company will be valuable – neither of us may like the extra accountability it brings, but we both recognize that it is the only way that the company can expand and grow! This company has grown out of the dynamic relationship between Yuriko and myself. We are now – frighteningly – entering our fifteenth year, so we must be doing something right!! Who knows what the future holds for it?!

(*Names and environs have been changed to protect confidentiality.*)

Unlike the founders in The Contemporary Dance Studios (Chapter 3) and The Museum (Chapter 3), this arts professional has made an honest appraisal of the organization's history and its potential future. Past events have not quelled his passion, energy or commitment; he recognizes how and why the company has changed and adapted over the years. He is self-aware enough to understand what he has invested in the enterprise and to know that his sense of personal success, and that of his colleague, is tied up with the fate of the company.

The process in which he has been engaged bears further analysis. In the beginning, he had an idea – a professional instinct, perhaps – that a particular piece of work he had developed had additional potential beyond the purpose for which it was originally created, albeit that this may be in an environment with which he was only partially familiar and which had drawbacks. At one level, this is his moment of 'inspiration' – not so much in creating the work itself, but in realizing that it could grow to become of greater significance. To implement this idea, he recognized that he needed help: someone with complementary skills that would allow him to turn a latent concept into reality. Yuriko's scepticism at the outset was a healthy force in this instance: it prompted the research upon which both parties embarked – the preparation for their proposed artistic endeavour. It is interesting that, in this account, the Artistic Director deems himself to be the more successful marketing/sales person, whereas passion and energy are attributed to the Administrative Director's role when, so easily and frequently, this is held to be valid only the other way around. Following this, there is a realization of the ambition: the creative work finds a wider audience and the Directors' aspirations are fulfilled.

In this account, the level and nature of internal tensions is acknowledged when the question of ownership of the company arises; in this case the drive to arrive at a shared vision for the future is successful and there is a meeting of minds. Then, external forces influence the effectiveness of internal working relationships. The Artistic Director acknowledges the difference that new employees, or the input of other personnel, make to the organization – the dynamics change, particularly when new people manipulate circumstances sowing distrust in the process. The Directors engage in collaborative role-play as a way of dealing with this: the Artistic Director adopting an empathetic approach, which he realizes left the Administrative Director operating as the disciplinarian – an unenviable part to play.

However, there has been no battle for power between them and no overriding charismatic personality seeks to lead this enterprise; this chimes with Kate Maddison's experience, as recorded later in this chapter. Instead, the continuing, mutually supportive relationship between the principals has helped this company through difficult times. They have learned their craft together over the years and arrived at a point where they are comfortable with their own roles and with the agreed operating principles of the company, so that the prospect of handing over to other staff and/or a Board of Directors has become less frightening and delegation has become a legitimate and viable exit strategy rather than something undesirable and alarming.

Outside his formal role, the Artistic Director has approached the whole business of running the company as a creative process in and of itself. When the organization moves on from being the Directors' 'little child' it manages to continue to thrive in a new environment. This is an interesting variation on Founder's Syndrome as, in this case, the founders positively welcome the opportunity to hand on their company to those newly responsible for its ongoing welfare and success.

The evolution of this creative company can be charted via the various stages of the Artistic Director's account, and could be represented, thus far, as in Figure 9.1.

In 2006, the Oxford English Dictionary Online (OED 2006) defined the adjective 'creative' as:

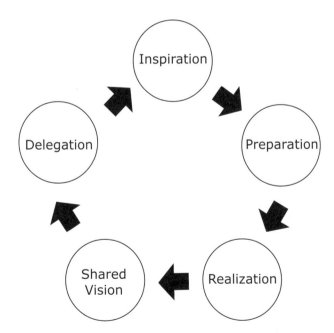

Figure 9.1 Life cycle of a healthy creative organization

a. Having the quality of creating, given to creating; of or pertaining to creation; originative.

b. Spec. of literature and art, thus also of a writer or artist: inventive (cf. INVENTION 3b), imaginative; exhibiting imagination as well as intellect, and thus differentiated from the merely critical, 'academic', journalistic, professional, mechanical, etcetera, in literary or artistic production.

A straightforward interpretation tells us that 'creative' describes producing original work, particularly in the fields of art and literature, that goes beyond scholarly pursuits, analytic judgement or reportage. This may be extended to all arts disciplines, so that where the production of new work is involved – for example, in choreography, film or the broadcast arts – we can also perceive this work as creative. Further, where a new production of an existing piece of work is concerned, such as a play or an opera, this too can be deemed creative on the grounds that it represents a new interpretation of a current oeuvre.

By 2010, however, the Cambridge Dictionary Online defines the adjective 'creative' as:

producing or using original and unusual ideas.

And the noun 'creative' as:

an employee whose imagination and artistic skills are very important for a company.

Whilst creative as an adjective is still extant in respect of the production of artworks, today we recognize 'the creative' as a type of employee with particular skills or expertise. Also, and perhaps as a result, organizational creativity has taken on a different meaning: it is a highly valued concept that has excited the imagination of employers across industrial, business and non-profit sectors. It may be understood as an organization's ability to innovate, by creating:

... a valuable, useful new product, service, idea, procedure, or process by individuals working together in a complex social system. (Woodman, Sawyer and Griffin, 1993)

So, as organizations operating outside the cultural sector increasingly aspire to become more creative and to capitalize on, and profit from, the benefits of creativity, researchers advocate the need to recognize that the development of creativity-friendly conditions in the working environment are part of a long-term process, rather than a short-term solution for current problems (Andriopoulos 2001). Whilst the capability of an organization to become more creative may start at the level of the individual, personal creativity in itself is not enough. Constantine Andriopoulos is an author and an expert on managing change, creativity and innovation, and he asserts that a vital, often ignored, component of creativity is that which occurs at the organizational level. Antonio Davila, an expert on management accounting and control systems, suggests that, in order to be competitive, successful organizations today rely to a larger extent on creativity and innovation than used to be the case. They also combine an environment that is:

supportive to this new competitive dimension with a relentless focus on execution. They manage this organizational duality of systems to maintain a delicate equilibrium between chaos and routine. (Davila 2010: 65)

Arts workers may, perhaps, be surprised to learn that organizations forced to manage chaos as well as routine exist outside the cultural sector, as well as inside it. Indeed, a model of typical contemporary perspectives behind making non-arts organizations more creative (Figure 9.2) does not look very much different to the lifecycle of a healthy creative organization such as Click Wheel.

Andriopoulos summarizes five key factors that influence organizational creativity – and hence that need to be taken into consideration when managing creativity in organizational settings – namely, leadership style, organizational culture, organizational climate, resources and skills, and the structure and systems of an organization. These five factors have an important bearing on the findings of the research into bullying in the arts, and are illustrated explicitly in the case studies.

For example, leadership style can dictate the way in which bullying situations are handled: where a positive leadership style is in place, negative behaviours can be stemmed, and vice versa. The CEO in The Theatre Project (Chapter 5) demonstrated poor leadership when he retreated from the incidents perpetrated by his Director of Fundraising, and this was compounded when eventually he distanced himself deliberately from his own staff. Undoubtedly, organizational culture affects perceptions of bullying behaviour, as was the case in the New Zealand employment courts when a complaint of bullying in a busy hotel kitchen was dismissed on the ground that it was to be expected in such an environment. In The Contemporary Dance Studios (Chapter 3) the immature and autocratic founders felt they were entitled to behave exactly as they wished towards their freelance business advisor – on the basis that this was their company – effectively inventing and putting in place an unpleasant, oppressive organizational culture as they went along.

The ability of individuals and management to deal adequately with bullying behaviour depends on available resources and skills; for example, the young members of The Ensemble (Chapter 5) were bemused by the situation in which they found themselves,

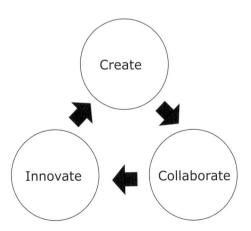

Figure 9.2   Factors in developing organizational creativity
Source: based on a description by Mauro Porcini (2009).

and were unable to withstand the bully's persistent intimidation, whereas the bully's external colleagues in The Creative Industry (Chapter 6) were able to distance themselves from the perpetrator and her behaviour, unlike her staff. The structure and systems of an organization relate to the organizational culture – even if bullying is not, knowingly, condoned by management, a lack of satisfactory procedures to address complaints makes it extremely difficult to resolve bullying situations in a fair and reasonable manner. In The Museum (Chapter 3), the Curator was disbelieved by his Board of Governors and – devoid of assistance from a trades union – found that he had no other recourse. In The Arts Service (Chapter 4) the supposed guardians of good practice in human resources management did their best to negate and to downplay the problem by discouraging staff from seeking access to legitimate complaints procedures.

The differentiation implicit in the use of the OED term 'merely critical', as part of the definition of the adjective creative (above), may be considered an outmoded reference from the nineteenth century: it sets artists apart from academics, journalists and others on the basis that they demonstrate 'imagination as well as intellect'. This infers that the two aspects rarely function together, and/or that academics, journalists and others are likely to have only one of these attributes, but not both – the latter being the preserve of the artist. It is tempting to surmise that the definition suggests that academics might have intellect, but no imagination; and that journalists may have imagination, but no intellect. This may appear to be the case if we view the world as a repository only for dry erudite papers and lurid tabloid journalism. Whilst this view is not without its attractions, on balance the equation appears too rudimentary to be taken seriously.

We have seen in Chapter 8 that some arts practitioners today hold the view that working in the arts is different, or special, implying or stating openly, that it is better than working in other employment sectors. This is not surprising given the notion that working in the arts is described by Peter Hewitt as tantamount to a vocation. By extension, then, creative people are also different and special; but do we think of them also as better than other people? As bullying behaviour not only exists, but actually appears to thrive, in arts workplaces, the connections and tensions amongst the creative personality, the creative environment and coercive behaviour demand further research and investigation.

The responses from arts practitioners portray the arts workplace as a centre of frenzied, energetic, creative activity where low-paid, emotionally charged employees, driven by a passion for the arts, continually strive for excellence. Arts executives are experts at multitasking and nowadays are required to spend considerable time on detailed quantitative reporting to meet the onerous demands of funders. Non-arts people may regard artists, and other creative people working in the arts, as idiosyncratic and scatterbrained. Many arts organizations are underfunded, and the arts workplace is an insecure environment; arts workers must constantly be inventive in their approach to their 'vocation', to the exclusion of all else, at personal cost and in the face of adversity, channelling all their energy into a creative task until it is accomplished: 'the show must go on'. This is exemplified by Peter Stark's candid comments on what can drive and sustain arts administrators, in Chapter 8.

Versions of this reality are valid for each of the arts practitioners who tell their stories; however, they do not provide evidence of an actuality that is, in truth, necessarily different from other workplaces. These ingredients could be facets of a shared arts mythology, particularly if viewed in the light of two other components of arts folklore with a particular relevance to arts workplace bullying – the concepts of creative genius and artistic temperament. The former might yield 'great art', but often at a terrible cost; the latter is the result of artists behaving badly and is indefensible in the true professional. The terms 'creative genius' and 'artistic temperament' are used not in the sense employed by Oscar Wilde, as something desirable possessed by great artists, but rather as interpreted by Bertrand Russell when in his essay 'On Youthful Cynicism' he talked about artists as:

> ... inspired by some kind of rage against the world so that they wish rather to give significant pain than to afford serene satisfaction. (Russell 1930: 125)

And by G K Chesterton when he said disparagingly:

> The artistic temperament is a disease that afflicts amateurs ... very great artists are able to be ordinary men – men like Shakespeare or Browning. There are many real tragedies of the artistic temperament, tragedies of vanity or violence or fear. But the great tragedy of the artistic temperament is that it cannot produce any art. (Chesterton 1905: 242–243)

According to arts mythology, then, at the heart of every great creative enterprise lies one or more stereotypical artistic genius personalities – these are people who work outside the ordinary milieu, in a flourish of uncontrolled creativity which can cause havoc in terms of normal operations or procedures, but which eventually yields great art. It is also understood that the creative periods of the artistic genius are frequently accompanied by interludes of depression, alcoholism or drug abuse, which may lead to suicide, and researchers such as Jamison (2001) have reported on strong links between the creative personality and manic depression or other mental illness.

Six years ago, a BBC Radio Four programme investigated 'Creative Genius' and journalist Ian Peacock described how the evolution of language and the use of metaphor kick started creativity; he found that creativity is unleashed by some kinds of brain damage and that neuroscience is now beginning to shed light on the mystery of creativity (BBC 2005b). There are examples in historical biographies of the phenomenon of the downside of the creative personality: many of our well-known artists have lived lives of great emotional turmoil, notwithstanding, or some would argue because of, their exquisite artistic genius – for example, Wolfgang Amadeus Mozart, George Gordon Byron, Vincent Van Gogh, Virginia Woolf, Ludwig van Beethoven, Emily Dickinson.

The literary world has gained poetry, short stories, plays and novels from writers such as Irishman Brendan Behan, and Welshman Dylan Thomas; they are remembered also for their damaging addiction to alcohol alongside their genius. The bad boys of rock 'n roll who exhibit self-destructiveness – such as Iggy Pop, Keith Richards and Jim Morrison – are by no means a feature of past decades. Contemporary celebrity culture is peopled with dysfunctional artists – in the music world, for example, the UK's own Pete Doherty and Amy Winehouse have received high praise for their creative work, and also achieved notoriety for their drug abuse.

Perhaps we can conclude, then, that creative genius is something of a mixed blessing. Undoubtedly society has gained marvellous artistic works and stunning, unforgettable performances from its cultural icons, and skilful, artistic people remain at the core of the very best work that is produced in the humanities and the fine arts. Sadly, society has lost too – artists have suffered, self-harmed and endured wretchedness in the throes of their creative processes, and often those close to them have been damaged too. If Ian Peacock is right, it may be that it is the neuroscientists who will teach us to understand creativity fully – already they have linked the capacity to imagine with perception, and identified the fact that new environments stimulate the brain to perceive things in a new way – triggering the imagination.

> *Creativity and imagination begin with perception ... how you perceive something isn't simply a product of what your eyes and ears transmit to your brain. It's a product of your brain itself. (Berns 2008: 1)*

A Union of Interests

We have seen from the experience of the directors of Click Wheel that working relationships between truly creative people in arts organizations do not always operate smoothly, but that they do not have to be fraught with artistic temperament, even when change has to be managed, difficult or key issues explored or significant decisions taken. Another example of an artistic organization successfully adapting to changing circumstances can be seen in the contribution below from Kate Maddison, one of the founder Directors of Chrysalis Arts, an artist-led public art company, training and arts development agency in the UK. This creative organization has grown and flourished over a substantial period of time and the company as it exists now has more directors than the original two founders, and broader partnerships and collaborations with other organizations.

> Rick and I originally formed Chrysalis Arts as a way of supporting our work as freelance artists and a way of collaborating or associating with other artists for larger projects or initiatives. This team approach led us to work regularly with other freelancers and has shaped the development and established the key personnel of the company.
>
> Many of the activities that Chrysalis Arts has initiated or undertaken do support arts development, training, community cohesion, sustainability, etcetera, but the underlying strength is continuity of personnel, long-term commitment, mutual support and conscientiousness rather than a shared belief in achieving a prefixed mission or specific objectives, and following a charismatic leader. Over the years, the organization has evolved into a broader partnership than the original founders, and a recognition of the skills and expertise that others can contribute, and a willingness to share responsibility to accommodate this, have helped us to develop into a stronger organization.
>
> Another strength is a continuing interest in adapting and reinventing the company as our surrounding circumstances change and develop. Chrysalis Arts Development is a recent company, constituted as a social enterprise in response to our desire to work in a different way and to generate resources to facilitate this change. This does change the way we work to some extent; there is now a Board of Directors which brings new skills and energy to the company, but I don't think the difference will outwardly be that great and it makes it easier for us to draw a distinction between commissioned arts activity, mostly undertaken by Chrysalis Arts Ltd and funded/development work, mostly undertaken by Chrysalis Arts Development.

Once again, the original founders of the company made a mature, long-term commitment to the development of their creative work. They wanted to work with others and they have retained this as a key goal. They believe it helped to strengthen their organization. As the company has grown, adaptation and change has remained at the core of their response. Stable, supportive and enlightened partnerships have been formed and artistic solidarity is a strong factor in how and why the company has changed and adapted over the years. Outside of their formal roles as Directors in different spheres of the company's work, the original founders have taken a creative approach to the development concept for their company.

Evidently, it is possible to be a creative individual and to work in an arts environment and not to bully or abuse others. Why, then, does bullying happen? By virtue of office, people working in the arts tend to subscribe to the value of great art, *per se*. We have seen that, as the art is revered, so, too, is the creator, and consequently the artist has the potential to assume a great deal of power and status, and often to inspire awe.

> *A work of art is the unique result of a unique temperament. Its beauty comes from the fact that the author is what he is. It has nothing to do with the fact that other people want what they want. Indeed, the moment that an artist takes notice of what other people want, and tries to supply the demand, he ceases to be an artist, and becomes a dull or an amusing craftsman, an honest or dishonest tradesman. He has no further claim to be considered as an artist.* (Wilde 1891 [2006]: 141–142)

Diva, Maestro, Prima Donna, Virtuoso: the terminology is testimony to the esteem in which is held the creative genius – a superior being in terms of the ability to deliver artistic excellence. The difficulty with the acceptance and acknowledgement of this superiority is that it can become generalized to other areas – generalized in the sense used in psychology, that a response learned to one stimulus is carried over to another stimulus, for example, in Pavlovian conditioning. This is a type of conditioned learning that occurs because of the subject's instinctive responses, and was developed by the Russian physiologist Ivan Petrovich Pavlov in the 1920s. Conditioned learning can be especially powerful in areas of emotional influence among humans and serves to tilt the balance of power in relationships and to substantiate the validity of artistic temperament: the master is always right; the diva must have her way; the artistic genius may be hell to work with, but the end result (the art) is exceptional so behaviour deemed unacceptable in normal circumstances must be tolerated and, indeed, excused.

Here, then, is a new slant on the issue of permissibility (Rayner 1999): if the corporate culture in the arts is in thrall to the concept of the artistic genius, then across the various disciplines within the creative sector, the prevailing mentality may be subscribing to a set of values that allows, even directly encourages, behaviour, or terms and conditions, that are abusive, in the name of the pursuit of creative excellence. This mindset has the capacity for a profoundly negative effect in performing arts organizations, allowing employees to be subjected to exploitative terms and conditions, and/or permitting managers and other staff to ignore bullying behaviour, as long as 'the show goes on', as it surely must. Attitudes in this vein are likely, therefore, to be a significant contributory factor to the high incidence of bullying behaviour in the performing arts. For arts managers to subscribe implicitly to the argument that the arts are different as a way of excusing bullying, both personal and corporate, is to undermine the integrity of the arts workplace and to perpetrate an injustice against its workers. In effect, this equates to sanctioning any sort of abusive behaviour, including the negative aspects of what we term artistic temperament, on the grounds that the end (great art) justifies the means.

So, do we in the arts cultivate bullies? Given some of the famous artists available to us as role models, it is not unnatural that we may have come to expect, or at least become used to, bullying behaviour from individuals deemed to be creative people. The relationships between creative artists and those who work with them, both one-to-one and within a team, can be complex and are often emotionally stirring, as the evidence from practitioners and the case studies indicates – for example, The Ensemble (Chapter 6), The Creative Industry (Chapter 5) and the reports from artistic directors and contributors. Beyond the histrionic outbursts that familiarly characterize the detrimental traits of artistic temperament, as exhibited by the founders of The Contemporary Dance Studios (Chapter 3), have we further developed a tendency to extend the excuse that the arts are different to everyone involved in any aspect of the production of artistic work? Can we make a convincing, and honest, argument that the arts environment is so special that the tenets of basic civilized behaviour simply do not apply?

Surely, there is no valid reason why arts workers, no matter in what role, should have to put up with insulting, belittling and demeaning behaviour from colleagues and/or unfair workplace terms and conditions. It is unacceptable to assume that they must do so in order to serve the core purpose of their arts organization and to assure its success. The contributions from Click Wheel and Chrysalis Arts, and doubtless the experiences of many other similar arts organizations that have weathered the years, demonstrate that it is possible to subscribe to a valid, shared artistic vision without giving up fundamental human rights to live and work in a safe, healthy environment – one that respects the dignity and well-being of the individual, just as much as their personal physical safety. There is no justification for creative to become coercive. Indeed, the capacity for coercion may be the converse of the capacity for true creativity. Here is a contribution from a respondent to the national survey:

In my previous job [in the arts] I had a manager who was guilty of all the sorts of [bullying] behaviour listed … and as his PA I had to suffer most of it.

Although I liked him – in his better moods – and believed in what he and his company were doing, I was forced to leave the job after two years, mainly due to being treated like this. I now work as an arts officer within a large NHS Trust which has a written policy to protect its employees from harassment by other staff, visitors and patients – it covers all the above [types of bullying behaviour] as far as I know – and I am confident that any bullying behaviour would be dealt with – but I haven't had any problems like that here.

The attitude at the small company where I used to work was 'if you can't stand the heat, get out of the kitchen'. So I did! My boss always claimed that there were many much more difficult people than him out in the 'real world'. If this is true I have yet to meet any of them, and I work for the NHS! I think there is a big problem in the small- and medium-sized arts companies as regards treating staff properly.

In this case, the 'big problem' of bullying behaviour in the arts has caused an employee to leave her job to work in another employment sector, although she is still involved in the promotion of the arts. This is not likely to be a lone incident, given the levels of stress and illness, absenteeism and high staff turnover recorded by targets of bullying behaviour elsewhere (for example, Turney 2003: 2) and among the respondents in the pilot study and in the arts case studies. The boss in the above arts worker's story labelled non-cultural sectors as 'the real world' – once again the arts are singled out as different or set apart. This individual admitted that he could be viewed as difficult, although how this is construed from his own viewpoint is not explicit, but this pales into insignificance alongside his opinion of the number of difficult people working outside the arts.

If we tolerate artists and creative people who behave badly because we regard them as superior due to their skill and talent, do we transpose this to others who work in the arts? For example, do we excuse abusive behaviour in those who are bosses, considering them to be representative of 'strong' management, whilst simultaneously condemning similar behaviour in those deemed to be underlings? Certainly, the latter would be in line with management's patent indifference to low-status complaints, as cited by so many arts workers.

The importance of status is reflected in The Art Gallery (Chapter 1), The Museum (Chapter 3) and The Arts Service (Chapter 4), where the bullies were all in positions of authority compared to their targets, and where the targets were either not believed or fobbed off with petty bureaucracy. In The Ensemble (Chapter 6) the bully manipulated himself into a position of increased power. In The Theatre Project (Chapter 5) she insidiously weakened the target's positive working relationship with his long-term colleague, ensuring her personal ascendancy and diminishing his power.

THE PLAYWRIGHT: THE DIVA IS ALWAYS RIGHT

A talented writer won a commission to create a new piece of performance art for a small, thriving theatre company – one whose creative team had been lauded for its collective talent and outstanding achievements. The new work was to be partially scripted: in each performance the creative team would then improvise additional dialogue and stage business, so that the performance changed every time it was performed. The company's Artistic Director was thrilled to be able to employ such a skilful artist, and entered into the contract with enthusiasm.

The performance piece was to be devised with the actors through a series of rehearsals. As these progressed, privately the cast and the production crew expressed to the Artistic Director the collective opinion that the writer was bullying and intimidating – she was frequently difficult and confrontational, taking upon herself a role that was highly directive and often autocratic. There were many tense and hostile moments during rehearsals, and several of the performers became upset on more than one occasion. The writer was manipulative and only one actor spoke up about her behaviour, which outraged her; the others were too frightened to comment. The writer frequently lost her temper with the production crew, complaining particularly about costumes and lighting and implying that the work of the crew members in technical areas was substandard. She also developed the habit of taking aside individuals to 'talk to them' about their performances. On every occasion she did this, the performers were extremely distressed afterwards and the Artistic Director had to work very hard to comfort them and to convince them to persevere with the project. It emerged that the writer's disrespect for the creative team and her scornful abuse of them was not confined to the rehearsal studio.

As the writer's behaviour continued to deteriorate, eventually the Artistic Director contacted the company's Board:

'There have been some difficulties dealing with the writer and on a couple of occasions I have been upset by her manner with members of staff and with me. This has been ongoing, and I have been dealing with a lot of it on my own. Most of the time it has been to do with intimidation rather than actual notable events so it has been difficult to pinpoint. I have had a couple of meetings with her about the situation during which I have felt very uncomfortable. I have outlined that staff and team had at times been upset by the way they were spoken to.

This morning her landlady, whom our company has used for years, phoned me in tears and wants her to leave her digs immediately as she has felt "bullied and intimated" by her during a particular conversation. The writer left saying that she would discuss "things" with the landlady later when she gets back. The landlady is so upset that she doesn't want to see her again and wants to avoid any unnecessary confrontation.

I feel that I am out of my depth here … I do not want the landlady to endure what I have had to experience and therefore have booked the writer into alternative accommodation. This obviously has cost implications for the company, which haven't been budgeted for.'

In one particular response to the Artistic Director, a Board member said:

'You can imagine my sadness in reading your email. The landlady has been on our digs list for many years and, I think I'm right in saying, there has never been one ounce of trouble on either her or our artists' side. If anything, she can be too kind and considerate and I am struggling to imagine a situation where anyone could find cause to upset her.

I am all too well aware there will be cost implications as, I am assuming, the company would still have to honour, at least in part, their financial commitment to the landlady. There is quite a large part of me that thinks that if the writer has been deliberately intimidatory that any overspend on the rehearsal digs should come from her in person. Tricky to prove, and, potentially, a very incendiary discussion to boot. I agree with the other Board members in that we need to approach this in a positive manner so that things don't escalate any further, resulting in a loss of artistic integrity and performance but, at the same time, we cannot stand by and allow staff, freelancers, landladies et al to be bullied and intimidated.'

The Board members consulted and confirmed that the writer's contract, like all the company contracts, contained a clause dealing with bullying and intimidation. The core of the work was complete and ready for the production process, so at this point the writer's contract had come to an end. Everyone breathed a sigh of relief.

As planned, the Artistic Director took up the task of rehearsing and directing the performers, preparing them for the different physical features and limitations they would meet in each of the varied venues for the tour. However, unexpectedly, the writer began to appear at rehearsals, frequently interrupting the Artistic Director and shouting her own set of instructions to the cast. Some of these stipulations directly countermanded those of the Artistic Director, who had researched the venues as part of the preparatory work and knew them well.

When the tour got under way, the writer again arrived at venues during pre-performance rehearsals and get-ins, issuing instructions about presentation, lighting, design and other aspects of the performance, often contrary to the Artistic Director's decisions. When asked not to do this, she reacted angrily, saying that she was involving herself 'in the interests of the performers and the piece'. Everyone (and no one could avoid listening) heard that she had an exceptionally special talent, being an experienced and mature creative artist – whilst they observed that she behaved in a petulant and immature fashion.

Copious emails and letters from the writer to the Board followed – sometimes up to eight pages long – containing accusations against the Artistic Director and details about why the writer was the best (and only) person to 'look after' the work. The Board found that it had no choice but formally to ask her to withdraw and not to attend before, during or after any performances due to the accompanying destructive impact her presence had on the performers and the production crew, and the negative results that inevitably ensued. It was necessary to make clear that this would be construed as hostile to the creative team, the Artistic Director and the organization as a whole, and that appropriate action would be taken.

The writer contributed a few final words along the lines of being the subject of minor dictatorship, but she stopped interfering, and the tour was able to proceed successfully. The Artistic Director and the Board considered that, in the end, the writer's work had reflected a good grasp of the themes, but that it had in no way been remarkable, exceptional or unique.

(Names and environs have been changed to protect confidentiality.)

In this instance, the writer's behaviour soured a potentially promising creative relationship; the psychological contract – the mutual perceptions, beliefs and informal obligations between an employer and an employee – was broken. The concept of the psychological contract, first introduced in the 1960s, is defined as:

> ... the perceptions of the two parties, employee and employer, of what their mutual obligations are towards each other. (Guest and Conway 2002)

The Artistic Director expected a positive working relationship with a colleague – one whose skills she admired. It is more difficult to ascertain the writer's expectations – she held a very high opinion of her own abilities and seemed to discount the capacity of any of her colleagues. Perhaps this was because she was relatively well known and the company was small; perhaps she expected to be unanimously revered. In this case, the arrogance of the writer destroyed any chance of productive collaboration, and her negative effect on the creative team seriously undermined company morale. Beyond the employment situation, she transposed her sense of self-importance to her relationship with an innocent bystander, the landlady in the digs, who suffered accordingly.

In the national survey, the problem with the psychological contract in cultural organizations is that arts workers perceive that they are adversely affected by the lack of effective 'people management' practices on the part of employers. They do not feel employers have listened to complaints, other than with indifference; they do not perceive that complainants have been treated fairly; they do not always trust their employers. This works against employers' interests: where arts workers are positive about the psychological contract they tend to be more committed and more satisfied – which undoubtedly has an impact on their personal and collective performance. This, in turn, may have the effect of increasing productivity and, in terms of creative impact, of realizing high quality work.

The key to ensuring that arts employees have a positive attitude to the psychological contract is good communication:

> ... and specifically of dialogue in which managers are prepared to listen to employees' opinions ... employee commitment and 'buy-in' come primarily not from telling but from listening. (Chartered Institute of Personnel and Development 2010)

If an example were required of how needlessly aggravating artistic temperament can be, then we have it here. No matter how talented the writer was, her behaviour cannot be vindicated. She appears to have a vastly inflated opinion of herself, so much so that she intimidated the Artistic Director, the creative team and even the hapless landlady in her digs: this is not behaviour of which anyone working in, and committed to, the arts, could claim to be proud.

CHAPTER **10** *Beating Bullying*

Research Summary

The original research carried out in a range of arts organizations in the UK included employees at every level within both commercial and subsidized performing arts organizations in England, Scotland and Northern Ireland. It demonstrates that bullying in UK performing arts organizations is common and increasing in frequency, and that bullying is damaging, oppressive and unacceptable. Clear evidence is presented of the failure of management to satisfactorily address bullying: some arts workers tolerate intimidating behaviour by powerful managers because they believe in, and are committed to, the arts.

Among managers, the notion of the arts as vocation persists. The widespread perception is that by choosing to work in an arts organization, rather than an office, factory or shop, for example, employees are outside the rules and limitations of the ordinary milieu – the arts are different and therefore exempt from normal rules and regulations. However, the research found that many aspects of working in the performing arts are not peculiar to the profession; they occur in other employment sectors and are more likely to be characteristic of the times in which we live, than specific to the sector in which we work. In assessing workplace stressors, it is the response of the organization, in coexistence with the individual response, which determines negative stress levels.

At the outset of the research into workplace bullying in the arts, the fundamental guiding question was whether the behaviour represented isolated, rare occurrences in specific creative environments or whether, as was suspected, it was indicative of a more widespread problem in the cultural sector. Initially, many arts managers intentionally or unintentionally disregarded the phenomenon, at the same time as other arts employees revealed that bullying in arts organizations was widespread and was being ignored by management. Eight individual case studies illuminate bullying by arts workers, arts managers, board members of arts organizations and a local authority department. Subsequently, in a major national survey, Broadcasting, Entertainment, Cinematograph and Theatre Union (BECTU) employees in Scotland, Northern Ireland and England, from theatres and arts centres of all sizes and scales, reported bullying behaviour as occurring 'commonly' or 'not uncommonly', including 62.9 per cent of participating arts managers. These employees, including managers, clearly perceive that their working terms and conditions are often unfair and stressful, and believe this to be unnecessarily so, and thus equivalent to organizational or corporate bullying. Anecdotal evidence from a wide variety of contributors has confirmed initial suspicions: bullying is ubiquitous in arts workplaces.

The Mythology of Creativity

Arts managers claim that the experience of working in arts environments with creative people is different from working elsewhere, and use this to explain the requirement for workplace terms and conditions that differ from the norm. Patently, however, as we have learned from the investigations carried out by neuroscientists, creativity is a function of the human brain, and therefore we must recognize that it is not the sole preserve of the cultural sector. Teresa Amabile is the Edsel Bryant Ford Professor of Business Administration in the Entrepreneurial Management Unit at Harvard Business School. She is also a Director of Research at the School, and has devoted her entire research programme to the study of creativity. Professor Amabile is one of the foremost explorers of business innovation in the USA, and she says:

> … almost all of the research in this field shows that anyone with normal intelligence is capable of doing some degree of creative work. Creativity depends on a number of things: experience, including knowledge and technical skills; talent; an ability to think in new ways; and the capacity to push through uncreative dry spells. Intrinsic motivation – people who are turned on by their work often work creatively – is especially critical. Over the past five years, organizations have paid more attention to creativity and innovation than at any other time … (Amabile 2004: 1)

In particular, it is interesting that Amabile identifies the ability to think in new ways as conducive to creativity, which correlates with the findings of the neuroscientists, and also that she touches upon 'dry spells' – analogous with writer's block. Given the neurological evidence to date, we could characterize these as periods when no new environments are available to the creator – so that familiarity breeds a paucity of ideas; or, 'same old, same old' prevails and prevents creativity. Amabile proposes six myths about creativity in the commercial world, and it is interesting to consider these in the context of the cultural sector, not least because they allow us to compare and contrast commercial and cultural values – ultimately supporting the argument that the arts are not so very different after all:

MYTH 1. CREATIVITY COMES FROM CREATIVE TYPES

Amabile reports that business managers lovingly cherish this belief, identifying advertising, marketing and research and development people as 'creatives' and, for example, accountants as not creative. However, perhaps we in the arts hold similar views – our performers, set designers and make-up artists may be considered creative, but do we consider the box office staff, the technicians and the clerical workers as being creative too? Do arts organizations treat differently those perceived as being less creative and, therefore, less important? The main complainant in The Arts Service (Chapter 4) was a junior employee – was she discouraged and rebuffed because she was *not* a manager?

MYTH 2. MONEY IS A CREATIVITY MOTIVATOR

Business people want to feel they are being compensated fairly; however, Amabile finds that they:

put far more value on a work environment where creativity is supported, valued, and recognized. People want the opportunity to deeply engage in their work and make real progress. (Amabile 2004: 1)

Many arts people regard their counterparts in commercial organizations as solely financially motivated; however, it seems that employees everywhere have similar goals ultimately: those working in commercial organizations actually care about what they do and, conversely, arts people too want fair pay and reasonable hours of work. It is possible to conclude that most people, given the option, would express the opinion that they want a supportive work environment.

MYTH 3. TIME PRESSURE FUELS CREATIVITY

Amabile records that business people often thought they were most creative when they were working under severe deadline pressure:

But the 12,000 aggregate days that we studied showed just the opposite: People were the least creative when they were fighting the clock. In fact, we found a kind of time-pressure hangover – when people were working under great pressure, their creativity went down not only on that day but the next two days as well. Time pressure stifles creativity because people can't deeply engage with the problem. Creativity requires an incubation period; people need time to soak in a problem and let the ideas bubble up. (Amabile 2004: 2)

This is familiar territory: it represents the Eureka! moment – the point at which a stray idea results in what we may call inspiration. Of course, the findings related to the 'time-pressure hangover' have implications for the longer hours of work reported in the arts, particularly where organizations are required to meet first-night and other deadlines, as it suggests that failing to ensure time off in lieu (TOIL) is taken will, in fact, have a detrimental effect on the arts workforce as a whole. There are lessons here, too, for how arts projects are planned and implemented; rather than deadlines themselves, it is the way in which deadlines are constructed (the timetables to meet them) that can have a negative effect on strategic management: this should teach us to work smarter, not harder.

MYTH 4. FEAR FORCES BREAKTHROUGHS

This myth is close to McGregor's Theory X, and Amabile's business research found that creativity:

is positively associated with joy and love and negatively associated with anger, fear, and anxiety. (Amabile 2004: 2)

This does not support the psychological literature linking creative genius with depression and other mental health issues, as examined in Chapter 9; however, the business research was correlating evidence of creativity contemporaneous with overt signs of happiness/unhappiness. Happiness briefly became a topical theme in the UK in May 2006 because of remarks made by the then Leader of the Opposition, David Cameron, at the Google

Zeitgeist Europe Conference, in which he insisted that there was more to life than making money, and that improving people's happiness was a key challenge for politicians. Amabile's research found that business people were more likely to come up with an innovative idea if they had been happy 'the day before'. In the arts, we also experience this 'virtuous cycle', and anecdotal evidence suggests that being enthused and excited about work improves our chances of making:

> a cognitive association that incubates overnight and shows up as a creative idea the next day … One day's happiness often predicts the next day's creativity. (Amabile 2004: 2)

Arts workers who are unhappy because they are bullied, especially where this is taking place over a prolonged period of time, are not likely to sustain either creativity or effectiveness.

MYTH 5. COMPETITION BEATS COLLABORATION

In finance and high-tech industries Amabile found that internal competition destroys innovation, and that when people compete for recognition they stop sharing information. The most creative teams are the ones that are confident enough to share and debate ideas. In this respect there has been a sea change since the Final Report of the Task Force set up by the Clore Leadership Programme in December 2002: we know that collaboration now forms part of the pattern for creativity in both arts and non-arts environments. This is also evident in the arts case studies – The Ensemble (Chapter 6), The Museum (Chapter 3), The Theatre Project (Chapter 5), The Playwright (Chapter 9) – and we have seen that where personal status is an issue, teamwork declines and bullying results. In terms of cultural leadership programmes, the principles of engagement have overtaken those of strong directorial management, and this is a positive and a welcome change. We have seen that leadership affects how bullying is handled, and the greater extent to which cultural sector leaders are engaged with their colleagues and employees, the less likely it is that bullying behaviour will go undetected in arts organizations.

MYTH 6. A STREAMLINED ORGANIZATION IS A CREATIVE ORGANIZATION

Amabile finds that creativity suffers greatly during restructuring and downsizing, and the arts case studies support this, particularly The Arts Service (Chapter 4). The following was written about Amabile's research in a 6,000-person division of a global electronics company during the entire course of a 25 per cent downsizing, which took an incredibly agonizing 18 months. It could have been written about The Arts Service case study (Chapter 4) instead:

> Every single one of the stimulants to creativity in the work environment went down significantly. Anticipation of the downsizing was even worse than the downsizing itself – people's fear of the unknown led them to basically disengage from the work. (Amabile 2004: 2)

Comparative Working Environments

There is insufficient evidence to sustain the claim that the arts are different on the basis implied by the arts managers in the pilot study – that is, that they are sufficiently unique in all that they do, so that normal rules and procedures do not apply. Whilst it is true that many arts workers believe that they are among the hardest-pressed employees in any sector, and that they are often deprived of employment rights that apply elsewhere, it is the author's belief that arts managers did not intend to endorse this – simply, they believed that different employment conditions within the performing arts come with the territory. Outside of negotiations with trades unions – where these have a presence in arts workplaces – alternative ways of working to resolve issues about terms and conditions appeared not to have been considered.

The percentage of respondents from theatres and arts centres who reported that they had been targets of bullying behaviour was higher than that previously recorded in any other single employment sector in the UK and, in this sense, the arts may be considered to be different – currently they are the market leaders in workplace bullying in the UK. This is not to deny the qualities and attributes of creative people and arts environments, as expressed, for example, by practitioners – it is necessary, simply, to state that there is no rationale for treating arts employees less well or less fairly than employees in any other sector.

The descriptors for bullying in the performing arts are the same as for other employment sectors; the definitions of mobbing, harassment and bullying are relevant to the arts experience and corporate bullying is a recognizable feature. The nature and circumstances of the behaviour in, for example, the health service and education, is replicated in arts organizations and has similar effects on individuals and organizations. The psychological profile of the arts bully, as far as this can be determined from the case studies and the reports of website respondents, is the same as other fields (for example, Einarsen et al. 2003: 168–73).

The combined methodology for the research incorporated quantitative and qualitative analysis, and enabled the recording of perceptions as well as the collection of empirical evidence. The investigative procedures sought to ensure that the approach was objective and fair to all participants, including guaranteeing complete anonymity to contributors. Arts workplaces share many of the characteristics of other professions; whether or not a nominal hierarchical structure exists – and in some format this is usually the case – there are both formal and informal interrelationships and communications constructs.

Arts bullies are found at every level and there is no significant variation from other professions in terms of reasons for bullying, with status/position, competence and popularity emerging as principal causes, as opposed to gender, age, disability, length of service, area of work, type of post, or geographical location. In the arts more women than men reported experiences of being bullied and said that it was increasing in frequency. In considering factors in the performing arts environment that might contribute to corporate bullying behaviour, such as hours of work and rates of pay, it was evident that dissatisfaction levels were high. More than half of the survey participants (52.6 per cent) said taking time off was either not possible due to workload or not encouraged. The same percentage was maintained among the bullied group (52.5 per cent), significant because in this instance, bullied people were *not* reporting negative behaviour more than non-bullied people (Rayner 1999). Given what Amabile has said about the 'time-pressure hangover', this inability to adequately recuperate following longer working hours has the potential to be disastrous for arts workers and arts organizations alike in terms of individual and organizational creativity, and also in terms of workplace health and safety.

The research sought to determine if the arts working environment is particularly conducive to the encouragement and tolerance of bullying behaviour. Previous studies of workplace bullying have taken place in non-arts environments and indicate that a number of constituents can be held to contribute towards circumstances in which bullying is likely to occur. Undoubtedly, in the cultural sector, for example, emotional responses play a part – practitioners comment freely on their perceptions of the emotional investment required when working in the arts. Hoel, Faragher and Cooper (2004) note the negative effects on witnesses to bullying and Lewis (2004) records feelings of shame and embarrassment experienced by targets of bullying in other, non-arts workplaces.

There is a requirement for team working in arts organizations or a 'high demand for co-operation', identified as an ingredient in the environment in which bullying occurs by Matthiesen and Einarsen (2001). Although arts organizations are not associated necessarily with command and control structures (as in, for example, prisons, armed forces, police forces), we have seen that power imbalance is a contributory factor in all the arts case studies: the arts perpetrator moves into a position of manipulating and dominating the arts target. Lewis (1999) identifies funding pressures as a feature of the bullying environment – an undeniable aspect of the arts, evinced by practitioners' experience of burdensome bureaucracy as an outcome of arts managerialism. The case studies provide examples of the existence in the arts of management as politics (Watson 1986; Bratton and Gold 1999), lack of constructive leadership (Rayner 1999) and conflicting goals and priorities (Einarsen, Raknes and Matthiesen 1994).

If these characteristics are supplemented by the concepts of creative genius and artistic temperament, bearing in mind the phenomenon of Founder's Syndrome as discussed in Chapter 3, the inevitable conclusion is that the arts workplace has all the hallmarks of a bully-friendly environment, and that bullying behaviour is likely to grow and to flourish where managements in arts organizations pursue a policy characterized by acquiescence and inertia.

Corporate Bullying

The research in performing arts organizations clearly identified a perception on the part of employees in theatres and arts centres that their working terms and conditions were often unfair and stressful, and unnecessarily so, and thus tantamount to organizational or corporate bullying. In the pilot study there was a perception among arts managers that terms and conditions are unavoidable because of the nature of the work in the sector. Yet the routes to prevent and/or to resolve bullying, as outlined by Hoel and Cooper, include reducing bullying by reducing stress levels:

> *Bullying is associated with a negative work-climate, high workload and unsatisfactory relationships. This suggests that organizations may be able to go some way towards resolving or at least minimizing the problem of bullying by reducing and controlling stress at work. (It follows that any risk-assessment strategy focusing on psychosocial work-hazards should include bullying and victimisation). (Hoel and Cooper 2000)*

Management appears to be failing to accept responsibility for institutional bullying, despite the work of the trades unions and other agencies in raising the profile of the issue. The excerpt below, for example, focuses on the difficulties experienced by a part-time fine arts lecturer, who felt that their terms and conditions were abusive:

> *The organizational strategy of the organization I worked for was bullying in that it used peoples' fear of losing their jobs and kept lecturers on one-day contracts. Part-time lecturers were given no staff meetings or professional support, had no formal process for finding out important information about students. We had no personal development opportunities or personal supervision. I left the college because my self-esteem was suffering. I am a good lecturer and contributed to the running of the fine art part of the foundation course at my local college for several years as one of a team of four (I never had a proper contract). (Respondent to pilot study)*

It is clear that a high level of job insecurity created a climate of fear among employees in this place of employment. Researchers have urged organizations to establish 'a culture free of bullying' (Hoel and Cooper 2000) and this is pertinent, especially, to performing arts organizations in the context of their creative genius/artistic temperament environment. The issue of permissibility has a particular, statistically significant, resonance and there is an onus on performing arts management to examine objectively the standard organizational *modus operandi*, which can directly or indirectly endorse the existence of bullying as routine.

Managing the Chaos

Increasingly, arts managers are acknowledging the existence of the bullying problem and there is a need for those agencies working with them also to recognize, confront and challenge aggressive and abusive management styles. The predictable and familiar breeding ground for bullying behaviour – management by command and control – does not sit comfortably alongside the image of an empathetic and caring system of governance in the arts which is frequently cited by managers. In a hierarchical management framework pressure imposed from above exhorts managers to exert pressure on those below; therefore governing bodies are also in the frame. We have seen that external, as well as internal, forces can cause pressure, and it is highly likely that the creeping influence of managerialism in the arts – the target culture – is playing a major part in creating burdensome bureaucracy.

In the UK it seems that all of the key professional agencies are conscious of bullying behaviour, and certainly some of them have received complaints from members. The ITC encourages well-being in performing arts companies and is aware that representatives of its member companies are keen that the subject of bullying should be explored. There is an appreciation that this is an issue for the cultural sector and that practical solutions are needed. Experienced arts manager Roger Lang briefly began to examine the issue two years ago on behalf of the ITC and recognizes that some employees feel pressurized and that this can cause bullying. He gave one example of a director who decided an employee who had been ill was not ready to come back to work, although she and her doctors felt that she was. There was a tussle but, happily, in his view, she prevailed. Lang felt that probably the director did not realize the kind of pressure he had exerted, which was tantamount to bullying.

Lang is also familiar with the concept of the target culture – that managers are working to meet targets set by funders, rather than to achieve the core purpose of their work. Many of Lang's observations smack of the burdensome bureaucracy described by the Artistic Director (Theatre) in Chapter 8. For example, some funders use monitoring forms that are complex to complete, demanding details that are irrelevant to arts organizations and data that is extremely difficult to collect and then to collate. Fundamentally, there seems to be a lack of understanding of the function of the arts, and arts organizations, in some quarters.

Bullying by individuals was more common, in Lang's view, than corporate bullying, although he has heard of instances in commercial arts organizations, principally due to attempts to make changes by people who are unfamiliar with the cultural sector in the UK. Lang's understanding of the competence issue is clear: in his experience many incompetent managers bully – 'somehow they just seem to need a whipping boy or girl' (personal email to the author). As a manager who has dealt with people who have set up their own arts organizations, Lang is also very familiar with Founder's Syndrome and has seen that some founders have a real problem 'letting go of the baby', or putting in place succession strategies; they find it difficult to delegate and difficult to manage change; they externalize – 'when things go wrong it's always somebody else's fault' (personal email to the author).

Although the Protection from Harassment Act (1997) has been used to deal with instances of bullying, and the Equality Act 2010 covers some, but not all, types of harassment, Lang is conscious that there is 'no specific law against bullying' (personal email to the author). He says we have adopted the word from the playground, and describes having witnessed fifty-year-old people in the boardroom 'acting like badly behaved teenagers' (personal email to the author). The Artistic Director (Theatre) described some people working in theatre as 'highly functional', whilst others are 'grossly under-functional'. Lang has also seen this function/dysfunction in the theatre – and believes it can lie at the heart of bullying. In his experience some successful people seem to be able to manage dysfunction and, ironically, often, very good work can come out of dysfunction. Directors, in particular, who are effective and succeed seem to learn how to work through difficulties and tensions so that nothing ever impacts on them sufficiently to divert them from their goal.

So, how is the element of dysfunction related to cultural leadership? In the larger arts organizations, Lang feels that top-level posts often do not allow for diversion – there is too much at stake. As implied in the contribution from the founder and partner in the Touring Theatre Company in Chapter 8, perhaps some aspects of cultural leadership are about successfully managing chaos. There are a number of ways in which this can be undertaken. Some theatre companies take a democratic approach. Lang cites an example of a theatre company in which each new production begins with the director assembling the team so that everyone has their say about how they want the production to go – they all feel involved in the decision-making and have a sense of ownership of the process. This same director still manages to get the end result he wanted all along.

It seems that it is possible to achieve a good result in the performing arts by managing the chaos without resorting to oppressive tactics: McGregor's Theory Y, then, rather than Theory X. Also, it must be hoped that the upsurge in the promotion of quality education and training in cultural leadership, which has burgeoned in the UK recently, will result in the development of more constructive leadership and management in the arts.

Managing Change

As the media continues to report that old-fashioned and incompetent management styles are failing the performing arts (for example, Higgins 2005), increasingly there is an emphasis on cooperative management styles and disdain for hard-line management techniques. So, we should be thankful that strong management has given way to engagement. Notwithstanding the image of 'successful' (that is, profit-making) management as aggressive and macho, as portrayed in television series such as The Apprentice (a series in which a number of competitive business-oriented events are staged to eliminate inept candidates, thus ultimately identifying a suitable 'apprentice' to a successful tycoon – NBC (USA) featuring Donald Trump and BBC (UK) featuring Sir Alan Sugar, it is increasingly likely that companies that refuse to change obsolete operating strategies will not survive in the rapidly changing world of work, and particularly in a difficult economic climate. This is true of creative organizations as much as any others.

Sally Bibb, Director of Group Sales Development for The Economist Group and author of several books about management issues, claims that the business hierarchy that seeks to monitor and control workers' methods and output is outmoded and must be changed, even at the risk of hurting those who have always benefited from hierarchical arrangements: the executives and managers (Bibb 2005). Like Bibb, McKeown and Whiteley (2002) assert that current management techniques, based on the myth that organizations are machines, stifle the ability of people and organizations to grow. They make a strong case that companies must re-envision themselves, or 'unshrink' their thinking, in order to survive and to thrive in tomorrow's business landscape.

This makes sense for the performing arts. In Watson's (1986) human resources management model, he proposed that managing people can be viewed as: an art – successful managers are born with appropriate traits; or as a science – successful managers have acquired appropriate knowledge or skills; or as politics – successful managers have worked out the unwritten laws of life in the organization; or as control – successful managers can exploit and control workers (as reported in Bratton and Gold 1999).

Salin (2003) found a clear relationship between bullying and organizational politics, and it seems an appropriate time to denounce 'management as control' as an unacceptable option: not only are controlling styles unjust and unethical but, as with organizational politics, according to many research findings they are also linked to negative organizational outcomes (Field 1996; Clifton and Serdar 2000; Hoel and Cooper 2000). In this context, performing arts organizations have an important choice to make: they can continue some of the current negative operating strategies until they are forced to make a change, as inevitably will be the case, or they can take the opportunity to revisit their roots as cooperative teams and opt for styles of management based on recognizing personal and professional qualities, such as integrity and respect for the needs both of the individual and of the company as a whole, thus embracing a transformational leadership style. This offers the added chance to rotate the kaleidoscope of creative genius and to acknowledge creativity inherent in every member of an arts organization, irrespective of designation or role.

The Role of Trades Unions and the Law

High-profile cases in the media undoubtedly serve to raise awareness generally about bullying behaviour; for example, that of UK TV presenter Esther Rantzen who admitted, in the national press in 2006, that she had previously bullied junior employees. In the UK, former Prime Minister Gordon Brown found himself in the midst of controversy as claims about his behaviour hit the headlines in February 2010. One of the UK's increasing number of anti-bullying organizations, the National Bullying Helpline, disclosed that complaints of bullying had been made by staff at 10 Downing Street, the Prime Minister's Office. This disclosure dismayed many other anti-bullying campaigners who publish information, use help lines and manage websites dedicated to dealing with the behaviour. Clearly, there is a growing public consciousness of adult bullying and its detrimental effects.

Trustees of The National Bullying Helpline Charity decided with regret at a meeting held on January 4, 2011, to discontinue the helpline service with immediate effect and take steps to close the Charity down. ... This last year, calls to our helpline have trebled and we have had to take on additional Volunteers and resources to meet demand. Without doubt, this demonstrates that a free anti-bullying helpline is a much needed and much valued life-line for the general public – adults and children alike. (National Bullying Helpline 2011)

In the UK, trades unions have played a significant part in raising the bullying issue and in researching strategies to address it. The most active have been the Manufacturing, Science and Finance Sector Union (MSF), which launched The Campaign against Bullying at Work with a conference (May 1994), and UNISON, which conducted a survey in 1997 and has commissioned reports and studies (for example, Rayner 1999) and a campaign in 1996 to change UK law (Dignity at Work Bill). In 1995 a survey showed that bullying was prevalent in the finance, health, sales professionals and voluntary sectors, and other umbrella bodies for trades unions, such as the TUC, have addressed the issue and created good-practice guidelines via factsheets and guides, which include bullying as a hazard in the workplace.

BECTU is an independent trades union for those working in broadcasting, film, theatre, entertainment, leisure, interactive media and allied areas. It represents arts workers, including contract and freelance workers, who are based primarily in the United Kingdom. BECTU offers a wide range of services to its more than 26,500 members, including:

- negotiations on pay, conditions and contracts with employers;
- personal advice and representation for individual members;
- advice and representation on health and safety;
- a range of benefits and services for members;
- a union journal, *Stage Screen and Radio*, published eight times a year;
- a website designed to improve access to the union's advice and support.

BECTU agreed to undertake the original research in the performing arts in partnership with the Department of Cultural Affairs, Policy and Management at the City University, and reported news of a further study to examine the extent of workplace bullying among people working in broadcasting media, to be undertaken by the University of Ulster. BECTU also asked the Society of London Theatre (SOLT), on behalf of members in the capital's West End, for a revision of the equal opportunities, harassment and bullying, and health and safety policies. It has created a series of education and training programmes for union representatives:

- One-day induction for new BECTU Reps;
- Branch Reps part 1 - 'How to Represent your Members' includes information on bullying and harassment;
- Safety Reps part 2 - includes a module on stress as a workplace hazard.

Training Officer Brian Kelly believes there is a demand for a short practical workshop about how to tackle bullying through grievance procedures, and another on identifying and tackling stress, and hopes to introduce these as one-day courses later in 2011.

Further, BECTU has worked on policy development and on ensuring that it has better complaints procedures to deal with bullying. In March 2006, the union supported a half-day seminar, Work to the Bone, organized by The Institute of Employment Rights, about regulating the UK's long-hours working culture. On behalf of its members, BECTU already negotiates with employers on terms and conditions, including hours of work and rates of pay.

Other bodies, such as the TUC, also take action on bullying behaviour in order to raise awareness and provide advice, information and training. Respondents (all of whom were members of BECTU) to the national survey were asked if there was also a function for BECTU in addressing bullying behaviour in the workplace, and 84.3 per cent of the members approved of the idea that the union should have a role. Just as agreements have been reached on pay and working hours, strong lobbying by Trades Unions might encourage more employers to introduce written policies promoting dignity at work, and 83.5 per cent of those who responded to the national survey were in favour of this. Respondents also wanted BECTU to represent employees who make complaints about bullying behaviour, both formally and informally, and to provide information, advice and assistance on the subject to all members (82.1 per cent).

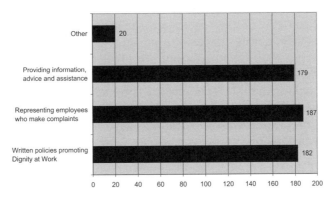

Values are citations based on 218 observations (31 non-respondents)

Figure 10.1   How BECTU can help to stamp out bullying behaviour

The number of citations is greater than the number of observations due to multiple answers, each respondent being able to give a maximum of 4.

Among comments from the bullied group, there was a call for BECTU to raise awareness of the subtle and degrading nature of bullying and to provide training for stewards to enable them to set an example in the workplace – which some at present do not. The fact that some do not was reflected in the text comments that identified some trades union representatives as bullies, an important fact for BECTU to recognize if it and other trades unions plan to position themselves to provide constructive leadership on this issue. The suggestions from non-bullied respondents included encouraging employees to approach management in confidence, and also focused on BECTU giving advice and assistance to members *only*. The former suggestion came, unsurprisingly, from a manager – perhaps keen to ensure that a joint employer-union partnership approach results in future action on the prevention of workplace bullying behaviour. The assertion that advice and assistance should be given to BECTU members only, reflects a wider concern about union activities generally, which was expressed by some respondents who appear to resent non-union members benefiting from legitimate union members' hard work and successes.

Professional Institutes

THE THEATRICAL MANAGEMENT ASSOCIATION

The Theatrical Management Association (TMA) is the principal UK-wide organization dedicated to providing professional support for the performing arts. Its members include repertory and producing theatres, arts centres and touring venues, major national companies and independent producers, opera and dance companies and associated businesses. The TMA has a number of training courses on offer and although none of these are specifically about bullying in the workplace, the TMA does hold a number of courses throughout the year on subjects such as managing conflicts at work, working with creative people, managing conflicts with customers and strategic marketing. Training events scheduled for 2011 include Effective Management – Walking the Tightrope, Negotiation Skills, and Managing Third Parties.

The TMA and BECTU have produced an agreement that includes a statement of their joint opposition to abusive behaviour (paragraph 1.16: Harassment, Bullying and Victimisation). In April 2003, a clause dealing with bullying and harassment appeared in two collective agreements issued by the Theatrical Management Association – one with Equity, the actors' union, and the other with the commercial theatres sector (TMA/Equity Subsidized Repertory Collective Agreement, 2003: section 3j, items 4 and 10 respectively).

In April 2004, the TMA produced a Legal Update, for circulation among members, which included the following:

Guidance on Bullying and Harassment

ACAS has updated its guidance on bullying and harassment at work. It provides two separate guides, one for employees and one for managers and employers. The guides can be found on the

ACAS [Advisory, Conciliation and Arbitration Service] website at www.acas.org.uk or ordered from 0870 242 9090. (Guidance on Bullying and Harassment: TMA Legal Update 2004)

THE ADVISORY, CONCILIATION AND ARBITRATION SERVICE

The Advisory, Conciliation and Arbitration Service (ACAS) helps with employment relations by supplying up to date information, independent advice and high-quality training, working with employers and employees to solve problems and improve performance. In 2011, ACAS is using advice leaflets, e-learning packages and regional training sessions to encourage employers to tackle workplace bullying.

In May 2006, ACAS had 34 items on its website which were overtly bullying-related, including guidance for employers and employees, action plans to counter bullying behaviour, legal advice, information on work-related stress and on Ban Bullying at Work day (formerly, annually in the UK in November). By 2011, the number of items has grown to 316 – an increase of more than 900 per cent. ACAS has also introduced a free-to-register e-learning course on bullying and harassment, and a range of training courses available at regional level.

THE MUSICIANS' UNION

In the UK, The Musicians' Union (MU), which represents over 30,000 musicians, has received several complaints of bullying over the years, particularly from orchestral musicians. The MU's Safety & Learning Official in the Live Engagements Department in 2010, Pauline Dalby, states:

> *Unfortunately, quite a few of complaints of bullying involve the Conductor, but there are also complaints from other individual musicians who, at one time or another, have experienced bullying from their colleagues within the orchestra. These situations have been dealt with as and when they arise, and have resulted in the Union assisting the relevant managements in developing a Bullying/harassment policy.*
>
> *These situations are always extremely difficult to deal with as some individuals don't realize that what they are doing is being perceived as bullying, and we have to make sure that all enquiries are dealt with in the most sympathetic and confidential manner. Our safety representatives are all trained to deal with issues such as bullying in the workplace, and the MU has developed an information sheet to help safety reps and individual members deal with bullying, as they are normally the first port of call for any member who is being bullied. (Personal email to the author: 2010)*

During the last two to three years, Dalby has not, personally, had to deal with a bullying case. She believes this might be due to the fact that most orchestras now have policies in place or that the MU's safety representatives are dealing with the problems on-site. Nevertheless, she thinks that awareness-raising training would be useful to members.

EQUITY

Equity is the UK trades union representing professional performers and other creative workers from across the spectrum of the entertainment, creative and cultural industries. In spring 2004, the Lesbian, Gay, Bisexual and Transgender Committee set up a bullying hotline following anecdotal evidence that members were experiencing bullying in the workplace. In election year, 2010, Equity launched a Respect Manifesto, focusing on the state of British theatre and broadcasting, and on how artists are treated:

> It is a manifesto that proposes radical change in many areas – greater artistic leadership in decision-making on the arts, a genuine focus on local production that represents the whole community, less bureaucracy and more investment in production, secure funding and fair pay for performers. (Equity 2010)

Equity wants to achieve 'an end to low wages', which the research in theatres and arts centres identified as a problem for many arts workers alongside long hours of work, and the two are often related. 'Increased production' is also called for – in terms of live theatre as well as broadcast drama: more work for more people. In demanding 'increased artistic leadership' and 'less bureaucracy', the union's requirements correlate with the arts bullying research findings – poor leadership in the arts, particularly by those who are unfamiliar with the role and function of the sector, for example managers drafted in from non-arts organizations, is a cause of bullying behaviour identified in The Art Gallery (Chapter 1), The Creative Industry (Chapter 6) and The Arts Service (Chapter 4), and the Artistic Director (Theatre) in Chapter 8 eloquently expresses the pressures on arts workers as a result of burdensome bureaucracy.

Finally, Equity makes a plea for a return to 'local focus', noting that the UK is culturally diverse with access to a rich and varied heritage. The union would like local authorities to have a mandatory duty to fund the arts in their area, and for television production to be 'genuinely decentralised'.

> Respect for the artist means recognizing the important role Equity members play in the wider economy and demanding a fair deal. We want fair pay but we also want artists to be given greater control of their working lives with less bureaucracy, more stable funding and a greater ability to contribute to the decisions about the future of the arts. (Equity 2010)

These are ambitious aims. In 2011 the cuts imposed on local authorities are resulting in local authorities paring back expenditure to fund services in line with statutory responsibilities, cutting many valuable areas in the process, including arts provision. Far from increasing production, the BBC is cutting back on drama productions both on radio and television. However, Equity's call for change is important and, although some issues are likely to remain out of reach well into the future (for example, secure funding as a reality), much could be done to improve working terms and conditions for Equity members, if government and employers act upon the CIPD's research findings:

> … employee commitment and 'buy-in' come primarily not from telling but from listening. (Chartered Institute of Personnel and Development 2006)

The Arts Councils

The arts councils in England, Northern Ireland, Scotland and Wales have internal policies dealing with dignity at work issues, including bullying and harassment. As might be expected, as key funders in the cultural sector their formal involvement with bullying, in terms of dealing with complaints from external organizations, appears to be non-existent. Individual arts employees are more likely to seek assistance from trades unions and/or professional institutes, than from funders. Similarly, arts organizations looking for help are highly unlikely to want to reveal a problem with bullying in the workplace to their funders.

ARTS COUNCIL ENGLAND

In defining its relationship with the creative individuals and organizations it supports financially, Arts Council England (ACE) states that it is a funding partner and not a regulator: it is not in a position, therefore, to act as an intermediary in clients' disputes or to control how they conduct their business. The Council does not have the internal capacity or expertise to supervise all aspects of the activity of funded organizations. There have been, however, a number of expectations of ACE's Regularly Funded Organizations (RFOs), including expectations of relevant legal requirements, such as health and safety, and specific mention of some duties, such as around safeguarding statutes. It is of note that ACE has discontinued subsidy to organizations where regulations have not been met.

Although bullying may not be mentioned specifically in the conditions that have been attached to agreements with RFOs, we have seen that it is recognized within health and safety laws, particularly in Scandinavian countries, and in North America and Australia. Were the Scandinavian models to become EU-wide (see Chapter 7), then explicit references to bullying and/or psychological harassment would be included in safeguarding legislation in the UK, and ACE would be obligated to implement this.

Notwithstanding the non-regulatory position that ACE adopts, the Council has been involved in discussions with clients about management issues. In the collective experience of staff, disputes within arts organizations have tended to arise between two employees, or accusations have been made against senior management. This supports the incidents of both one-on-one and corporate bullying reported by arts workers in the national survey. If ACE has a concern about a particular area of senior management that has been brought to the Council's attention, often a conversation with a higher echelon would ensue. However, the Council's employees are aware that, within arts organizations, junior members of staff may not be involved with ACE at any level and so would not know whom to approach in the funding body in the event of a problem with bullying occurring.

In terms of finding ways to tackle bullying behaviour in the cultural sector, the lack of voice of arts employees is an important feature of the current arts infrastructure. Consider the employees in The Arts Service (Chapter 4), who were deflected by the local authority's HR department on the spurious grounds that their complaints were technically invalid. Consider also the voicelessness of employees who find themselves without trades union support – such as those employees featured in the case studies The Ensemble (Chapter 6) and The Art Gallery (Chapter 1); those without an understanding CEO – The Theatre

Project (Chapter 5); and those without a knowledgeable governing body – The Museum (Chapter 3).

ACE's position as a funding partner, rather than a regulatory body, means that it is required to insist that funded clients comply with regulations in which ACE has been named as having an obligation, such as those ensuring racial equality. Other people have approached ACE to make a complaint about a Council client; however, the Council intervenes only if ACE is directly involved; that is, if the complaint is concerned specifically with ACE's financial support. ACE has precise duties under the UK's racial equality legislation, and also in regard to its responsibility concerning people with disabilities, and the Council has required the RFOs it funds to abide by these duties, checking compliance on an annual basis. In 2010, the Council was reviewing whether the requirements of RFOs are as robust as they should be, and promoting a self-evaluation framework to assist the process of distinguishing between what is appropriate for larger- and smaller-scale organizations. However, the system of funding is changing. Those arts companies that have made successful applications to the new National Portfolio Funding scheme for 2012 onwards are likely to have to comply with the same or similar terms and conditions that apply to previously funded RFOs.

Dignity at work, *per se*, is not incorporated into current agreements with clients; however, ACE has stated that it would be willing to give consideration to the development of an appropriate policy and to make a statement about how it regards bullying behaviour in the arts.

ARTS COUNCIL OF NORTHERN IRELAND

The HR Officer at the Arts Council of Northern Ireland (ACNI) states:

> *As far as I know we haven't been asked to deal with any complaints of bullying from individual artists or from arts organizations/other clients … (Personal email to the author: 2010)*

Making reference to the council's own internal Dignity at Work Policy, she goes on to say:

> *In terms of our overall policy/approach, we … advise that we would encourage arts organizations/ clients to follow the same sort of guidelines as those in it, if they were to encounter bullying. (Personal email to the author: 2010)*

ACNI's Dignity at Work Policy and Procedures guidelines are enshrined in a comprehensive document, which distinguishes harassment from bullying in terms of the status of the target, rather than the extent of the psychological distress. Harassment is therefore described as being linked to aspects of social identity, such as disability, age, race, etcetera, and a familiar definition of bullying is used, indicating non-status-based suffering.

ARTS COUNCIL WALES

The Arts Council of Wales has various internal policies but can recall no occasion where it has been asked to deal with:

external issues of bullying and harassment. (Personal email to the author: 2010)

A spokesperson reports:

> *There have been occasions over the years where we've been asked to intervene over broader staffing and HR matters, but that's something different. It's not unusual for there to be tensions between a Chair and Chief Executive, or within a staff team. (Personal email to the author: 2010)*

This recalls the problems outlined in the case study The Museum (Chapter 3) and the behaviour of the disbelieving Founder/Chair in The Art Gallery (Chapter 1).

> *However, this is usually a matter of organizational culture. There have also been occasions where we've been asked to intervene over unpaid bills and invoices, though this again is different. (Personal email to the author: 2010)*

CREATIVE SCOTLAND

Like the other Arts Councils, Creative Scotland (formerly the Scottish Arts Council) has a range of HR policies for internal use. In 2010, the Scottish Arts Council confirmed that its Compliance Officer had no external complaints held on file regarding bullying.

> *Relationships between a funded organization and its employees remain a matter for the Board and management of that organization. General principles of good governance would suggest that any issues surrounding workplace bullying would be dealt with using the appropriate channels within the organization. The Scottish Arts Council has received no complaints from its funded organizations on the issue of workplace bullying. (Personal email to the author: 2010)*

Third-Party Assistance

The importance of the involvement of trades unions and professional institutes in dealing with bullying needs to be highlighted, as well as the participation of specialist support agencies and ACAS. Beyond the remit to raise awarenes, taken together these are organizations that understand employers, employees and the arts environment – they must be key players in terms of promoting best practice in the workplace, and it may be that they are needed as conduits for arts workers who find themselves in difficulties and effectively voiceless (Lewis and Rayner 2003: 370–382). Evidently, internal policies and procedures are not always enough: consider the situation in the The Arts Service (Chapter 4), where the very people meant to assist with human resources problems in the organization instead blocked and dismissed a genuine complaint of bullying.

BECTU membership is equivalent, at most, to 45 per cent of those eligible to join. It is likely that the reality is that members represent a much smaller proportion than this, as the broadcasting, film, video and digital media sectors have grown enormously in the last decade due to constantly developing technology. Therefore, a minimum of 33,000 non-union members working in live and broadcast arts are unrepresented currently and may be without a champion of any sort.

Legislation alone will not remove the problem of bullying at work; however, it has the potential to act as a catalyst, place emphasis on human resources issues in the workplace and mend loopholes in existing laws. As Roger Lang noted, there is inadequate statutory provision to deal with bullying behaviour in the UK and the campaign to introduce a Dignity At Work Act, or to amend the Equality Act 2010, should continue to press the coalition government on this issue. Unite the Union (formed as a result of a merger in 2007 of Amicus and the Transport and General Workers' Union) is Britain's largest union and led the Dignity at Work partnership. In 2010, Unite publicized the plight of many clergy in the UK who had been subjected to bullying by parishioners and received little or no support from the church authorities. The Andrea Adams Trust was the world's first non-political, non-profit-making charity operating as the focus for the diverse and complex problems caused by bullying behaviour in the workplace. It provided specialist technical advice to the Dignity at Work Partnership until the Trust closed in 2009. The Dignity at Work Partnership was led by Unite the Union, and other launch partners included:

- Connect: the Union for Professionals in Communications;
- Legal and General Insurance;
- BAE Systems;
- The Chemical Industries Association;
- Remploy;
- Royal Mail;
- BT.

Baroness Anne Gibson, who introduced the Dignity at Work Bill in Parliament, chaired a steering group which comprised representatives from the Health and Safety Executive, ACAS, the TUC and the former Department of Trade and Industry (DTI – now the Department for Business, Innovation and Skills (BIS)). Leading academic and practitioner experts on bullying and related issues have acted as advisers to the Dignity at Work Partnership. Via its website, the Dignity at Work partnership still provides advice and guidance for anyone suffering from workplace bullying or harassment and remains intent on advocating cultural change in the workplace to develop a code of conduct where respect for individuals is regarded as integral to the behaviour of employees and managers.

It is clear that adult bullying in the workplace is a global issue. Particularly in the United Kingdom, Australia, Canada, France, Sweden and the United States, the profile of bullying behaviour in a number of sectors continues to be highlighted regularly, although not yet in performing arts organizations. Different strategies are being adopted to address workplace bullying in different parts of the world. The approaches tend to be external to the organization, occurring at a sociopolitical level, as individuals or groups, often people who have suffered at the hands of a bully, attempt to confront, and to deal with, the problem. Some success has been achieved, notably in Sweden where specific legislation has been introduced. In particular, the approaches adopted in Australia and the UK have been collaborative processes between responsible employers, trades unions, politicians, university researchers and voluntary and community groups seeking the introduction of meaningful and effective legislation (Sheehan, Barker and Rayner 1999). Clearly, further collaboration is required and highlighting some of the legal and economic aspects of the problem may serve to promote additional change.

In advancing the cause of dignity at work, we have the potential to reduce stress and related health problems, and also absenteeism, among those who are suffering as a result of, and/or being a close witnesses to, bullying behaviour. According to advocates of the Dignity at Work Bill, time spent on the promotion of dignity at work policies is often better in terms of outcomes than time spent on dealing with individual complaints of bullying and harassment (Dignity at Work Partnership: 2011). Developing a proactive, integrated organizational approach to the problem is likely to be the most effective way forward (Leather et al. 1999).

Funding Issues

Secure funding, or more properly perhaps, *insecure* funding, has always been a problem in the cultural sector. Those individuals and companies who may be experiencing the uncomfortable economic climate in the UK for the first time may be unaware that we in the arts have lived this way for a long, long, long time. For example, although in the past Arts Council England's regularly funded organizations have gained some sense of security and a limited ability to plan longer-term, most individual artists and project-funded companies continue to exist hand to mouth, year-on-year – that is, if they are lucky enough to be awarded funding on an annual basis.

Notwithstanding past hardships, in the first half of 2010, Arts Council England lost 4 per cent of its funding from government, totalling some £19 million, which it could not recoup from running costs alone – these were already pared back during the previous 12 months – so that cuts had to be apportioned to various schemes and to individual arts organizations, including RFOs. The Comprehensive Spending Review in October 2010 then announced that the Arts Council's grant in aid would be reduced to £349.4 million by 2014–15 – a 29.6 per cent cut. ACE Chief Executive Alan Davey commented:

> *The Secretary of State has asked us to try to ensure that funding for arts organisations is not cut by more than 15% over the next four years – the tipping point that we identified to the Chancellor some months ago. We will see what we can do, but the fact that we are receiving a larger cut in the first year will make managing the impact even more challenging.*
>
> *These cuts will inevitably have a significant impact on the cultural life of the country. There will be some tough decisions but we are determined to manage the cuts in the best possible way for the benefit of the arts and cultural sector overall. (Arts Council England 2010)*

With greater competition for funds – Davey expects 100 arts organizations to lose all their public sector funding – comes greater pressure on already under-resourced cultural organizations and their workforces and, as we have seen in Chapter 8, with increased pressure and stress comes the increased likelihood of the eruption of hostile and abusive behaviour. More than ever before, arts organizations and the professional bodies operating in the UK cultural sector need to be aware of the necessity to promote and encourage constructive leadership and team-working, and to effectively deal with destructive and oppressive behaviour.

Professional Ethics and Research into Bullying

The early chapters of this book outline some of the issues highlighted in previous research into bullying in non-arts workplaces, including the debates about terminology – bullying/mobbing/harassment and victim/target. In the English-speaking literature, the term bullying continues to be used alongside new appellations, such as emotional abuse (Einarsen et al. 2003). Increasingly, researchers are examining workplace bullying within a broader context – beyond that of health and safety at work – as outlined in Chapter 2. As the quest for understanding the causes of, and ways to mitigate or prevent, bullying behaviour continues, organizational structures are being revisited with a view to determining how bullying is positioned within paradigms for a range of operational activities, including 'conflict escalation' and 'conflict resolution' (Keashly and Nowell 2003), 'undesirable interaction' (Hubert 2003), risk management (Spurgeon 2003) and human resources management (Lewis and Rayner 2003).

Another issue which arose during the research journey, and is explored in Chapter 2, was one of professional ethics when conducting research with humans and in the knowledge that there is a need for researchers to protect participants from stress, however this might be created (Eysenck 2004). Inevitably, targets and witnesses of bullying, in participating in interviews and in the construction of case studies, relive their negative experiences to a certain extent. The identification of appropriate interview techniques assisted with minimizing distress during the research; however, some participants became emotionally upset or shaken as they recounted their personal histories and, as an interviewer, it was impossible to be entirely unmoved by some of these narratives. On balance, the ability to establish a good understanding of the person being interviewed, to adopt a non-judgemental approach and to develop good listening skills (Coolican 1994) assisted with the delicate process of gathering information that evoked unhappy experiences, and in every case that has been reported the individuals were proactive in this process and exhibited a positive desire to impart their personal knowledge. Where participants took a decision *not* to re-engage with distressing episodes, this was instantly accepted and, in all cases, rights to absolute confidentiality were protected and honoured.

From the point of view of the author, it is important to make it clear that those who did not want their stories to be told need not be concerned about their decision – such a worry was expressed by one or two individuals who felt that, in not telling their stories, they have in some way failed to support colleagues. However, historian and philosopher Isaiah Berlin proposed a concept that there are two types of freedom – negative and positive. We can characterize these as, respectively, freedom 'from' and freedom 'to'. In the author's view, an individual who has gained freedom *from* bullying is wholly entitled to freedom *to* decline to revisit it, particularly given the pain that revisiting can incur. In this respect, the student aspiring to be a careful and caring researcher will take steps to gain appropriate skills before embarking on evaluations of sensitive issues through structured and semi-structured interviews. Of course, researchers continue to seek other ways to examine the issue of bullying, apart from through evidence from targets and witnesses, and incidence studies dealing with both bullied and non-bullied people continue to offer useful opportunities for data comparison from a variety of sources (Rayner 1999).

Victims, Targets and Survivors

The victim/target/survivor issue is highly significant, particularly when considering the information gathered during the research. The models in Chapter 5 (Figures 5.1 and 5.2) illustrate respectively the 'self-help' model prevalent in the early 1990s and the 'victimhood is temporary' variation suggested by Field (1996). These offer inadequate ways to understand the complex factors that contribute to 'successful' bullying behaviour, predicated as they are on the philosophy of describing routes to help the victim to be more assertive, so that they become, merely, a target.

The alternative model, presented in Figure 5.4, aims to ensure that arts workers are equipped to be survivors of bullying; it emerged from a body of evidence demonstrating that it is necessary to look beyond changing the behaviour of, or finding reasons for bullying among, victims/targets alone. Often, the presenting problem is how to handle what appears to be a purely interpersonal negative relationship. In fact it may be entirely wrong only to consider the individuals who appear to be directly involved. If serial bullying is taking place, for example, this is likely to be because the work environment allows this to happen. Certainly, assertiveness training may help the victimized person, and awareness training may help the bullying person. However, besides the bully-target relationship, the underlying problem, in the author's view, is inextricably connected with the context: positive interventions are likely to have minimal impact unless they happen within a work environment in which management overtly acknowledges that bullying is unacceptable; provides help, advice and action if bullying occurs; has, or can call on, skills and expertise to deal with harassment or bullying issues. We can begin to get a sense of how powerful that work environment is: literally, it has the power to let bullying happen – through inaction or permissibility – or to prevent or stop it from happening – through affirmative action that supports dignity at work.

Permissibility and Prevention

The concept of permissibility – a belief among staff within an organization that bullying is condoned, as it is perceived to be permitted regardless of whether bullying is actually tolerated – has taken on increased significance. Permissibility has become a multidimensional reference describing, in addition to the original meaning according to Rayner (1999):

- accessories to bullying: onlookers/witnesses who are empowered to act, but fail to do so, thereby condoning the actions of the bully (Chapter 1);
- arts organizations in thrall to creative genius: whereby behaviour that is unfair to staff is excused in the name of the pursuit of creative excellence (Chapter 9);
- arts workers who continue to tolerate poor terms and conditions: thereby condoning the arts corporate culture (Chapter 4);

- the lack of more effective measures at national level to deal
  with workplace bullying, beyond the Equality Act 2010: thereby
  exhibiting tolerance of the behaviour (Chapter 7).

It is the sense that bullying is being allowed to happen in many different ways and at all levels that has proved both a fascinating and a discouraging aspect of attempts to find routes towards a solution. Hoel et al. (2003) consider a number of ways forward for researchers in Europe and the US and recommend that:

academics and practitioners would benefit from shared insight into key aspects of the issues as an alternative to allowing research to sub-divide into separate concepts covering what is virtually common ground (Hoel et al. 2003: 412–413)

The call for further dialogue and cooperation across academic disciplines and among practitioners is well made: there is much understanding to be gained from considering the bullying issue from a wide variety of perspectives. Cooperation and collaboration within and between employment sectors will also assist progress. In the wake of this research, there is a need for arts organizations and arts managers to set aside the notion of the arts as different in this respect, and to acknowledge the existence of workplace bullying and its personal, organizational, legal and economic consequences for the arts. Further research is required to better understand the psychological profile of the arts bully and those aspects particular to the variety of arts environments, which contribute to the climate in which bullying happens. The case studies and the quantitative research are a beginning – a signpost rather than a destination. People working in the arts need to have an input into the development of collaborative processes and methods for tackling bullying behaviour, including policy development and appropriate training for managers. They need to campaign and lobby alongside colleagues in other disciplines for improved legislation at national and European levels. In this respect, the performing arts could lead the way in identifying routes to prevent and eradicate workplace bullying, rather than topping the league tables for its high prevalence.

In considering 'antagonism and rivalry in the field of workplace bullying' Crawford (1999) warns of the need for each interest group to respect the status of the other as all move forward to contribute to the resolution of a major problem. By this he means that academic and scientific studies have their place, providing research and analysis methods that help to unravel the complexities of the subject; also, that campaigners and lobbyists bring influence and knowledge to bear so as to instigate political and legal changes; and, further, that the carers and hands-on workers alleviate suffering. In his view, even the sceptics challenge assumptions to concentrate our thinking. It would be a Utopia, indeed, if internationally concerted, collaborative approaches to beating bullying behaviour were instigated and supported at an appropriate level.

Martin Luther King Jr believed that injustice anywhere is a threat to justice everywhere, and Einstein declared that:

in matters of truth and justice, there is no difference between large and small problems, for issues concerning the treatment of people are all the same. (Albert Einstein, 1879–1955)

Workplace bullying in the arts is an injustice, and a real threat to the cultural sector. The records of poor treatment of arts workers present us with a problem we cannot ignore. If we in the arts can set aside endorsement of artistic temperament as valid behaviour, and focus instead on being inventive, resourceful and imaginative in our approach to this issue, perhaps this will enable us to help each other to tackle arts bullying honestly and successfully. Perhaps we can reverse the process and convert coercive to creative once again.

Appendix: Bullying Help and Support Groups

The Independent Police Support Group (IPSG) is available to police officers and police staff.

The IPSG is a voluntary support organization dedicated exclusively to providing support to Police Officers and Police Staff.

We deal with and research the more complex issues affecting individuals including bullying, harassment, whistleblowing, mental health and suicide.

Volunteers for the IPSG have accumulated considerable experience and training in this field over a number of years and are happy to raise issues with your force to assist you if necessary.

If we don't have the answers we will find out or point you in the right direction for you to seek appropriate levels of support and advice.

Source: http://www.ipsg.org.uk/

BALM (Bullied & Abused Lives in Ministry) offers support to church ministers and their close family.

Following our own experience of being bullied in ministry we have set up the BALM website as a resource for bullied and abused ministers, and for anyone else concerned about these issues.

We hope too that BALM will raise awareness of the plight of bullied and abused ministers, and encourage better practice in churches.

There is also a BALM e-mail group providing a forum for mutual support and understanding.

Source: http://www.balmnet.co.uk/

Bullying, Conciliation & Advisory Service (BCAS)

Aims

Provide advice and assistance to all IT contractors/recruitment agencies and clients with bullying issues and employment issues.

To assist people who feel that they have suffered from any form of mistreatment from Sunguard Sherwood Systems, DEFRA and Atos Origin.

To encourage corporate responsibility and tackle any form of workplace abuse.

Source: www.jfo.org.uk/support/bcas/index.htm

Scotland

Buchan Teacher Support Group

A support group for teachers in Aberdeenshire

Source: http://www.jfo.org.uk/support/btsg

England

Dignity At Work Now (DAWN) is a mutual support and campaign group in the West Midlands that was established in 2002. The group's website states:

Membership is open to those who believe they have been, or are being, bullied at work their partners, relatives, friends and supporters, advocates and professionals working in the field, and those interested and/or active in identifying, eradicating and raising awareness of issues associated with bullying in the workplace.

Support group meetings are held on the first Wednesday of each month.

Source: www.dignityatworknow.org.uk

Wales (Powys & Mid Wales)

Our support group covers Builth Wells, Brecon, Llandrindod Wells in Powys, mid-Wales. Email bullied_at_work@hotmail.com

Northern Ireland

The Adult Bullying Clampdown (ABC), a support group for adults who have been bullied at work, invites Northern Irish employees to contact them if they would like more information. Email abclampdown@btinternet.com

UK Wide

There are several organizations that work throughout the UK, and sometimes further afield. Bully OnLine is perhaps the most famous and the most familiar. It was founded by the late Tim Field, and is now run by his son, Michael. It was one of the first websites created to provide online information and advice on workplace bullying, and was a huge undertaking. It is crammed with information drawn from myriad sources about every aspect of bullying behaviour.

Bully OnLine is the world's leading web site on workplace bullying and related issues which validates the experience of workplace bullying and provides confirmation, reassurance and re-empowerment

Source: www.bullyonline.org

The Dignity at Work Partnership is described as the world's largest anti-bullying project, made possible thanks to just under £1million worth of funding from the Department for Business, Enterprise and Regulatory Reform.

Unite the Union is heading this vital initiative. With the help of industry leaders ... we aim to encourage employee representatives and employers to build cultures in which respect for individuals is regarded as an essential part of the conduct of all those who work in the organization. The project will also increase awareness and knowledge of 'dignity at work' issues, and encourage the development of partnership working in the workplace through the promotion of joint working on dignity at work.

Source: www.dignityatwork.org

Just Fight On! Against Workplace Bullying and Abuse (JFO)

... aims to be the ultimate resource for victims by bringing together information, ideas, people and groups so that we truly make a difference. The website provides information and articles; a hosting service for bullying support groups, for example B.C.A.S and the Buchan Teacher Support Group above; and a moderated, interactive online support forum. JFO also runs the Centre Against Workplace Bullying UK (CAWBUK) in Slough and provides a range of services to employees focusing on prevention, intervention and recovery.

Source: www.jfo.org.uk

The UK National Work Stress Network consists of many hundreds of like-minded people, some of whom have suffered the consequences of work-related stress.

Amongst these are experienced caseworkers, counselors, occupational health workers, trades union lay and paid officers and those who are just determined to see effective management which recognizes the needs of the workforce as well as of business.

The Network calls for:

Employers, Company Directors and managers at all levels to acknowledge their duty of care for and their acceptance of their health and safety responsibilities to the workforce;

Legislation and enforcement procedures to outlaw all forms of workplace stress, bullying and victimisation; also to ensure full corporate liability for workplace injury; and

The creation of a caring, supportive workplace culture with 'Dignity at Work' for all and for worker sensitive procedures for all.

Source: www.workstress.net

Public Concern at Work, founded in 1993, is the independent authority on public interest whistleblowing. Since 2004, the charity has funded all its own activities from the income it raises through helpline subscriptions, training and consultancy. It has four activities and will:

offer free, confidential advice to people concerned about crime, danger or wrongdoing at work;

help organizations to deliver and demonstrate good governance;

inform public policy; and

promote individual responsibility, organizational accountability and the public interest.

Source: www.pcaw.co.uk

Some Anti-bullying Movements Elsewhere

Worldwide, there are many support organizations working in similar ways to those in the UK. Their collective aim is to counter workplace bullying and support targets of harassment. In Chapter 9, the assistance specific to arts workers from both trades unions and professional institutions is examined further.

AUSTRALIA

Reach Out provides information, including factsheets, legal information and links to other related sites. As with its Irish counterpart, it is run by the Inspire Foundation. (website: au.reachout.com)

BELGIUM

SASAM is the Belgian movement against bullying. The organization is focused on four points: battling bullying, prevention, information for the media and the public and political lobbying about improving the law. (website: www.sasam.be)

CANADA

No Bully For Me was a campaign started in Vancouver and run by two volunteers. Its website, which still provides resources and useful links for people who have been bullied, became static at the end of April 2010 because its owners stated they were simply too swamped with the volume of contacts and requests for personal help, so that they became unable to offer the level of service and response that people were looking for. www.nobullyforme.org.

There are a range of other organizations in Canada, many of which focus on bullying among young people, including mobbing.ca (website: http:// members.shaw. ca/mobbing/mobbingCA/index.htm) and OvercomeBullying.org (website: http://www. overcomebullying.org).

FRANCE

Harcèlement Moral Stop (HMS) is the French association for the fight against bullying at work. The website provides information on the subject, legislation, advice and different ways to make contact. The aim of HMS is to assist anyone who considers themselves to have been harassed. It operates both in the private and public sectors. (website: www. hmstop.com)

GERMANY

Mobbing-web, founded as an online citizens' initiative in 1999, has a website that provides information and advice, plus details of the current case law in Germany. (www. mobbing-web.de)

HOLLAND

Stop Mobbing stil verdriet op de werkvloer. See also www.pesten.net. and Psychische terreur op het werk, a Dutch website on workplace bullying.

IRELAND

Reach Out is run by the Inspire Ireland Foundation. Inspire's mission is to help young people lead happier lives. The Inspire Ireland Foundation is a nationally registered charity. It has produced a factsheet about bullying at work, and runs a helpline. (website: ie.reachout.com)

SPAIN

A multilingual website containing information, advice and links: www.mobbing.nu

SWITZERLAND

An anti-workplace bullying website, accessible in either German or French: www. mobbing-zentrale.ch

USA

The Workplace Bullying Institute runs a number of websites combining help for individuals, research, public education, consulting for employers, and legislative advocacy. (website: www.workplacebullying.org)

Bibliography

Abu-Lughod, L. (1991) 'Writing Against Culture', in Richard G. Fox, ed., *Racapturing Anthropology: Working in the Present* (Santa Fe: School of American Research Press), 137–162.

Adams, A. with Crawford, N. (1992) *Bullying at Work: How to Confront and Overcome It* (London: Virago).

Aesop (2006 [1912]) *Fables*, 'Afterword' by Anna South (London: Collector's Library), 1.

Alimo-Metcalfe, B. and Alban-Metcalfe, J. (2005) 'Leadership: Time for a New Direction?' *Leadership* 1(1), 51–71.

Amabile, T. (2004) quoted by B. Breen, 'The 6 Myths of Creativity', *Fast Company* No. 89.

Amicus-MSF Union (1994) *Definition of Workplace Bullying*. http://www.bullyonline.org/workbully/defns.htm accessed 15 January 2006.

Amicus MSF (2006) *Amicus and DTI Launch the World's Largest Anti-bullying Project*. http://www.unitetheunion.com/news__events/2006_archived_press_releases/amicus_and_dti_launch_the_worl.aspx accessed 15 June 201].

Amnesty International (1975) 'Biderman's Chart of Coercion', in *Report on Torture* (London: Gerald Duckworth and Co), 53.

Andriopoulos, C. (2001) 'Determinants of Organisational Creativity: A Literature Review', *Management Decision Journal*.39(10), 834–841.

Appelberg, K., Romanov, K., Honkasalo, M. and Koskenvuo, M. (1991) 'Interpersonal Conflicts at Work and Psychosocial Characteristics of Employees', *Social Science & Medicine* 32(9), 1051–1056.

Aquino, K., Grover, M., Bradfield, M. and Allen, D. G. (1999) 'The Effects of Negative Activity, Hierarchical Status, and Self-determination on Workplace Victimization', *The Academy of Management Journal* 442(3), 260–272.

Archer, D. (1999) 'Exploring "Bullying" Culture in the Paramilitary Organisation', *International Journal of Manpower* 20(1–2), 94–106. http://www.Worktrauma. Org/research/research10.htm accessed 18 February 2011.

Arts Council England (2010) http://www.artscouncil.org.uk accessed 15 January 2011.

Ashforth, B. E. (1994) 'Petty Tyranny in Organisations', *Human Relations* 47(7), 755–778.

Asthana, A. (2006) 'This Week We Want to Know All About … Mobbing', *The Observer*, 30 April, 12.

Australian Council of Trade Unions (2010) http://www.actu.org.au/About/ACTU/default.aspx accessed 15 June 2010.

Australian Human Rights Commission (2004) *Workplace Bullying*. http://www.hreoc.gov.au/info_for_employers/fact/workplace.html accessed 10 June 2010.

Ball, C. (1998) 'Trade Union Action on Bullying at Work: The Campaign of the Technical and Professional Union', in P. McCarthy, ed., *Vital People, Viable Workplaces – Beyond Victimisation* (London: MSF).

Barham, C. and Begum, N. (2005) 'Sickness Absence from Work in the UK', *Office for National Statistics Labour Market Trends*, April (London: HMSO), 149–158.

Bates, S. (2004) 'Archbishop's Despair over Anglican Infighting', *The Guardian*, 2 November. http://www.guardian.co.uk/uk/2004/nov/02/religion.gayrights accessed 15 June 2010.

Batty, D. (2004) 'Personality Disorders, which Cover a Wide Range of Behavioural Abnormalities, Affect up to 13% of the UK Population. What Kinds are There and How are They Treated?' *The Guardian*, 15 December.

Baumgartner, C. (2006) *Bullying: From Victim to Target*. News item: Youth Development Specialist for Iowa State University (Buchanan Extension), 30 April. http://www.extension.iastate.edu/buchanan/news/Bullying.htm accessed 15 May 2006.

BBC (2005a) 'Gay Jibe Theatre Worker Wins Case', 4 May. http://news.bbc.co.uk/1/hi/england/wear/4514485.stm accessed 15 June 2010.

BBC (2005b) *Creative Genius*. Three programmes by Ian Peacock. Repeated 2006. http://www.bbc.co.uk/radio4/science/creativegenius.shtml accessed 15 June 2010.

BBC (2006a) 'Japan pupil in "suicide warning"'. http://news.bbc.co.uk/1/hi/world/asia-pacific/6124646.stm accessed 15 June 2010.

BBC (2006b) 'Make People Happier, Says Cameron'. http://news.bbc.co.uk/1/hi/uk_politics/5003314.stm accessed 15 June 2010.

BBC (2010) 'Manchester Head Teacher Sacked After Bullying Claims', 21 May. http://news.bbc.co.uk/1/hi/england/manchester/8697029.stm accessed 26 May 2010.

BECTU (2000) *Bring Back Annual Pay Negotiations*. http://www.bectu.org.uk/news/ae/na0030.html accessed 4 June 2000.

BECTU (2005) *News Release*, 'Spotlight on Media Industry Bullying'. http://www.bectu.org.uk/news/gen/ng0230.html accessed 15 March 2006.

Bennett, J. and Lehman, W. (1999) 'The Relationship Between problem Co-workers and Quality Work Practices: A Case Study of Exposure to Sexual Harassment, Substance Abuse, Violence and Job Stress', *Journal of Work & Stress* 13(4), 299–311.

Berns, G. (2008) 'Neuroscience Sheds New Light on Creativity', *Fast Company Magazine*. http://www.fastcompany.com/magazine/129/rewiring-the-creative-mind.html?page=0%2C1 accessed 15 June 2010.

Bibb, S. (2005) *The Stone-Age Company: Why the Companies We Work for Are Dying and How They Can Be Saved* (London: Cyan Communications).

Björkqvist, K., Österman, K. and Lagerspetz, K. (1994) 'Sex Differences in Covert Aggression Among Adults', *Aggressive Behaviour* 20(1), 27–33.

Blake, H. (2009) 'Zoë Wanamaker Demands Equal Pay for Actresses', *The Telegraph*, 27 July.

Bowers, S. (2002) 'Judge Hits at Both Sides in Poaching Case', *The Guardian*, 30 July. http://www.guardian.co.uk/business/2002/jul/30/10?INTCMP=SRCH accessed 15 February 2011.

Bratton, J. and Gold, J. (1999) *Human Resource Management: Theory and Practice* (Hampshire and London: Macmillan).

Bridgewater State College (2009) *MARC Statement of Purpose*. http://www.bridgew.edu/MARC/purpose.cfm accessed 15 May 2009.

Brown, C. (2010) 'Whelan Denies Bullying Officials at Unite Union', *The Independent*, 15 April. http:www.independent.co.uk/news/uk/politics/whelan-denies-bullying-officials-at-unite-the-union-194535/html accessed 26 May 2010.

Brown, D. (2004) *Bully the Bully?* http://www.lbwf.gov.uk/bully-the-bully.pdf accessed 15 May 2006.

Brown, R. S. (2007) 'Enhancing Student Employability? Current Practice and Student Experiences in HE Performing Arts', *Arts and Humanities in Higher Education* 6(1), 28–49.

Bully, director Larry Clark (StudioCanal 2001) [film].

Bully Online (2005) *Developing a Policy to Deal with Bullying at Work*. http://www.bullyonline.org/action/policy.htm accessed 15 January 2011.

Burns, S. (2007) *Mapping Dance*. http://www.palatine.ac.uk/publications/project-research/ accessed 15 June 2010.

Callahan, T. C. (1998) *Research Ethics. Ethics in Medicine*. http://depts.washington.edu/bioethx/topics/resrch.html accessed 15 March 2006.

Cambridge Dictionary Online (2010). http://www.dictionary.cambridge.org/ accessed 15 June 2010.

CBI (2010) *Absence Costs UK Economy £17 billion – CBI/Pfizer Survey*. News release, 7 June. http://www.cbi.org.uk/ndbs/press.nsf/0363c1f07c6ca12a8025671c00381cc7/adb2dcd8d9455258802577350036dcf0?OpenDocument accessed 15 June 2010.

Chadwick, E. (1997) 'Surveillance, and the Politics of Workplace Difference', *The International Journal of Comparative Labour Law and Industrial Relations* 3(3), 199–210.

Chartered Management Institute (2005a) *Bullying at Work: The Experience of Managers* (by Woodman and Cook). http://www.managers.org.uk/research-analysis/research/current-research/bullying-work-experience-managers-2005 accessed 15 June 2010.

Chartered Management Institute (2005b) *Best Practice: Bullying in the Workplace: Guidance for Managers*. http://www.managers.org.uk/content_3.aspx?id=3:2433&id=3:125&id=3:33&id=3:14 accessed 15 February 2011.

Chartered Institute of Personnel and Development (2004) *Employee Absence: A Survey of Management Policy and Practice*, July. http://www.cipd.co.uk (accessed 15 February 2011).

Chartered Institute of Personnel and Development (2006) *Harassment at Work*. http://www.cipd.co.uk/subjects/dvsequl/harassmt/harrass.htm?IsSrchRes=1 accessed 15 May 2006.

Chartered Institute of Personnel Development (2010) *The Psychological Contract*. http://www.cipd.co.uk/subjects/empreltns/psycntrct/psycontr.htm accessed 15 February 2011.

Chesterton, G. K. (1905) *Heretics* (12th edn,Massachusetts: The Plimpton Press), Chapter XVII.

Childnet International (2007) *Cyberbullying: A Whole-School Community Issue*. http://old.digizen.org/cyberbullying/overview/default.aspx accessed 15 February 2011.

Chong, D. (2002) *Arts Management* (Abingdon, Oxon: Routledge).

City University (2010) *Harassment and Dignity at Work Policy Guidelines*. http://www.city.ac.uk/hr/policies/harassment.html accessed 15 December 2010.

Clifford, J. (1986) 'Partial Truths', in James Clifford and George E. Marcus, eds, *Writing Culture. The Poetics and Politics of Ethnography* (Berkeley: University of California Press), 1–29.

Clifton, J. and Serdar, H. (2000) *Bully Off: Recognising and Tackling Workplace Bullying* (Lyme Regis, Dorset: Russell House Publishing Ltd).

Clore Foundation (2002) *Task Force Final Report, December 2002*. http://www.cloreleadership.org/page.php?id=79 accessed 15 January 2011.

Colvin, G., Tobin, T., Beard, K., Hagan, S. and Sprague, J. (1998) 'The School Bully: Assessing the Problem, Developing Interventions, and Future Research Directions', *Journal of Behavioral Education* 8(3), 293–319.

Commission des normes du travail (2007) 'Psychological Harassment in the Workplace – Prevention Remains the Solution for Québec's Employers!' (News Release, June 4). http://www.newswire.ca/en/releases/archive/June2007/04/c8475.html accessed 15 June 2010.

Cook, T. and Payne, M. (2002) 'Objecting to the Objections to Using Random Assignment in Educational Research', in F. Mosteller and R. Boruch, eds, *Evidence Matters: Randomized Trials in Education Research* (Washington: Brookings Institution).

Coolican, H. (1994) *Research Methods and Statistics in Psychology* (London: Hodder and Stoughton).

Costigan, L. (1998) *Bullying and Harassment in the Workplace: A Guide for Employees, Managers and Employers* (Blackrock, Co Dublin: Columba Press).

Cox, H. (1987) 'Verbal Abuse in Nursing: Report of a Study', *Nursing Management* 18, 47–50.

Crawford, N. (1999) 'Conundrums and Confusion in Organisations: The Etymology of the Word "Bully"', *International Journal of Manpower* 20(1–2), 86–94.

Creative and Cultural Skills (2010) *Performing Arts Blueprint*. http://www.ccskills.org.uk/Research/Publications/tabid/81/Default.aspx accessed 15 December 2010.

Crown Prosecution Service (2009) *Harassment: Protection from Harassment Act 1997*. Legal Guidance. http://www.cps.gov.uk/legal/h_to_k/harrasment/ accessed 15 May 2010.

Davenport, N., Elliott, G. and Schwartz, R. (1999) *Mobbing: Emotional Abuse in the American Workplace* (Ames, Iowa: Civil Society Publishing).

Davies, R. and Lindley, R. (2003) *Artists in Figures*. Study conducted by the Institute of Employment Research, University of Warwick (London: Arts Council England).

Davila, A. (2010) 'Thoughts on the Structure of Management Systems to Encourage Creativity and Innovation', *Studies in Managerial and Financial Accounting* 20, 65–78. http://www.emeraldinsight.com/books.htm?chapterid=1852806&show=pdf accessed 15 July 2010.

De Bono, E. (1991) *I am Right, You are Wrong* (London: Penguin).

Dignity at Work Partnership (2011). http://www.dignityatwork.org/default/htm accessed 15 February 2011.

Directgov (2010) *Cyberbullying – An Introduction*. http://www.direct.gov.uk/en/YoungPeople/HealthAndRelationships/Bullying/DG_070501 accessed 15 May 2010.

Douglas, A. (2010) 'The Cost of Bullying', *The Gladstone Observer* [Australia], 3 March.

Edgar,I. and Russell, A. (1998) *Anthropology of Welfare* (London: Routledge).

Einarsen, S. (1999) 'The Nature and Causes of Bullying at Work', *International Journal of Manpower: International Manpower Forecasting, Planning and Labour Economics* 20(12), 16–27.

Einarsen, S. (2000) 'Harassment and Bullying at Work: A Review of the Scandinavian Approach', *Aggression and Violent Behaviour* 5(4), 379–401.

Einarsen, S. and Hoel, H. (2001) 'The Negative Acts Questionnaire: Development, Validation and Revision of a Measure of Bullying at Work', paper to the 10th European Congress on Work and Organisational Psychology, Prague, May 2001.

Einarsen, S. and Mikkelsen, E. (2003) 'Individual Effects of Exposure to Bullying at Work', in S. Einarsen, H. Hoel, D. Zapf and C. Cooper, eds, *Bullying and Emotional Abuse in the Workplace: International Perspectives in Research and Practice* (London: Taylor & Francis), Chapter 6.

Einarsen, S. and Raknes, B. (1997) 'Harassment in the Workplace and the Victimisation of Men', *Violence and Victims* 12: 247–263.

Einarsen, S., Hoel, H., Zapf, D. and Cooper, C., eds (2003) *Bullying and Emotional Abuse in the Workplace: International Perspectives in Research and Practice* (London: Taylor & Francis).

Einarsen, S., Matthiesen, S. and Skogstad, A. (1998) 'Bullying, Burnout and Well-being Among Assistant Nurses', *Journal of Occupational Health & Safety, Australia and New Zealand* 14(6), 562–568.

Einarsen, S., Raknes, B. and Matthiesen, S. (1994) 'Bullying and Harassment at Work and Their Relationship to Work Environmental Quality – An Exploratory Study', *European Work and Organizational Psychologist* 4, 381–401.

Einarsen, S. and Skogstad, A. (1996) 'Bullying at Work: Epidemiological Findings in Public and Private Organisations', *European Journal of Work and Organisational Psychology* 5, 185–201.

Englander, E. (2006a) *Cyberbullying: A Guide for Parents* (Bridgewater, MA: MARC).

Englander, E. (2006b) *Social Networking Online: A Guide for Parents to Xanga, MySpace, and Similar Websites* (Bridgewater, MA: MARC).

Englander, E. (2009) *Massachusetts Statistics on Bullying & Cyberbullying: 2008–2009*, Research Brief (Bridgewater, MA: Massachusetts Aggression Reduction Center, Bridgewater State College).

Eysenck, W. (2004a) *Ethical Issues* (Hove: Psychology Press Ltd), 5. www.cranepsych.edublogs.org/files/2009/06/PIP_Ethical.pdf accessed 20 February 2011.

Eysenck, W. (2004b) *Research Methods: Psychological Enquiry*. www.grajfoner.com/Research%20methods%20paper%20mbff.pdf accessed 15 June 2010.

Field, T. (1996) *Bully in Sight: How to Predict, Resist, Challenge and Combat Workplace Bullying* (Didcot, Oxfordshire: Success Unlimited).

Field, T. (1999) 'Definition of Workplace Bullying by Tim Field'. http://www.bullyonline.org/workbully/defns.htm accessed 4 May 1999.

Field, T. (2001) *Twelve Types of Bullying*. http://www.bullyonline.org/workbully/bully.htm accessed 15 June 2010.

Field, T. (2002) 'The Hidden Cost of a Bully on the Balance Sheet', *Accounting & Business Magazine*, 1 February.

Gardener, L. (2010) 'Arts Internships: Chance of a Lifetime or Cut-price Labour?' *The Guardian*, 23 February. www.guardian.co.uk accessed 15 March 2010.

Gaupp, A. C. (1997) 'Founder's Syndrome: The New Theatre's Dilemma', *TD&T* (Spring), 48–56.

Giacalone, R. and Greenberg, J., eds (1997) *Antisocial Behavior in Organizations. A Management Development Guide* (Thousand Oaks, CA: Sage Publications).

Giga, S. and Hoel, H. (2003), 'Ethnic Difference in the Experience of Bullying', in *Proceedings of the Fifth Conference of The European Academy of Occupational Health Psychology*, Berlin, Germany, 20–21 November, 98.

Giga, S., Hoel, H. and Lewis, D. (2008) *The Cost of Workplace Bullying and Bullying at Work*. News release from Unite the Union. http://unitetheunion.com/news__events/2008_archived_press_releases/unite_the_union_exposes_the_co.aspx accessed 15 June 2010.

Glasl, F. (1994) *Konfliktmanagment. Ein Handbuch Für Führungskäfte und Berater*. [Conflict Management: A Handbook for Managers and Consultants] (4th edn, Bern, Switzerland: Haupt).

Glazier, L. (2005) 'When the Office Bully is a Woman', *The Bay Street Bull*, February 2005, 1–2. http://www.paintedred.com/portfolio/BSB/archive_feb_05_Office_Bully_01.php accessed 15 June 2010.

Gorard, S. and Taylor, C. (2004) *Combining Methods in Educational and Social Research* (Oxfordshire: OUP).

Guest, D. E. and Conway, N. (2002) *Pressure at Work and the Psychological Contract* (London: CIPD). http://www.cipd.co.uk/subjects/empreltns/psycntrct/psycontr.htm accessed 15 July 2010.

Gustavsson, B. and Leymann, H. (1984) *Psykiskt våld i arbetslivet – Två explorativa intervjuundersökningar* [Physical Force in the Working Sphere – Two Explorative Interview Investigations]. Investigation Report, 42. (Stockholm: Arbetarskyddsstyrelsen [Swedish management for employee protection]).

Hall, B. L. (2001) *Methods: What is Ethnography?* http://www.sas.upenn.edu/anthro/CPIA/METHODS/Ethnography.html accessed 6 November 2001.

Harder, D., Cutler, L. and Rockart, L. (1992) 'Assessment of Shame and Guilt and Their Relationship to Psychopathology', *Journal of Personality Assessment* 59(3), 584–604.

Health and Safety Commission (2006) *Health and Safety Statistics 2006–2006* (London: HMSO).

Health and Safety Executive (2010) *Self-reported Work-related Illness and Workplace Injuries in 2008/09: Results from Labour Force Survey*. http://www.hse.gov.uk/statistics/lfs/0809/hubresults.htm accessed 15 February 2011.

Herman, M. (2010) 'Bullying "Did Not Apply" to PwC Partner', *The Times*, 8 May. http://business. timesonline.co.uk/tol/business/law/article 7120122.ece accessed 26 May 2010.

Herman, N. and Reynolds, L. (1994) *Symbolic Interaction: An Introduction to Social Psychology* (Maryland: Altamira Press).

Higgins, C. (2005) 'Open Letter Calls for ENO Boss's Head', *The Guardian*, 16 December.

Hirigoyen, M-F. (1998) *Le Harcèlement moral, La violence perverse au quotidien* [Moral Harassment: Perverse Violence within a Daily Newspaper] (Paris: Editions Syros).

Hirigoyen, M-F. (2000) *Stalking the Soul: Emotional Abuse and the Erosion of Identity* (New York: Helen Marx Books).

Hoel, H. and Cooper, C. (2000) *Destructive Conflict and Bullying at Work*. Survey report. http://www. workplacebullying.org/research/further-studies.html accessed 15 June 201].

Hoel H., Cooper C. L., and Faragher, B. (2001) 'The Experience of Bullying in Great Britain: The Impact of Organisational Status', *European Journal of Work and Organizational Psychology* 10. 443–65.

Hoel, H., Einarsen, S., Keashly, L., Zapf, D. and Cooper, C. (2003) 'Bullying at Work: The Way Forward', in S. Einarsen, H. Hoel, D. Zapf and C. Cooper, eds, *Bullying and Emotional Abuse in the Workplace. International Perspectives in Research and Practice* (London and New York: Taylor & Francis).

Hoel, H., Faragher, B. and Cooper, C. (2004) 'Bullying is Detrimental to Health, but All Bullying Behaviours are Not Necessarily Equally Damaging', *British Journal of Guidance & Counselling* 32(3), 367–387.

Hoel, H., Rayner, C. and Cooper, C. (1999) 'Workplace Bullying', *International Review of Industrial Organizational Psychology* 14, 195–229.

Hoel, H. and Salin, D. (2003) 'Organisational antecedents of Workplace Bullying', in S. Einarsen, H. Hoel, D. Zapf and C. Cooper, eds, *Bullying and Emotional Abuse in the Workplace. International Perspectives in Research and Practice* (London: Taylor & Francis), Chapter 10.

Hoel, H. (2003) 'Bullying at Work. The Way Forward', in S.Einarsen, H. Hoel, D. Zapf and C. Cooper, eds, *Bullying and Emotional Abuse in the Workplace. International Perspectives in Research and Practice* (London: Taylor & Francis), Chapter 25.

Hubert, A. (2003) 'To Prevent and Overcome Undesirable Interaction: A Systematic Approach Mode', in S. Einarsen, H. Hoel, D. Zapf and C. Cooper, eds, *Bullying and Emotional Abuse in the Workplace. International Perspectives in Research and Practice* (London and New York: Taylor & Francis).

Hubert, A. and Van Veldhoven, M. (2001) 'Risk Sectors for Undesirable Behaviour and Mobbing', *European Journal of Work and Organizational Psychology* 10(4), 415–424.

Ishmael, A. with Alemoru, B. (1999) *Harassment, Bullying and Violence at Work* (London: The Industrial Society).

Jamison, K. R. (1993) *Touched with Fire: Manic Depressive Illness and the Artistic Temperament* (New York: Free Press Paperbacks).

Janes, C. (2010) 'Bully for You: Intimidation at Work', *The Guardian*, 27 February. http://guardian. co.uk/money/2010/feb/27/bullying-at-work accessed 26 May 2010.

Keashly, L., Hunter, S. and Harvey, S. (1997) 'Abusive Interaction and Role State Stressors: Relative Impact on Student Residence Assistant Stress and Work Attitudes', *Work & Stress* 11, 175–185.

Keashly, L. and Jagatic, K. (2003) 'By Any Other Name: American Perspectives on Workplace Bullying', in S. Einarsen, H. Hoel, D. Zapf and C. Cooper, eds, *Bullying and Emotional Abuse in the Workplace. International Perspectives in Research and Practice* (London: Taylor & Francis), Chapter 2.

Keashly, L. and Nowell, B. (2003) 'Conflict, Conflict Resolution and Bullying', in S. Einarsen, H. Hoel, D. Zapf and C. Cooper, eds, *Bullying and Emotional Abuse in the Workplace. International Perspectives in Research and Practice* (London: Taylor & Francis), Chapter 20.

Kelly, S. (2004) 'Workplace Bullying: The Silent Epidemic'. www.nzma.org.nz/journal/117-1204/1125. accessed 15 June 2010.

Kennedy, B. (2001) 'The Arts! Who Gives a Rats?' Address to Canberra Business Council Dinner, 8 November. http://www.nga.gov.au/AboutUs/press/artsRats.cfm accessed 15 February 2011.

Kivimaki, M., Eovanio, M. and Vahterra, J. (2000) 'Workplace Bullying and Sickness Absence in Hospital Staff', *Occup Environ Med* 57 (October), 656–660.

Kling, R. (1991) 'Cooperation, Coordination and Control in Computer-Supported Work', *Communications of the ACM* 34(12), 83–88.

Knorz. C. and Zapf, D. (1996) 'Mobbing – eine extreme Form socialer Stressoren am Arbeitsplatz' [An Extreme Form of Social Stressor in the Workplace], *Zeitschrift für Arbeits & organisationspsychologie* 40, 12–21.

Labour Research Department (1997) *Stress, Bullying and Violence: A Trade Union Action Guide* (LRD booklet series, London: Labour Research Department).

Lambert, T. (1994) *High Income Consulting: How to Build and Market Your Professional Practice* (London: Nicholas Brealey Publishing Ltd).

Lathan, P. (2001) *The Eyre Report: A Summary Part IV*. http://www.britishtheatreguide.info/articles/050798e.htm accessed 5 March 2006.

Lawrence, D. H. (1994 [1923]) 'The Captain's Doll', in *The Fox, The Captain's Doll and The Ladybird* (new edn, London: Penguin Books Ltd).

Leather, P., Beale, D., Lawrence, C., Brady, C. and Cox, T. (1999) *Work-Related Violence: Assessment and Intervention* (London and New York: Routledge).

Lee, D. (2000) 'An Analysis of Workplace Bullying in the UK', *Personnel Review* 9(5), 593–612.

Lee, M. B. (2001) 'Oppression and Horizontal Violence: The Case of Nurses in Pakistan', *Nursing Forum* 36(1), 15–24.

Lewis, D. (1999) 'Workplace Bullying – Interim Findings of a Study in Further and Higher Education in Wales', *International Journal of Manpower* 20(1/2), 106–118.

Lewis, D. (2002) 'The Social Construction of Workplace Bullying – A Sociological Study with Special Reference to Further and Higher Education'. PhD thesis, University of Wales, Cardiff.

Lewis, D. (2003) 'Voices in the Social Construction of Bullying at Work: Exploring Multiple Realities in Further and Higher Education', *International Journal of Management and Decision Making* 4(1), 65–81.

Lewis, D. (2004) 'Bullying at Work: The Impact of Shame Among University and College Lecturers', *British Journal of Guidance & Counselling* 32(3), 281–299.

Lewis, D. (2006) 'Recognition of Workplace Bullying: A Qualitative Study of Women Targets in the Public Sector', *Journal of Community & Applied Social Psychology* 16 2), 119–135.

Lewis, D. and Rayner, C. (2003) 'Bullying and Human Resources Management: A Wolf in Sheep's Clothing?', in S. Einarsen, H. Hoel, D. Zapf and C. Cooper, eds, *Bullying and Emotional Abuse in the Workplace. International Perspectives in Research and Practice* (London: Taylor & Francis), Chapter 22.

Leymann, H. (1987) *Mobbing I arbeidslivet* [Bullying in Working Life] (Oslo: Friundervisningens Forlag), as cited in Hoel, H., Faragher, B. and Cooper, C. (2004).

Leymann, H. (1990) 'Mobbing and Psychological Terror at Workplaces', *Violence and Victims* 5(2), 119–126.

Leymann, H. (1993) *Mobbing – Psychoterror am Arbeitsplatz und wie man sich dagegen wehren kann* [Bullying – Psycho-terror at Work and How One Might Protect Oneself] (Rowolt: Reinbeck).

Leymann, H. (1996) 'The Content and Development of Mobbing at Work', in D. Zapf and H. Leymann, eds, *A Special Issue of The European Journal of Work and Educational Psychology* 5(2), 165–184.

Leymann, H. and Gustafsson, A. (1996) 'Mobbing at Work and the Development of Post-Traumatic Stress Disorders', *Journal of Work and Educational Psychology* 5(2), 251–276.

Liefooghe, A. and Olafsson, R. (1999) '"Scientists" and "Amateurs": Mapping the Bullying Domain,' *International Journal of Manpower* 20(1–2), 39–49.

Liefooghe, A. and Mackenzie Davey, K. (2003) 'Explaining Bullying at Work: Why Should We Listen to Employee Accounts?', in S. Einarsen, H. Hoel, D. Zapf and C. Cooper, eds, *Bullying and Emotional Abuse in the Workplace* (London: Taylor & Francis), Chapter 11.

London School of Economics (2010) *Guidance on Managing Pressure at Work*. http://www2.lse. ac.uk/intranet/LSEServices/divisionsAndDepartments/humanResources/employmentRelations/ policiesAndProcedures/pressureAndStress/guidanceOnManagingPressureAtWork.aspx accessed 15 June 2010.

Lundin, W. and Lundin, K. (1995) *Working with Difficult People* (The WorkSmart Series, 1st edn, New York: Academy of Management).

Mann, R. (1996) 'Psychological Abuse in the Workplace', in P. McCarthy, M. Sheehan, and W. Wilkie, eds, *Bullying: From Backyard to Boardroom* (Alexandria, New South Wales: Millennium Books), Chapter 7.

Markus, M. (1994) 'Finding a Happy Medium: Explaining the Negative Effects of Electronic Communication on Social Life at Work,' *ACM Transactions on Information Systems* 12(2), 119–149.

Matthiesen, S. and Einarsen, S. (2001) 'MMPI–2 Configurations Among Victims of Bullying at Work', *European Journal of Work and Organizational Psychology* 10(4), 467–484.

Matthiesen, S., Aasen, E., Holst, G., Wie, K. and Einarsen, S. (2003) 'The Escalation of Conflict: A Case Study of Bullying at Work', *International Journal of Management and Decision-Making* 4(1), 96–112.

McCarthy, P. (1996) 'When the Mask Slips: Inappropriate Coercion in Organisations Undergoing Restructuring', in P. McCarthy, M. Sheehan, and W. Wilkie, eds, *Bullying: From Backyard to Boardroom* (Alexandria, New South Wales: Millennium Books).

McCarthy, P., Sheehan, M. and Kearns, D. (1995) 'Managerial Styles and Their Effects on Employees Health and Well-being', in *Organisations Undergoing Restructuring*, Report for Worksafe Australia (Brisbane: Griffith University).

McCarthy, P., Sheehan, M. and Wilkie, W., eds (1996) *Bullying: From Backyard to Boardroom* (Alexandria, New South Wales: Millennium Books).

McKeown, M. and Whiteley, P. (2002) *Unshrink Yourself – Other People – Business – The World* (London: Pearson Education Ltd).

McNamara, C. (1999) *Founder's Syndrome: How Corporations Suffer – and Can Recover*, adapted from *Nuts-and-Bolts Guide to Leadership and Supervision*. http://managemenhelp.org/misc/founders. htm accessed 7 June 2010.

MFL Occupational Health Centre (2010) 'Bullying at Work', in *Factsheet*. http://www.mflohc.mb.ca/ fact_sheets_folder/index.html accessed 30 June 2010.

MGHK Ltd (GoKunming) (2009) *Kingdom of the Dwarfs – Blog*. http://www.gokunming.com/en/ forums/thread/1836/kingdom_of_the_dwarfs accessed 15 June 2010.

Mikkelsen, E. and Einarsen, S. (2001) 'Bullying in Danish Work-life: Prevalence and Health Correlates', *European Journal of Work and Organizational Psychology* 10(4), 393–413.

Mikkelsen, E. and Einarsen, S. (2002) 'Basic Assumptions and Symptoms of Post-Traumatic Stress Among Victims of Bullying at Work', *European Journal of Work and Organizational Psychology* 11(1), 87–111.

Missouri State University (formerly the Southwest Missouri State University) (2010) *Welcoming the 21st Century, Performing Arts*, Details of performing arts courses. http://www.missouristate.edu accessed 15 March 2010.

Morse, J. and Chung, S. (2003) 'Toward Holism: The Significance of Methodological Pluralism', *International Journal of Qualitative Methods* 2(3),.

Namie, G. and Namie, R. (1999) *Bullyproof Yourself at Work! Personal Strategies to Stop the Hurt from Embarrassment* (Benicia, CA: DoubleDoc Press).

Namie, G. and Namie, R. (2000) *The Bully at Work: What You Can Do to Stop the Hurt and Reclaim Your Dignity on the Job* (Naperville, IL: Sourcebooks).

National Bullying Helpline (2011) *Trustee Statement*, 5 January. http://nationalbullyinghelpline. co.uk/ accessed 15 January 2011.

National Institute for Health and Clinical Excellence (2009) *Promoting Mental Wellbeing at Work. Guidance for Employers*. http://reveiew2009-2010.nice.org.uk/public_health/ accessed 15 February 2011.

Neilson, G., Pasternack, B. and Van Nuys, K. (2005) 'The Passive-Aggressive Organization', *Harvard Business Review*, October.

Neuberger, O. (1999) *Mobbing: Übel Mitspielen in Organisationen* [Mobbing: Unfair Play with People in Organizations] (3rd revised edn, München: Rainer Hampp Verlag), as cited in Salin (2003).

Neuman, J.H. and Baron, R.A. (1997) 'Aggression in the Workplace', in R. Giacalone and J. Greenberg, eds, *Antisocial Behaviour in Organizations* (Thousand Oaks, CA: Sage), 33–67.

New Zealand Department of Labour/*Te Tari Mahi* (2009) *Workplace Bullying: An Update*. http://ers. govt.nz/law/case/themes/aug-09.html accessed 15 June 2010.

Niedl, K. (1995) 'Wem Nützt Mobbing? Psychoterror am Arbeitsplatz und die Personalwirtschaft von Unternehmen', in H. Leymann. ed., *Der neue Mobbing-Bericht: Erfahrungen and Iniativen, Auswege und Hilfsangebote* (Reinbck bci Hamburg: Rowohlt Taschenbuch Verlag GmbH), as cited in Salin (2003).

Niedl, K. (1996) 'Mobbing and Well-being: Economic and Personnel Development Implications', *European Journal of Work and Organizational Psychology* 5(2), 239–249.

O'Donnell, G. (2010) 'Brown Bullying Claims: Allegations and Non-denials', *The Guardian*, 23 February. http://www.guardian.co.uk/politics/2010/feb/23/brown-bullying-claims-allegations-non-denials accessed 15 June 2010.

Office of National Statistics (2001) *Census Statistics 2001*. http://www.statistics.gov.uk/census2001/census2001.asp accessed 15 May 2006.

Office of the United Nations High Commissioner for Human Rights (2007) *Good Governance Practices for the Protection of Human Rights*. www2.ohchr.org/English/issues/development/governance/ accessed 15 June 2010.

Olweus, D. (1991) 'Bully/Victim Problems Among Schoolchildren: Basic Facts and Effects of a School-Based Intervention Program', in D. J. Pepler and K. H. Rubin, eds, *The Development and Treatment of Childhood Aggression* (Hillsdale, NJ: Erlbaum), 411–448.

Olweus, D. (1993) *Bullying at School: What We Know and What We Can Do* (London: Blackwell).

O'Moore, M. (2000) 'Critical Issues for Teacher Training to Counter Bullying and Victimisation in Ireland', *Aggressive Behaviour* 26, 99–111.

Oxford University (1998) *Oxford Studies Bullying in Prisons*, News release. http://www.ox.ac.uk/ gazette/1997-8/weekly/260698/news/story_5.htm accessed 15 June 2000.

Oxford English Dictionary Online (2006) http://www.oed.com/ accessed 15 June 2006.

Parris, T. (2010) *Costs of Bullying: The Business Cost of Bullying in the Workplace.* http://www.overcomebullying.org/costs-of-bullying.html accessed 15 April 2010.

Porcini, M. (2009) 'Review of *Corporate Creativity: Developing an Innovative Organization,* edited by T. Lockwood and T. Walton'. http://www.dmi.org/dmi/html/publications/books/reviews/corporate_creativity.htm accessed 15 May 2010.

Press Association (2005) 'Bullying Costs MoD More than £895,000 in Payouts', *The Guardian,* 15 October. http://www.guardian.co.uk/uk/2005/oct/15/military.immigrationpolicy accessed 15 February 2011.

Protherough, R. and Pick, J. (2002) *Managing Britannia: Culture and Management in Modern Britain* (Norfolk: Edgeways).

Quine, L. (1999) 'Workplace Bullying in NHS Community Trust: Staff Questionnaire Survey', *British Medical Journal* 23(January), 228–232.

Raffalli, P. (2010) 'Bullying and Cyberbullying: Beneath the Radar No More', *Thrive: Children's Hospital Boston's Health & Science Blog.* http://childrenshospitalblog.org/bullying-and-cyberbullying-beneath-the-radar-no-more/ accessed 15 December 2010.

Randall, P. (1997) *Adult Bullying: Perpetrators and Victims* (London: Routledge).

Rantzen, E. (2006) 'I Was Not Only Tough but Rough: Esther Rantzen Confesses to Being a Bully as a Boss', *Media Guardian,* 27 February, cover story and p. 2.

Rathus, Z. (1996) 'Domestic Violence: Bullying at Home', in P. Mc Carthy, M. Sheehan and W. Wilkie, eds, *Bullying: From Backyard to Boardroom* (Alexandria, New South Wales: Millennium Books).

Rayner, C. (1997) 'The Incidence of Workplace Bullying,' *Journal of Community and Applied Psychology* 7, 199–208.

Rayner, C. (1998) 'Workplace Bullying: Do Something!', *The Journal of Occupational Health and Safety – Australia and New Zealand* 14(6), 581–585.

Rayner, C. (1999) 'From Research to Implementation: Finding Leverage for Prevention,' *International Journal of Manpower* 20(1/2), 28–38.

Rayner, C., Hoel, H. and Cooper, C. (2002) *Workplace Bullying. What We Know, Who Is to Blame and What Can We Do?* (London: Taylor & Francis).

Rayner, C., Sheehan, M. and Barker, M. (1999) 'Theoretical Approaches to the Study of Bullying at Work,' *International Journal of Manpower* 20(1–2), 11–15.

Reynolds, P. (1994) *Dealing with Crime and Aggression at Work: A Handbook for Organizational Action* (a Management Development Guide, London and New York: McGraw-Hill).

Richards, H. and Freeman, S. (2002) 'A Summary of the Literature Relating to Workplace Bullying,' *Journal of Community and Applied Social Psychology* 7(3), 181–191.

Richter, E. (2001) 'Efforts to Stop Repression Bias by Protecting Whistleblowers', *International Journal of Occupational and Environmental Health* 7(1), 68–71.

Ritzer, G. and Goodman, D. (2004) *Sociological Theory* (6th edn, London and New York: McGraw-Hill).

Romm, C. and Pliskin, N. (1999) 'The Office Tyrant – Social Control Through E-mail', *Information Technology and People* 12(1), 27–43.

Russell, B. (2004 [1932]) 'Essay: On Youthful Cynicism', in *In Praise of Idleness: And Other Essays* (new edn, London: Routledge Classics).

Safe Workers (2010) *Cyber-bullying at Work.* http://www.safeworkers.co.uk/cyber-bullying-work.html accessed 15 May 2010.

Salin, D. (2001) 'Prevalence and Forms of Bullying Among Business Professionals: A Comparison of Two Different Strategies for Measuring Bullying', *European Journal of Work and Organization Psychology* 10(4), 425–441. http://hdl.handle.net/10227/282 accessed 15 February 2011.

Salin, D. (2003) 'Bullying and Organisational Politics in Competitive and Rapidly Changing Work Environments,' *International Journal of Management and Decision Making* 4(1), 35–46.

Salin, D. (2005) 'Workplace Bullying Among Business Professionals: Prevalence, Gender Differences and the Role of Organizational Politics', *Perspectives Interdisciplinaires Sur le Travail Et la Santé* 7(3).

Schein, L. (2003) 'A Selection of Ethnographies of Gender and Sexuality in Asia, Recommended by Professor Louisa Schein', Departments of Anthropology and Women's Studies, Rutgers University, New Brunswick, NJ, USA. http://anthro.rutgers.edu/courses/378schein2003.htm accessed 15 May 2006.

Schell, B. and Lanteigne, N. (2000) *Stalking, Harassment, and Murder in the Workplace: Guidelines for Protection and Prevention* (Westport, CT: Quorum Books).

Scottish Arts Council (2008) *Care, Diligence and Skill* (6th revised edn, London: HMSO). http://www.scottisharts.org.uk/1/information/publications/1000877.aspx accessed 15 June 2010.

Seigne, E. (1998) 'Bullying at Work in Ireland', in C. Rayner, M. Sheehan and M. Barker, eds, *Bullying At Work 1998 Research Update Conference Proceedings*, (Stafford: Staffordshire University).

Semmer N. K. (1996) 'Individual Differences, Work Stress, and Health', in M. Schabracq, J. Winnubst and C. Cooper, eds, *Handbook of Work and Health Psychology* (Chichester: Wiley), 51–86.

Sheehan, M. (1996) 'Case Studies in Organizational Restructuring', in M. McCarthy, M. Sheehan and W. Wilkie, eds, *Bullying: From Backyard to Boardroom* (Alexandria, New South Wales: Millennium Books), 67–82.

Sheehan, M. (1999) 'Workplace Bullying: Responding with Some Emotional Intelligence', *International Journal of Manpower* 20(1–2), 57–69.

Sheehan, M., Barker, M. and Rayner, C. (1999) 'Applying Strategies for Dealing with Workplace Bullying', *International Journal of Manpower* 20(1/2), 50–56.

Silverman, D., ed. (2000) *Qualitative Research* (London: Sage).

Smith, S. G. and Sprague, J. (2003) *The Mean Kid: An Overview of Bully/Victim Problems and Research-Based Solutions for Schools* (Institute on Violence and Destructive Behavior, College of Education, University of Oregon). http://darkwing.uoregon.edu/~ivdb/doc/mean_kid.pdf accessed 15 June 2010.

Spurgeon, A. (2003) 'Bullying from a Risk Management Perspective', in S. Einarsen, H. Hoel, D. Zapf and C. Cooper, eds, *Bullying and Emotional Abuse in the Workplace. International Perspectives in Research and Practice* (London: Taylor & Francis).

Starland, T. (2002) 'Shoestring Publishing Company Marks 15 Years of Producing an Arts Newspaper', *Carolina Arts* [USA], July.

Swedish Work Environment Authority (1993) *Victimisation at Work* (AFS 1993: 17) (Stockholm: National Board of Occupational Health and Safety). http://www.av.se/inenglish accessed 15 March 2010.

Swinton, L. (2010) *Douglas McGregor – Theory X /Theory Y*. http://www.mftrou.com/douglas-mcgregor.html accessed 15 June 2010.

Switalski, G. (2009) 'City Lawyer £12m Action Following 18 Months of Workplace Bullying'. http://news.bbc.co.uk/1/hi/uk/8156637.stm accessed 3 June 2010.

Tapaleao, V. (2010) 'Bullying Thriving in the Workplace', *The New Zealand Herald*, 15 April. http://www.nzherald.co.nz/nz/news/article.cfm?c_id=1&objectid=10638499 accessed 15 June 2010.

Tattum, D. and Tattum, E. (1996) 'Bullying: A Whole School Response', in P. McCarthy, M. Sheehan and W. Wilkie, eds, *Bullying: From Backyard to Boardroom* (Alexandria, New South Wales: Millennium Books), 13–23.

Teachtoday (2010) 'What Laws are There to Help Protect Me from Cyberbullying?' http://www. teachtoday.eu/en/Teacher-advice/Cyberbullying/What-laws-are-there-to-help-protect-me-from-cyberbullying.aspx accessed 15 May 2010.

The Daily Mail (2006). 'NHS staff "bullied by patients and colleagues"', 19 May. http://www.dailymail. co.uk/health/article-386903/NHS-staff-bullied-patients-colleagues.html accessed 15 June 2010.

The Guardian (2005) 'Bullying Costs MoD More than £895,000 in Payouts', 15 October 2005. http:// www. Guardian.co.uk/uk/2005/oct/15/military.immigrationpolicy?INTCMP=SRCH accessed 15 February 2011.

The Telegraph (2010) 'Dwarves Found "Theme Park" Commune to Escape Bullying'. http://www. telegraph.co.uk/news/worldnews/asia/china/6245665/Dwarves-found-theme-park-commune-to-escape-bullying.html accessed 15 June 2010.

Theatrical Management Association (2004) *Legal Update: Guidance on Bullying and Harassment.*

Tolstoy, L. (2004 [1806]) *War and Peace* (new edn, London: CRW Publishing Ltd), Book Four, Chapter IV. http://www.online-literatur.com/tolstoy/war_and_peace/72/ accessed 15 February 2011.

Trades Union Congress (1999) *Beat Bullying at Work: A Guide for Reps and Personnel Managers Showing How Unions and Managers Have Worked Together to Reduce Bullying* (London: TUC).

Trumbull, D. (2003) 'Shame: An Acute Stress Response to Interpersonal Traumatization', *Psychiatry* 66, 53–64.

Turney, L. (2003) 'Mental Health and Workplace Bullying: The Role of Power, Professions and "On the Job" Training', *Australian e-journal for the Advancement of Mental Health* 2. http://www. auseinet.com/journal/vol2iss2/turney.pdf accessed 15 February 2006.

UCEA (2009) *Managing Performance and Respecting Dignity at Work.* Event programme. http:// www.ucea.ac.uk/en/Seminars/index.cfm?1=1&page+6&obj_id+4F3DE204-8DF04A8C-9718C614F3B1A3E2 accessed 15 December 2010.

UK Support Group Network (2010) www.jfo.org.uk accessed 15 January 2011.

UNISON (1997) *Bullying Report* (London: UNISON).

UNISON (2003) *Bullying at Work* (London: UNISON).

Van Dam, Y. and Engelen, M. (2004) *Evaluation of the Effectiveness of the Working Conditions Act with Respect to Undesired Behaviour* (The Hague: Ministry of Social Affairs and Employment), reported in *Workplace Violence Stabilising in the Netherlands* (European Foundation for the Improvement of Living and Working Conditions). http://www.eurofound.eu.int/ewco/2005/10/NL0510NU03. htm accessed 15 May 2006.

Van Veelen, W. (2007) 'The Making of a New Working Conditions Act in the Netherlands', *European Trade Union Institute Newsletter*, March. http://hesa.etui-rehs.org/uk/newsletter/files/NWL32-EN-p5-8.pdf accessed 15 May 2010.

Vartia, M. (1996) 'The Sources of Bullying – Psychological Work Environment and Organizational Climate', *European Journal of Work and Organizational Psychology* 5(2), 203–214.

Vartia, M. (2001) 'Consequences of Workplace Bullying with Respect to Well-being of its Targets and the Observers of Bullying', *Scandinavian Journal of Work Environment and Health* 27(1), 63–69.

Vartia, M. and Hyyti, J. (2002) 'Gender Differences in Workplace Bullying Among Prison Officers', *European Journal of Work and Organizational Psychology* 11(1), 113–126.

Vartia-Väänänen, M. (2003) 'Workplace Bullying – A Study on the Work Environment, Well-being and Health', *People and Work Research Reports* 56 (Helsinki: Finnish Occupational Health).

Von Heussen, E. (2000) 'The Law and Social Problems: The Case of Britain's Protection from Harassment Act 1997', *The Web Journal of Current Legal Issues*. http://webjcli.ncl.ac.uk/2000/issue1/vonheussen1.html accessed 15 May 2010.

Walmsley, C. (1991) *Assertiveness, the Right to Be You* (London: BBC Books Publication).

Watson, T. (1986) *Management, Organization and Employment Strategy* (London: Routledge and Kegan Paul).

WBI–Zogby International (2007) *Results of Workplace Bullying Survey*. http://www.workplacebullying.org/research/WBI-Zogby2007Survey.html accessed 15 February 2011.

Wetfeet (2006) *Performing Arts Career Overview* (Wetfeet Recruitment Agency). http://www.wetfeet.com/Careers-and-Industries/Careers/Performing-Arts.aspx accessed 7 February 2006.

Wheatley, R. (1999) *Dealing with Bullying at Work in a Week* (Institute of Management Series, London: Hodder and Stoughton).

Wilde, O. (2001 [1891]) 'Essay: The Soul of Man Under Socialism', in *The Soul of Man Under Socialism and Selected Critical Prose* (London: Penguin Books Ltd).

Wilkie, W. (1996) 'Understanding the Behaviour of Victimised People, in P. McCarthy, M. Sheehan and W. Wilkie, eds, *Bullying: From Backyard to Boardroom* (Australia: Millennium Books), 1–11.

Wilson, S. and Pringle, S. (2010) *Bullying, Banter or Brusque Management?* http://www.duncancotterill.com/index.cfm/1,159,613,43,html/Bullying-Banter-or-Brusque-Management accessed 15 February 2011.

Woodman, R., Sawyer, J. and Griffin, R. (1993) 'Toward a Theory of Organizational Creativity', *Academy of Management Review* 18(2), 293–321.

Wright, L. and Smye, M. (1997) *Corporate Abuse: How 'Lean and Mean' Robs People and Profit* (New York: Simon and Schuster).

Zapf, D. (1999) 'Organisational, Work Group Related and Personal Causes of Mobbing/Bullying at Work', *International Journal of Manpower: International Manpower Forecasting, Planning and Labour Economics* 20(1–2), 70–85.

Zapf, D., Dormann, C. and Frese, M. (1996) 'Longitudinal Studies in Organisational Stress Research: A Review of the Literature with Reference to Methodological Issues', *Journal of Occupational Health Psychology* 1, 145–169.

Zapf, D. and Einarsen, S. (2001) 'Bullying in the Workplace: Recent Trends in Research and Practice – An Introduction', *European Journal of Work and Organisational Psychology* 10(4), 369–373.

Zapf, D. and Einarsen, S. (2003) 'Individual Antecedents of Bullying', in S. Einarsen, H. Hoel, D. Zapf and C. Cooper, eds, *Bullying and Emotional Abuse in the Workplace. International Perspectives in Research and Practice* (London: Taylor & Francis), 165–173.

Zapf, D., Einarsen, S., Hoel, H. and Vartia, M. (2003) 'Empirical Findings on Bullying in the Workplace, in S. Einarsen, H. Hoel, D. Zapf and C. Cooper, eds, *Bullying and Emotional Abuse in the Workplace. International Perspectives in Research and Practice* (London: Taylor & Francis), Chapter 5.

Zapf, D. and Gross, C. (2001) 'Conflict Escalation and Coping with Workplace Bullying: A Replication and Extension', *European Journal of Work and Organisational Psychology* 10(4), 497–522.

Zapf, D., Knorz, C. and Kulla, M. (1996) 'On the Relationship Between Mobbing Factors, and Job Content, Social Work Environment and Health Outcomes', *European Journal of Work and Organizational Psychology* 5(2), 215–237.

Zapf, D. and Warth, K. (1997) 'Mobbing: Subtile Kriegsführung am Arbeitsplatz', *Psychologie Heute* August, 20–25, 28–29, as cited in Salin (2003).

Useful Online Resources

https://obs.acas.org.uk/ViewEvent.aspx?EventId=183687 (training courses in dealing with bullying and harassment at work)

http://www.andreaadamstrust.org/

http://www.anti-bullyingalliance.org.uk/tackling_bullying_behaviour/research.aspx

http://www.bullyonline.org/ (also links to The Field Foundation)

www.carolinaarts.com (USA)

http://www.city.ac.uk/hr/policies/harassment (City University, London)

http://www.cloreleadership.org/index.php (Clore Foundation Leadership Programme)

http://dictionary.cambridge.org/dictionary/british/creative_1

http://www.dignityatworknow.org.uk/index.php?option=com_frontpage&Itemid=32

http://www.digizen.org.uk/cyberbullying/overview/ (Education)

http://www.encyclo.co.uk

http://www.equalities.gov.uk/equality_act_2010.aspx

http://www.equity.org.uk/article.aspx?id=307 (Respect for the Arts Manifesto, 2010)

http://www.hmstop.com/ (France)

http://www.icu.edu.au/eo/bullying (James Cook University, Australia)

http://ww.jfo.org.uk/ (Support Group Network)

http://www.mediationworks.com

http://www.overcomebullying.org

http://statemaster.com/encyclopedia

http://www.teachernet.gov.uk/wholeschool/behaviour/tacklingbullying/cyberbullying/

http://www.workplacebullying.org/ (Workplace Bullying Institute, since 2002; formerly Workplace Bullying and Trauma Institute)

Index

If you have found this book useful you may be interested in other titles from Gower

The Cultural Leadership Handbook
Robert Hewison and John Holden
Hardback: 978-0-566-09176-6
e-book: 978-0-566-09177-3

Diversity in the Workplace
Stefan Gröschl
Hardback: 978-1-4094-1196-3
e-book: 978-1-4094-1197-0

Imaginative Muscle
Victoria Ward and Julie Reynolds
Hardback: 978-1-4094-2108-5
e-book: 978-1-4094-2109-2

Understanding Creative Business
Jim Shorthose and Neil Maycroft
Hardback: 978-1-4094-0714-0
e-book: 978-1-4094-0714-0

Gender, Negotiation and Human Potential In Organizations
Teresa L. Smith and Jean-Luc Grosso
Hardback: 978-1-4094-2272-3
e-book: 978-1-4094-2273-0

Visit **www.gowerpublishing.com** and

- search the entire catalogue of Gower books in print
- order titles online at 10% discount
- take advantage of special offers
- sign up for our monthly e-mail update service
- download free sample chapters from all recent titles
- download or order our catalogue